# GREAT BRITISH PLANS

Can the British plan? Sometimes it seems unlikely. Across the world we see grand designs and visionary projects: new airport terminals, nuclear power stations, high-speed railways, and glittering buildings. It all seems an unattainable goal on Britain's small and crowded island; and yet perhaps this is too pessimistic. For the British have always planned, and much of what they have today is the result of past plans, successfully implemented.

Ranging widely, from London's squares and the new city of Milton Keynes, to 'High Speed One', the motorways, and the secret first electronic computers, Ian Wray's remarkable book puts successful infrastructure plans under the microscope. Who made these plans and what made them stick? How does this reflect the defining characteristics of British government? And what does that say about the individuals who drew them up and saw them through?

In so doing the book casts refreshing new light on how big decisions have actually been made, revealing the hidden sources of drive and initiative in British society, as seen through the lens of 'plans past'. And it asks some searching questions about the mechanisms we might need for successful 'plans future', in Britain and elsewhere.

Ian Wray is a Visiting Professor in Geography and Planning and Visiting Fellow in the Heseltine Institute for Public Policy and Practice, University of Liverpool. He was Chief Planner, Northwest Development Agency, 2000–2010. He has written for *The Architects' Journal*, *Management Today* and *The Guardian* and is currently a trustee of the Town and Country Planning Association and of World Heritage UK, and a member of the general assembly of the Royal Town Planning Institute.

# *Planning, History and Environment Series*

**Editor:**
Ann Rudkin, Alexandrine Press, Marcham, UK

**Editorial Board:**
Professor Arturo Almandoz, Universidad Simón Bolivar, Caracas, Venezuela and Pontificia
  Universidad Católica de Chile, Santiago, Chile
Professor Nezar AlSayyad, University of California, Berkeley, USA
Professor Scott A. Bollens, University of California, Irvine, USA
Professor Robert Bruegmann, University of Illinois at Chicago, USA
Professor Meredith Clausen, University of Washington, Seattle, USA
Professor Yasser Elsheshtawy, UAE University, Al Ain, UAE
Professor Robert Freestone, University of New South Wales, Sydney, Australia
Professor John R. Gold, Oxford Brookes University, Oxford, UK
Professor Michael Hebbert, University College London, UK

## *Selection of published titles*

*Planning Europe's Capital Cities: Aspects of nineteenth century development* by Thomas Hall

*Selling Places: The marketing and promotion of towns and cities, 1850–2000* by Stephen V. Ward

*The Australian Metropolis: A planning history* edited by Stephen Hamnett and Robert Freestone

*Utopian England: Community experiments 1900–1945* by Dennis Hardy

*Urban Planning in a Changing World: The twentieth century experience* edited by Robert Freestone

*Twentieth-Century Suburbs: A morphological approach* by J.W.R. Whitehand and C.M.H. Carr

*Council Housing and Culture: The history of a social experiment* by Alison Ravetz

*Planning Latin America's Capital Cities, 1850–1950* edited by Arturo Almandoz

*Exporting American Architecture, 1870–2000* by Jeffrey W. Cody

*The Making and Selling of Post-Mao Beijing* by Anne-Marie Broudehoux

*Planning Middle Eastern Cities: An urban kaleidoscope in a globalizing world* edited by Yasser Elsheshtawy

*Globalizing Taipei: The political economy of spatial development* edited by Reginald Yin-Wang Kwok

*New Urbanism and American Planning: The conflict of cultures* by Emily Talen

*Remaking Chinese Urban Form: Modernity, scarcity and space, 1949–2005* by Duanfang Lu

*Planning Twentieth Century Capital Cities* edited by David L.A. Gordon

*Planning the Megacity: Jakarta in the twentieth century* by Christopher Silver

*Designing Australia's Cities: Culture, commerce and the city beautiful, 1900–1930* by Robert Freestone

*Ordinary Places, Extraordinary Events: Citizenship, democracy and urban space in Latin America* edited by Clara Irazábal (**paperback 2015**)

*The Evolving Arab City: Tradition, modernity and urban development* edited by Yasser Elsheshtawy

*Stockholm: The making of a metropolis* by Thomas Hall

*Dubai: Behind an urban spectacle* by Yasser Elsheshtawy (**paperback 2013**)

*Capital Cities in the Aftermath of Empires: Planning in central and southeastern Europe* edited by Emily Gunzburger Makaš and Tanja Damljanović Conley (**paperback 2015**)

*Lessons in Post-War Reconstruction: Case studies from Lebanon in the aftermath of the 2006 war* edited by Howayda Al-Harithy

*Orienting Istanbul: Cultural capital of Europe?* edited by Deniz Göktürk, Levent Soysal and İpek Türeli

*Olympic Cities: City agendas, planning and the world's games 1896–2016*, 2nd edition edited by John R. Gold and Margaret M. Gold

*The Making of Hong Kong: From vertical to volumetric* by Barrie Shelton, Justyna Karakiewicz and Thomas Kvan (**paperback 2014**)

*Urban Coding and Planning* edited by Stephen Marshall

*Planning Asian Cities: Risks and resilience* edited by Stephen Hamnett and Dean Forbes (**paperback 2013**)

*Staging the New Berlin: Place marketing and the politics of reinvention post-1989* by Claire Colomb

*City and Soul in Divided Societies* by Scott A. Bollens

*Learning from the Japan City: Looking East in urban design*, 2nd edition by Barrie Shelton

*The Urban Wisdom of Jane Jacobs* edited by Sonia Hirt with Diane Zahm (**paperback 2014**)

*Of Planting and Planning: The making of British colonial cities*, 2nd edition by Robert Home

*Healthy City Planning: Global health equity from neighbourhood to nation* by Jason Corburn

*Good Cities, Better Lives: How Europe discovered the lost art of urbanism* by Peter Hall

*The Planning Imagination: Peter Hall and the study of urban and regional planning* edited by Mark Tewdwr-Jones, Nicholas Phelps and Robert Freestone

*Garden Cities of Tomorrow? A new future for cottage estates* by Martin Crookston

*Sociable Cities: The 21st-century reinvention of the Garden City* by Peter Hall and Colin Ward

*Modernization, Urbanization and Development in Latin America, 1900s–2000s* by Arturo Almandoz

*Planning the Great Metropolis: The 1929 Regional Plan of New York and Its Environs* by David A. Johnson (**paperback 2015**)

*Remaking the San Francisco–Oakland Bay Bridge: A case of shadowboxing with nature* by Karen Trapenberg Frick

*Great British Plans: Who made them and how they worked* by Ian Wray

# GREAT BRITISH PLANS
Who Made Them and How They Worked

Ian Wray

LONDON AND NEW YORK

First published 2016
by Routledge
2 Park Square, Milton Park, Abingdon, Oxfordshire OX14 4RN

and by Routledge
711 Third Avenue, New York, NY 10017

*Routledge is an imprint of the Taylor & Francis Group, an informa business*

© 2016 Ian Wray

This book was commissioned and edited by Alexandrine Press, Marcham, Oxfordshire

The right of the authors has been asserted in accordance with sections 77 and 78 of the Copyright, Designs and Patents Act 1988.

All rights reserved. No part of this book may be reprinted or reproduced or utilized in any form or by any electronic, mechanical or other means, now known or hereafter invented, including photocopying and recording, or in any information storage or retrieval system, without permission in writing from the publishers.

The publisher makes no representation, express or implied, with regard to the accuracy of the information contained in this book and cannot accept any legal responsibility or liability for any errors or omissions that may be made.

*Trademark notice:* Product or corporate names may be trademarks or registered trademarks, and are used only for identification and explanation without intent to infringe.

*British Library Cataloguing in Publication Data*
A catalogue record of this book is available from the British Library

*Library of Congress Cataloging in Publication Data*
A catalog record has been requested for this book

ISBN: 0978–0–415–71141–8 (hbk)
ISBN: 0978–0–415–71142–5 (pbk)
ISBN: 0978–1–315–64483–7 (ebk)

Typeset in Aldine and Swiss by PNR Design, Didcot

Printed and bound in Great Britain by
TJ International Ltd, Padstow, Cornwall

For my late mother, Winifred Wray, who had to leave school early, but encouraged me to learn.

# Contents

| | |
|---|---|
| Foreword<br>   The Right Honourable the Lord Heseltine CH | ix |
| Preface | xi |
| Acknowledgements | xiii |
| List of Illustrations and Sources | xv |

**PART ONE: CONTEXT**

| | |
|---|---|
| 1   Manoeuvre Well Executed? On Rational Plans and British Plans | 3 |

**PART TWO: CASE STUDIES**

| | |
|---|---|
| 2   Landlords and Objectors: London's Roads and Squares | 25 |
| 3   The Making of an English Landscape: Capability Brown and the New Aesthetic | 45 |
| 4   Urban Pastoral: The Building of Birkenhead Park | 60 |
| 5   The Uses of Disorder: Bletchley Park and the World's First Computer | 71 |
| 6   The Cambridge Paradox: Phenomenal Growth; Planned Restraint | 84 |
| 7   Driving Ambitions: Engineering the British Motorways | 104 |
| 8   The City as Chessboard: Constructing the New City of Milton Keynes | 119 |
| 9   The Dream of Caligula: The Channel Tunnel and Its Rail Link | 138 |
| 10  The Pedaller's Tale: Pioneering the National Cycle Network | 155 |

**PART THREE: EXPLANATIONS AND IMPLICATIONS**

| | |
|---|---|
| 11  The Common Threads: Drawing Together the Case Studies | 171 |
| 12  Who's in Charge? The British Government Machine | 180 |
| 13  How Britain Works: Pluralism, Autonomy and Individualism | 194 |
| 14  British Futures, British Plans: Conclusions and Implications | 208 |
| Index | 218 |

# Foreword by
# The Rt Hon the Lord Heseltine CH

I hope it does not appear ungracious but Ian Wray's painstaking and detailed account of some of Britain's largest postwar projects made me cross. As he faithfully records time and again, I was there and as I read his account and revisit past battle scenes I could feel the blood begin to flow at the frustration of it all.

This book could have been a blueprint for the report *No Stone Unturned* which David Cameron invited me to write three years ago examining the sort of issues Ian reveals. Why does everything take so long and why do we find it so difficult to reach strategic conclusions and carry them out? Of course there is no one simple solution and yet on the positive side at least one reason has to be that this is a wonderful country in which to live, with individual rights that are protected and respected, a rule of law open to every citizen and traditions of fairness inscribed in our history. Governments cannot treat the individual person or community with improper haste or disregard.

If this is a reasonable answer to the question it is not wholly comforting. Within the massive concentration of power in London there is a fragmentation of decision taking that has irked all the Prime Ministers I have watched or worked for. They pulled on the levers of power only to find that the connecting rods were made of elastic. Frequently they have tried to put in place machinery to improve their ability to get results. The most ambitious was Harold Wilson's decision to split the Treasury, which had found it difficult to combine its responsibility for financial discipline within long-term strategic planning, by creating the Department of Economic Affairs. Ted Heath recruited Lord Rothschild, Mrs Thatcher, John Hoskins and David Cameron appointed a team of top businessmen under Lord Browne of Madingley. There have been conspicuous examples of success. Harold Macmillan used Ernest Marples to drive the motorway and housing programmes. The most interesting of recent times was the decision of George Osborne to break out from the negative tradition of the Treasury and personally lead the negotiations that led to the very imaginative programme for Manchester and the Northern Powerhouse. It can be done but the exceptions merely reveal the indifference of usual practice.

My hope is that this tolerance of unimaginative and pedestrian performance based on monopoly power in London is about to end. The city deals and local growth deals with the Local Enterprise Partnerships are based on local strengths and opportunities led by the leaders in industry, academia and local authorities. The government is committed to transfer the administration and execution of service to those close to the point of delivery, leaving central government to pursue quality and excellence.

Ian's book is a timely arrival at an interesting moment in the debate about devolution in the United Kingdom.

And the diversity of it, the chaos! … How can one make a pattern out of this muddle?

George Orwell, *England Your England*, 1941

# Preface

Can the British plan? Sometimes it seems doubtful. We look overseas at gleaming new airports, high-speed railway lines and massive engineering projects and ask ourselves why we cannot do it here. Over 30 years as a professional planner one question came to haunt me: how did we ever get anything done in this country? Our whole system of town and country planning seemed to become ever more complex, centralized and 'process driven', with planners ticking boxes rather than using their own initiative and ideas. So the thought occurred that it might be constructive to look back, not at failure, but at implementation and positive achievement, which (with the honourable exception of management schools), seems to be something which academics do less often than they might, focused as they are on problems and criticism.

These are the practical concerns at the heart of this book. But the intellectual impetus comes from another book with a related theme: Peter Hall's *Great Planning Disasters*, written in the late 1970s, as Western societies first began to question the technocratic planning which had taken them through the three decades after the Second World War. It is still worth reading today, not just for the case studies – British politicians are still arguing about a third London airport – but for the clarity of Hall's prose as he introduces us to such gems as Anthony Downs's theory of why bureaucrats operate as they do.

This book inverts Hall's disasters theme, by investigating success and achievement, asking how we actually managed to get things done in the past. And that immediately prompts a question: what do you mean by success? We will return to that thorny problem. Of course, it is much easier to identify failure than success. A plan that does not get implemented is self-evidently a failure; although I should caution that remark, having seen examples of some fairly atrocious plans in my time. Sometimes it seems that a planner's biggest, and most paradoxical, contribution to the future can be failing to get that plan implemented.

In looking for examples I have focused largely on physical plans – those which create new infrastructure, new green space, and transport, and those which help to shape future physical and economic development. Occasionally the account strays into other fields, including military strategy. For one case study I have stretched a point, focusing on the creation of the electronic computer. If the pundits are to be believed, it is the infrastructure of information technology that will shape our destinies in the twenty-first century, so it would seem churlish to ignore the foundation stone for a virtual, rather than physical, world.

I have focused on British plans, from the seventeenth century through to the 1980s (and occasionally touching the present day) without dwelling too much on the sensitivities of the UK's newly devolved nations. Several of the case studies directly or indirectly impinge on the devolved nations (such as motorways, new towns, the national cycle network, and, perhaps one day, high-speed rail) but I have not chosen my case studies in order to achieve a strict geographical balance. My concern is to find out how the case studies have worked and why, and later to see whether they reflect a dominant British culture of decision-making and government. For this I tender my apologies in advance to the Welsh, Scots and Northern Irish. Perhaps as political devolution develops they will develop a different style of decision-taking.

In the third and closing part of the book I look for explanations. What have the case studies in common? How does British experience in infrastructure planning relate to its political institutions and national culture? How has this in turn been shaped by British history?

Though the book started out as an investigation of great plans, it has developed its own momentum. One might look on it as a work of geography, answering that fundamental geographical question: why is this feature located in this particular place? Alternatively one could see it as an exploration of the characteristics of British society (and of British innovation) viewed through the lens of plans past. It is essentially a work of synthesis and analysis, yet planning now runs so deeply in my veins that I cannot resist the temptation to briefly offer some advice and guidance in the closing pages.

The British have planned successfully in a culture without centralized diktat. Planners elsewhere may have the advantage of powerful government bureaucracies and determined political machines. But as incomes rise and the power of the middle classes grows they may find it necessary to take a different course. Perhaps our idiosyncratic experience in getting things done without the benefit of a Napoleonic, Prussian or Chinese Imperial tradition will have some useful wider lessons to offer.

*Ian Wray*
*Liverpool, 2015*

# Acknowledgements

Without the advice and encouragement of the late Professor Sir Peter Hall this book might not exist. I met Peter through the Town and Country Planning Association in London and he generously gave this aspiring (and slightly awe struck) author half an hour of his time, to advise on structuring and on the ways of the publishing trade. On structure, he said, follow the advice of the broadcaster Alistair Cooke: 'Say what you are going to do, do it, and draw your conclusions'. Months later, when I first e-mailed a draft chapter and proposal to Peter, the response was immediate and enthusiastic. He swiftly put me in touch with his friend and editor Ann Rudkin, who has done a wonderful editorial job, responding to successive draft chapters with the same enthusiasm as did Peter to the first.

Another debt must be acknowledged, this time to an institution rather than an individual. To my surprise, the University of Liverpool's Department of Civic Design (now Geography and Planning) appointed me as a Visiting Professor the very week my career as a planning practitioner ended. A later appointment as Visiting Fellow at the University's Heseltine Institute for Public Policy and Practice was equally appreciated. Both opened the door to the services of the University's Sydney Jones Library, whose librarians and staff could not have been more helpful and friendly, as I blew the dust off long forgotten tomes in their Abercrombie Store.

Many others have helped with advice, encouragement, constructive criticism, information and photographs. I would particularly like to thank the following individuals: Peter Batey, Alan Harding, David Massey, Cecilia Wong, Alan Townsend, David Lock, Philip O' Brien, Lee Shostak, Harry Dimitriou, Chia Lin Chen, Chris Couch, Michael Hebbert, John Harrison, Nicholas Falk, Katie Wray, Frankie Wray, Alan Chape, John Grimshaw, Pam Ashton, Robert Lee, Ian Thompson, Peter Hewitt, Daniel Imade, Geoff McDonald, Karen Potter, Philip Insall, Jane Healey Brown, and Nuno Gil.

Permission to use photographs was kindly supplied by the following organizations: the National Trust, Friends of Birkenhead Park, the Bletchley Park Trust, the Motorway Archive Trust, Arup, Sustrans and Wikicommons.

Lastly my thanks to Christine, who has probably learned more about British plans than she ever expected to, as this minor obsession has followed us round over the last four years, even accompanying us on holiday to Sri Lanka, New York and Stowe. I hope she will appreciate the result, though I fear she may share the views of Huckleberry Finn on writing books: 'So there ain't nothing more to write about, and I am rotten glad of it, because if I'd a knowed what a trouble it was to make a book I wouldn't a tackled it, and ain't a going to no more'.

I do know how Huck feels, but can't really share his conclusions.

# List of Illustrations and Sources

**Figure 1.1.** *Admiral Sir Andrew Cunningham.* A brilliant admiral, Cunningham did not suffer planners gladly, comparing his methods with those of Nelson, that skilled improviser and 'discoverer of advantages as they arose'. (*Source*: Dutch National Archives, The Hague, Fotocollectie Algemeen Persbureau (ANEFO), 1945–1989)

**Figure 1.2.** *Nassim Nicholas Taleb.* Taleb claimed that forecasting is a delusion and that the future cannot be extrapolated from the past. (*Photo*: Sarah Josephine Taleb)

**Figure 1.3.** *Karl Popper.* Popper attacked the notion that there can be any prediction of the course of history by scientific method. (*Source*: LSE Library)

**Figure 1.4.** *Robert McNmara (right) with President Lyndon Johnson and Dean Rusk, in 1968.* McNamara and his statistical 'whiz kids' pioneered technocratic planning during the Second World War; as US Defence Secretary during the Vietnam War, protests and failure caused his breakdown. (*Photo*: Yoichi Okamoto)

**Figure 2.1.** *Sir Patrick Abercrombie.* Abercrombie's wartime plan was only successful beyond London's built up area. (*Source*: Collection of Sir Peter Hall)

**Figure 2.2.** *Westway and Harrow Road.* One small implemented fragment of the proposals for inner London roads. (*Source*: CC Justinc)

**Figure 2.3.** *Lincoln's Inn Fields.* Created in the early seventeenth century, this is perhaps the earliest example of open space secured by environmental objectors. (*Photo*: Frankie Wray)

**Figure 2.4.** *Bedford Square.* A town planning masterpiece, created in the eighteenth century by the Duke of Bedford's Estate. (*Source*: CC Russ London)

**Figure 2.5.** *Regent's Park.* A single exercise in urban design, with most of the façades around the park designed by John Nash; the park was the creation of the Crown Estate. (*Photo*: Frankie Wray)

**Figure 2.6.** *Langham Place.* It proved impossible to align the Crown Estate's plan for a new central spine for London; instead the street line was swung across and pieced together over the years. (*Photo*: Frankie Wray)

**Figure 2.7.** *King's Cross.* An entirely new district is being created by one of the 'new great estates' on a 67 acre (26 hectare) formerly disused site. (*Photo*: Alan Chape)

**Figure 2.8.** *Raymond Revue Bar Neon Sign.* The sign was reinstated by the late Paul Raymond's two granddaughters (pictured here), owners of Soho Estates, valued at £300 million in 2010. (*Photo*: © Charlotte Fielding/Soho Estates)

**Figure 3.1.** *Grecian Valley, Stowe, Buckinghamshire.* Brown used subtle planting to turn a slight undulation into the impression of an Arcadian Valley at Stowe, now a National Trust property. (*Photo*: Andrew Butler, by courtesy of the National Trust)

**Figure 3.2.** *Croome Church, Worcestershire.* Brown heightened a low hill with belts of planting, demolishing the existing church and rebuilding a new tower on the ridge, the rest of the village being peremptorily cleared. (*Photo*: Arnhel de Serra, by courtesy of the National Trust)

**Figure 3.3.** *Croome Landscape Park Lake.* Archetypal components of Brown's style: the serpentine lake and isolated Cedar. (*Photo*: David Notan, by courtesy of the National Trust)

**Figure 3.4.** *Peradeniya Royal Botanic Gardens, Sri Lanka.* Created by British colonialists, the lawns sweeping towards boundary woodlands and gently curving paths faithfully replicate Brown's formula. (*Photo*: Ian Wray)

**Figure 3.5.** *Temple of British Worthies, Stowe Landscape Park.* Landscape as iconography: the Temple of British Worthies included busts of Shakespeare, Milton, Newton, and Locke, being figures revered by the Whig establishment. (*Photo*: Andrew Butler, by courtesy of the National Trust)

**Figure 4.1.** *Lake, Central Park New York.* Surrogate nature set in the rectilinear grid of Manhattan. (*Photo*: CC Ed Yourdon)

**Figure 4.2.** *Central Park Users.* Central Park's Literary Walk is a more formal element, found only on the edges of Birkenhead Park. (*Photo*: CC Ahodges7)

**Figure 4.3.** *Birkenhead Park, Swiss Bridge.* One of several original architectural features repaired in the recent restoration. (*Source*: Friends of Birkenhead Park)

**Figure 4.4.** *Cricket in Birkenhead Park.* Olmsted, Central Park's designer, noticed gentlemen playing cricket on his visit to the newly opened Birkenhead Park; and it is played today. (*Source*: CC Rept0n1x)

**Figure 5.1.** *General Eisenhower speaks to US paratroopers before D Day.* Eisenhower had just received a decoded message from Hitler to General Rommel, assuring Rommel that the invasion of Normandy was a feint. (*Source*: Library of Congress Prints and Photographs Division)

**Figure 5.2.** *Bletchley Park.* Nerve centre of the British code breaking operations, Bletchley Park was purchased by Admiral Sir Hugh Sinclair, using personal funds, after the War Office turned the project down. (*Source*: CC Draco2008)

**Figure 5.3.** *Thomas Flowers.* Flowers and his team of post office engineers designed and constructed the world's first electronic computer, turning Alan Turing's concept into reality. (*Source*: CC history-computer.com)

**Figure 5.4.** *Colossus.* Flowers's thermionic valve based electronic computer, in operation during the Second World War, its existence kept secret for over half a century. (*Source*: Bletchley Park Trust)

**Figure 6.1.** *Sir Isaac Newton.* Appointed to the Lucasian Chair in Mathematics in 1669, the scientific impetus from Newton's school was not sustained into the eighteenth century. (*Source*: From the 1689 portrait by Godfrey Kneller)

**Figure 6.2.** *Entrance to Original Cavendish Laboratory.* Crucial to the growth of scientific excellence in Cambridge, the Laboratory owes its existence to an act of personal philanthropy. (*Source*: CC William M. Connolley)

**Figure 6.3.** *Clare College.* The Holford plan protected the collegiate buildings and their setting to promote conservation, compactness and personal interaction. (*Source*: CC Dmitry Tonkonog)

**Figure 6.4.** *Apple/ARM A5 Chip in iPad Mini.* ARM is a descendant of Cambridge's Acorn Computers: 95% per cent of mobile phones across the world contain at least one ARM chip. (*Source*: CC Henrick)

**Figure 6.5.** *Maurice Wilkes.* As Head of the University's Mathematical Laboratory, Wilkes persuaded Charles Lang to move from MIT's Computer Assisted Design (CAD) team, establishing a new CAD centre in Cambridge. (*Source*: Computer Laboratory Archive, University of Cambridge)

**Figure 6.6.** *Laboratory of Molecular Biology.* Funded by the Medical Research Council, the Laboratory is a critical element in the Cambridge research base, moving into this new £200m facility in 2012. (*Source*: CC Cmglee)

**Figure 7.1.** *Monument recording the construction of the M6 Motorway, Charnock Richard Service Area, Lancashire.* A forlorn totem, hidden away behind signs and waste bins, records the first stages in the greatest public works programme since the departure of the Roman Legions. (*Photo*: Ian Wray)

**Figure 7.2.** *Sir James Drake, County Surveyor and Bridgemaster, Lancashire County Council.* Intelligent, forceful and assertive, civil servants in the Ministry of Transport warned each other when Drake was in the building. (*Source*: Motorway Archive Trust)

**Figure 7.3.** *The Prime Minister's Convoy on the Preston By Pass, 1958.* More than 50 years after the first Private Members Bill for construction of a motorway style road, the first section of British motorway is opened. (*Source*: Motorway Archive Trust)

**Figure 7.4.** *Newly constructed M6 motorway near Salmesbury.* Not built to relieve congestion, the motorway plans were essentially visionary. (*Source*: Motorway Archive Trust)

**Figure 8.1.** *Prime Minister Harold Wilson.* Wilson embraced modernity and the use of state planning; the passing of the second New Towns Act in 1965 paved the way for the creation of Milton Keynes. (*Photo*: Erich Koch)

**Figure 8.2.** *Dansteed Way, Milton Keynes.* By turning the back of development onto the main road grid, behind lavish landscaping, a remarkable garden city appearance is conjured, as too is the realisation of Melvin Webber's 'non place urban realm'. (*Photo*: CC Tom Walker)

**Figure 8.3.** *Central Milton Keynes.* Further homage is paid to architectural modernism (and to the rationality of grid squares). (*Photo*: CC Concrete Cowboy)

**Figure 9.1.** *Trackbed of the former Great Central Railway, Culworth.* The heroic scale of construction is evident even in dereliction, as is the unpopulated landscape through which this failed gamble ran. (*Photo*: CC Ben Brooksbank)

**Figure 9.2.** *Ove Arup.* Failed philosopher and brilliant structural engineer, Arup's lack of interest in management helped to found a business which was at once idiosyncratic, liberating and individualistic. (*Photo*: By courtesy of Arup)

**Figure 9.3.** *Medway Viaduct under construction.* Arup's route diverted from the British Rail proposal in mid Kent, running sharply north-west through the North Downs and across the chalk pits of Kent Thameside. (*Photo*: By courtesy of Arup)

**Figure 9.4.** *Eurostar high-speed train in mid Kent.* The Channel Tunnel Rail Link (now known as High Speed One) was the first, and only, new British railway route constructed in the twentieth century. (*Photo*: Daniel Clements, by courtesy of Arup)

**Figure 9.5.** *St Pancras International Station.* The quality of engineering, conservation and design achievement is widely regarded as a triumphant success. (*Photo*: Daniel Imade, by courtesy of Arup)

**Figure 10.1.** *National cycle network route on the Kennet and Avon Canal towpath.* The Network links together ancient paths, drovers' roads, disused railways, towpaths and minor roads. (*Photo*: Chandra Prasad, by courtesy of Sustrans)

**Figure 10.2.** *The Two Tunnels, Bath.* The longest cycling and walking tunnel in Britain.

**Figure 10.3.** *Manchester Road Bridge, Bradford.* Opening of new bridge for walking and cycling across a busy road in 2012. (*Photo*: By courtesy of Sustrans)

**Figure 10.4.** *Diglis Bridge.* Cyclists on National Route 46 beside the Worcestershire riverside. (*Photo*: J. Bewley, by courtesy of Sustrans)

**Figure 10.5.** *Andy Goldsworthy's 'Lambton Worm', County Durham.* Sculptures were commissioned along the Network to add interest: Andy Goldswothy's Lambton Worm was formed from reshaped spoil heaps. (*Photo*: By courtesy of Sustrans)

**Figure 10.6.** *David Kemp's 'Lost Legion', Glasgow to Greenock Cycleway.* Kemp's mysterious sculpture used old gas bottles and transformers. (*Photo*: By courtesy of Sustrans)

**Figure 12.1.** *Lloyd George.* On becoming Prime Minister in 1916, Lloyd George created pressure for strategic thinking, establishing a personal policy team known as the 'garden suburb'. (*Source*: Library of Congress Prints and Photographs Division)

**Figure 12.2.** *Tony Blair.* Like others before him, Blair came to believe that 'the traditional skill set of the civil service is not what is required if you want to drive change'. (*Source*: CC Gryffindor)

**Figure 13.1.** *Ralf Dahrendorf* (to left). Sociologist, anglophile and former LSE Director, Dahrendorf saw the autonomy of its institutions as a defining characteristic of British society. (*Source*: Bundesarchiv, B 145 Bild-F031122-0017/Engelbert Reineke/CC-BY-SA)

**Figure 13.2.** *Margaret Thatcher.* A committed centralizer, Thatcher's target was local government, whose traditional role as a bulwark of democracy was not accepted. (*Source*: Chris Collins, Margaret Thatcher Foundation)

**Figure 13.3.** *John Prescott, former Deputy Prime Minister.* Prescott promoted regionalism whilst practising centralism, imposing 2,500 central targets for transport and local government. (*Photo*: CC Steve Punter)

**Figure 14.1.** *Alex Salmond, Former Leader of the Scottish National Party.* Salmond came close to winning the Scottish referendum on independence; in the 2015 general election his Party swept aside all opposition in Scotland. (*Source*: Scottish Government)

**Figure 14.2.** *Elinor Ostrom.* Nobel prize winner and political scientist, Ostrom argued the case for polycentric and non-hierarchical forms of governance. (*Photo*: © Holger Motzkau 2010/Wikipedia/Wikicommons)

# Part One

# CONTEXT

# 1

# Manoeuvre Well Executed?
## On Rational Plans and British Plans

*Nations begin by forming their institutions, but in the end are continuously formed by them…*

Lord Hailsham, 1987

At 1900 hours on 11 November 1940 the British aircraft carrier *Illustrious*, with its escort of four destroyers and four cruisers, steamed towards its final 'flying off' position, 170 miles south east of the Italian port of Taranto. On deck, gleaming in the moonlight, was the first flight of twenty-one Swordfish biplanes, antiquated yet resilient aircraft, with a cruising speed of only 130 mph, each carrying a single torpedo. After supper and a final briefing the first wave of aircraft took off at 2040 hours into a lightly cloud covered sky. Less than two hours later the biplanes were nearing their target – the main capital warships of the Italian Navy, moored in the harbour of Taranto.

Their audacious torpedo attack crippled much of the Italian fleet; the battleship *Conte di Cavour* lay beached with her decks under water; two other battleships were badly damaged and out of action for months; a cruiser, several destroyers and oil storage facilities sustained damage. Admiral Andrew Cunningham, Commander in Chief of the Mediterranean Fleet, sent a terse signal: 'Manoeuvre well executed'. Britain's most respected Second World War Admiral had pulled off his first masterstroke. In six hours flying time, twenty aircraft had inflicted more damage on the enemy than was sustained in the First World War by the German Fleet at the Battle of Jutland (Barnett, 1991).

Cunningham's leadership style was direct and to the point. He had

Figure 1.1. *Admiral Sir Andrew Cunningham*. A brilliant admiral, Cunningham did not suffer planners gladly, comparing his methods with those of Nelson, that skilled improviser and 'discoverer of advantages as they arose'.

formidable personal authority: 'A stern visage ruddy from the sun, a rim mouth and a jawline like a battleship's bow, a searching stare … an impatience often manifested to his wary staff by a tigerish pacing of the deck' (*ibid.*, p. 221). His approach to plans and decisions was in marked contrast to his predecessor Admiral Sir Dudley Pound. On taking command of the Mediterranean fleet in May 1939 his staff presented Cunningham with detailed plans and orders for his first sea exercise. Cunningham wrote on the top of the thick document: 'too long, too complicated, cut' and returned them to his team. They duly returned a set of orders reduced to only 15 pages of text. On the revised orders Cunningham inscribed another note: 'I agree with the second sentence of paragraph 29, and little else'. Feverishly no doubt, his planning staff turned to paragraph 29, where the second sentence simply read: 'The Fleet will be manoeuvred by the Commander in Chief' (*ibid.*, p. 222).

Writing later about his individualistic and devolved decision-making style, Cunningham compared his approach to Admiral Nelson, whose instructions, given days before Trafalgar, were as follows: 'In case ships cannot be seen or clearly understood, no captain can do very wrong if he places his ship alongside that of the enemy' (Nelson, quoted in *ibid.*, p. 222). It was an instructive parallel. Commenting on Nelson's leadership style, his friend Admiral Collingwood had remarked on the huge importance of his flexibility: 'Without much previous preparation or plan he has the faculty of discovering advantages as they arise, and the good judgment to turn them to a use … but it was the effect of system and nice combination, not chance' (Rodger, 2004, p. 538).

## British Plans

This is not a book about naval or military strategy, though occasionally such matters may intervene (and at this stage some readers may be wondering whether they have picked up the wrong book). It is about the central questions of how the British plan, how the balance is struck between individuals and central power, the role of British institutions as well as objectors, and how these have changed (or remained constant) over time. Was Cunningham's style (admittedly a special style in a singular and especially important British institution) that of a wild one-off maverick, or does it have deeper lessons and implications for how the British organize themselves and plan successfully?

Our focus will be on great British plans – plans which delivered nationally significant infrastructure or profoundly shaped the physical environment (and sometimes both). These are almost always physical plans, although one of the case studies takes us into the realm of infrastructure for information technology, and another into what is increasingly known as the 'knowledge economy'. By British is meant plans prepared and delivered within Great Britain. By great is meant plans which have been successfully implemented, have stood the test of time and are still widely regarded as achievements (or at the very least are not criticized as failures). These plans often incorporate high levels of innovation and act as pioneers and path breakers, triggering change and sometimes imitation. It is an exploration of achievement and of the conditions for achievement.

It is widely believed that Britain does not excel at the planning or execution of major projects. An independent review of Britain's long-term infrastructure planning by Sir John Armitt concluded that its infrastructure has not been renewed or improved as it should. In 2012 Britain was ranked twenty-fourth in the world for the overall quality of its infrastructure; a study in 2006 warned that rising congestion could cost the country £36 billion per annum by 2025; lack of runway capacity in south-east England is threatening the country's position as an international air hub; with a fifth of the country's electricity generating capacity due to be retired in 10 years, we face the risk of power shortages. Governments are not planning for a projected rise in population to 73 million by 2035 (Armitt, 2013).

Another recent report claimed that the lack of a comprehensive planning framework to deal with issues across local authority and regional boundaries threatened the nation's capacity to deal with environmental shocks, whilst reducing efficiency and increasing inequality. Unlike Scotland and Wales, England has no government department, or agency, charged with addressing strategic problems across the country (TCPA, 2012). No less than 60 per cent of the country's infrastructure is now in private ownership – the highest proportion in the world – and this clearly poses an additional obstacle for state intervention. There is a high degree of policy uncertainty and too much silo thinking and bureaucratic drift within the confines of one or another Department of State (Armitt, *op. cit.*).

This depressing litany is not new. In his seminal book on great planning disasters, Peter Hall dissects four celebrated examples – London's third airport, London's motorways, the Anglo French Concorde, and the British National Library (Hall, 1980). Some of these *causes célèbres* failures are still with us. In 2012 the British government launched a Commission chaired by Sir Howard Davies, to once again examine the options for an expansion of London's airport capacity, making its first report by the end of 2013, and reporting finally after the next general election in 2015 (Simmons, 2013). By February 2015 the Commission had considered fifty-eight options and received 50,000 submissions. Having narrowed the choice to only three options – two at Heathrow and one at Gatwick – it planned to consider the submissions behind closed doors, before making its recommendation to government after the May 2015 general election (Hollinger, 2015).

An explanation for these problems lies in economic and political history. As the historian Peter Mathias puts it: 'Britain saw an industrial revolution by consent. It owed nothing to planners and nothing to policemen' (Mathias, 1969). Yet the resonance for British strategic planning and political decision-making is clear enough: Britain has few of the characteristics of a 'developmental state' (Johnson, 1982), by which is meant a state which concerns itself with setting and achieving social and economic goals. In Britain big infrastructure planning can be frustrating and frustrated. We shall return to Johnson's concepts later in the book.

## Success and Uncertainty

Judging success is difficult. For it is usually the case that projects which flow from great plans have a long-term impact and a long shelf life. And as time goes by the context for judging them can change. What exactly do we mean by success and how can we define it? As if to balance its message, an admirable recent book on British government mistakes set out several examples of British policy success: the National Health Service, post-war public house building, the Clean Air Act, the Green Belt, seat belt legislation, the sale of council houses, inward investment in the automotive sector, the Trade Union Act 1994, the privatization of public utilities, and others. But no rationale was offered for the selection of these examples (about whose success there has sometimes been legitimate debate). Tellingly, the examples focused on central government initiative by regulation, rather than action (King and Crewe, 2013).

Planning is by nature riddled with risk and uncertainty. It operates over long time scales in plan-making and implementation, and even longer timescales in terms of impact on outcomes and wider effects. In a seminal book on strategic choice, the operational research specialists Friend and Jessop identified three key sources of instability and uncertainty: uncertainty about the relevant planning environment; uncertainty about decisions in related decision areas; and uncertainty in value judgements (Friend and Jessop, 1969)

Uncertainty related to the *planning environment* includes everything in the world outside the decision-making unit, the expected patterns of future change in the external environment and expected responses to future policies. This is a conventional kind of uncertainty which finds expression in forecasts of costs and forecasts of demand. Uncertainty in *related decision areas* includes future intentions and choices in all sorts of fields outside the problem under consideration. It relates to external agents who may have considerable independence. Uncertainties related to *value judgements* reflect the importance which decision-makers attach to consequences, either because these are of a fundamentally different nature, because they relate to different sections of the community or because they relate to different periods of time. Different groups in society may have different values and these values are likely to change over time, even within the same group. During the 1960s for example political leaders in Britain widely believed that high-rise flats were the ideal solution to housing problems. Within little more than a decade high-rise public building was seen as a failure; partly through experience, and partly through the emerging view which favoured conservation and refurbishment.

The density of uncertainty leads Friend and Jessop to see planning as a process of strategic choice, where decisions are made between alternative courses of action on the basis of an inadequate picture of their total implications. Throughout the process there is the possibility that decision-makers will place too much emphasis either on value judgements, on external decision areas, or on their own planning environment.

As Hall points out (Hall, 1980) even this tangled web of uncertainties may underestimate the problem, for the three types of uncertainty may not be quite as separate as they seem. Problems with the planning environment and related decision areas, he argues, can all be traced to changes in values. Thus population projections are reduced because the birth rate falls, partly because of changes like abortion law reform, but in turn reflecting changes in social values like feminism or pessimism about the future. Plans for London's motorways, unveiled in the 1960s and finally dropped in the early 1970s, failed partly because of inadequate demand forecasts and partly because of changes in external policy that made investment in public transport more attractive. But the main explanation was almost certainly a major shift in values (Hall, *op. cit.*).

With hindsight we can see the 30 year era between 1945 and 1965 as a golden age for technocratic planning and mega-projects – an era the French refer to as *Les Trente Glorieuses*. In the Western world there was stable and predictable economic growth built on suburban expansion and new consumer industries, and stable energy supplies. Economic forecasting in this climate was effective; trends could be extrapolated with some certainty. The systems approach to planning, based on rational goal setting and forecasts of demand, was a logical consequence (McCloughlin, 1969).

In the United States four distinct phases in the history of urban public investment can be identified (Altshuler and Luberoff, 2003). Prior to 1950 localities were reactive rather than visionary in their investments, received little aid from federal government and never imposed disruption on communities. Between 1950 and the late 1960s cities carried out massive investment projects with large-scale federal support, in order to restructure the urban fabric. Starting in the late 1960s and into the 1970s there was a backlash, with increasing popular and community protest. Beyond the mid-1970s public investment in big projects remained high, but projects without environmental mitigation or with serious disruption were much harder to advance. A similar pattern was experienced in Britain, France and many other Western countries. For some reason in the mid-1970s, popular support for the products of technocratic planning fell away, though the techniques and ideology still remain, notably in the importance of cost benefit analysis and demand forecasts in the evaluation of big investment projects.

## Plans, Forecasts and Assessments

There are those who are sceptical about the benefits of strategic planning in general, and mega-projects in particular. These sceptics tend to fall into two camps: first, there are the 'forecasting doubters', who doubt whether long-term planning is possible at all; second, the 'project doubters', who argue that those involved in planning large-scale projects very often overestimate their benefits and underestimate their costs. Nassim Nicholas Taleb is a 'forecasting doubter'. His provocative book argues that forecasting is a delusion, that the future cannot be extrapolated from the past, and that massive discontinuities, 'outliers' and random events play a much bigger role in the future than we might like to believe. Taleb argues that:

> When I ask people to name three recently implemented technologies that impact most on our world today they usually propose the computer, the internet and the laser. All three were unplanned, unpredicted, and unappreciated upon their discovery. They were consequential. They were Black Swans… We tend to tunnel when looking into the future, making it business as usual, Black Swan free, when in fact there is nothing usual about the future. (Taleb, 2007, 135)

Taleb argues that we cannot really plan because we do not understand the

Figure 1.2. *Nassim Nicholas Taleb*. Taleb claimed that forecasting is a delusion and that the future cannot be extrapolated from the past.

future; the inability to predict 'outliers', he argues, implies the inability to predict the course of history. He quotes research by Tetlock,[1] who had systematically put expert advice under the microscope, by asking 300 specialists (and others) to judge the likelihood of specific economic and military events occurring within a specific time period. Economists were a quarter of the sample. The expert's error rates proved to be high. Indeed there seemed to be no difference in results between those with PhDs and graduate degrees. The only consistent regularity was that individuals with a strong reputation proved to be worse at predicting the future than those with none. Taleb found no comprehensive review of the fallibility of expert projections in the economics journals. Reviewing the papers he could find he concluded that:

> They collectively show no convincing evidence that economists as a community have an ability to predict, and if they have some ability their predictions are at best slightly better than random ones – not good enough to help with serious decisions. (*ibid.*, p. 154)

Taleb's view is that the only rational response is to rely less on top down planning and more on 'tinkering' and recognizing opportunities as they arise; the reason free markets work, he says, is because they allow people to be lucky, thanks to the process of trial and error.

John Kay, economist and former director of the Oxford Said Business School, reaches similar conclusions. If the environment is uncertain and constantly changing the product of adaptation and evolution may be better adapted than the product of conscious design. Forecasting is fraught: often we cannot imagine what the future might be like. People who are today concerned about the Iraq war, the rise of China and climate change would not have been worrying about these 20 years ago. They would have been worrying about the Cold War, Japan's unstoppable growth, and AIDS. President Roosevelt achieved his objectives through pragmatic improvisation in the face of circumstances he could not predict or control: 'Try something. If it fails, admit it frankly, and try another' (Roosevelt, quoted in Kay, 2011, p. 128). According to Kay it is true of many successful business ventures. Honda triumphed through improvisation and adaptation. Steve Jobs improvised and adapted endlessly. Most of Marks and Spencer's diversifications failed, with one critical exception – food. It became their strongest product range. The Boeing 737, the most successful airliner in history was developed through 'love of planes', not profit projections; indeed when a non-Executive Director asked about studies of the potential return on the plane's investment, he was brushed off by management.

These arguments suggest that the best we can hope for is a cautious incrementalism; and this is certainly what Martin Simmons implies in his persuasive consideration of current options for the expansion of London's airport capacity (Simmons, 2013). Simmons argues that the development of a new mega-project airport for London in the Thames Estuary cannot possibly open before 2030, by which time competitor airports elsewhere will have reacted to London's capacity shortage, casting doubt on potential demand, and thus funding. He argues in favour of an incremental strategy which expands existing facilities such as Stansted, and does not disrupt or close Heathrow, with the risk of economic damage to its buoyant sub-region.

In the wake of the 2008 financial crisis Taleb's apparently extreme point of view has been influential. Yet it reflects the treatment of risk and uncertainty set out in a seminal book first published in 1921. In 'Risk, Uncertainty and Profit' Frank Knight was equally sceptical about the art of forecasting: 'We live only by knowing *something* about the future; while the problems of life, or of conduct at least, arise from the fact that we know so little' (Knight, 1971, p. 199). Knight argued that we do not perceive the present in its totality, we cannot infer the future from the present with any high level of dependability, and that we cannot accurately know the consequences of our actions, which in any event may not be executed in the form we have willed. Thus he distinguished between measurable uncertainty (or risk) and unmeasurable uncertainty (or uncertainty). In the case of risk, a measure of probability can be assessed; in the case of sheer uncertainty this cannot be done.

Doubts about forecasting were advanced by a philosopher of knowledge Taleb clearly admires – Karl Popper. In his book 'The Poverty of Historicism'

Figure 1.3. *Karl Popper.* Popper attacked the notion that there can be any prediction of the course of history by scientific method.

Popper attacks the notion that there can be prediction of the course of history by any scientific or rational method. He argues that 'only a minority of social institutions have been consciously designed, while the rest have just grown as the undesigned results of human activities' (Popper, 1960, p. 65). Thus the preferred approach to social change should be by 'piecemeal social engineering', which proceeds by continual small adjustments, made step by step, and always on the lookout for the unintended consequences of reform. This pragmatic piecemeal tinkering is the obverse of sweeping or revolutionary change, or as Popper terms it 'utopian engineering'. Popper's book was conceived as an intellectual rebuttal of the ideologies which underlay fascism and communism. But his arguments have resonance for Taleb's phobic scepticism of forecasts and 'scientific' plans.

Bent Flyvbjerg is a 'project doubter'. In his world view rational planning may be possible, if only we could do it with sufficient integrity. With his colleagues Nils Bruzelius and Werner Rothengatter, he argues that we cannot trust the mega-project promoters and their consultants (Flyvbjerg *et al.*, 2003) who operate self-servingly, misinforming governments, the public and the media, in order to get their projects approved and constructed. Cost estimates are regularly understated and underestimated, demand is over stated, there is spin as well as substance in mega-project economics, environmental impacts are undervalued, and delusion is used by politicians and promoters alike, in order to get high risk projects started. Flvybjerg *et al.* argue that governments should reduce these risks by taking a more active role in engaging stakeholders and the public in mega-projects; by refusing to give sovereign guarantees to lenders or to act as promoter; by increasing the involvement of private consortia and private risk capital; and by reducing the opportunities for influence by private lobbying groups. They should promote transparency, as public scrutiny is the main and most effective means of enforcing accountability. Since the role of government is to represent and protect the public interest, all relevant government documents should be made available to the public. Thus Flyvbjerg embraces the techniques of forecasting, prediction and economic assessment, but bewails their flawed and inadequate use.

## Planning versus Analysis

The planning styles attacked by Taleb and Flyvbjerg are rooted in economics and forecasting techniques – a world, so it seems, of hard numbers, costs and benefits expressed in monetary values, and scientific thinking. Cost benefit analysis – the central technique – is a product of welfare economics. Its key tendencies or characteristics are detailed disaggregated techniques, economic quantification, analysis and measurement, economic tests of welfare, and the effect on different interests. Its political style is arbitrative or partisan and its political base populist and democratic (Self, 1975). In Self's words, cost benefit analysis is: 'biased to those articulations of individual wants which can be isolated, observed and measured, and its mathematical approach is congenial to elaborate forecasting exercises' (Self, *op. cit.*, p. 168).

But there is another approach to rational decision-making, which Self refers to simply as 'planning'. Its key tendencies are empirical studies, imaginative synthesis, medium- to long-term time scales, generalized physical and social effects, and most notably the use of goals and policies. Its political base is authoritarian democratic and its style consensus building. There are distinct echoes here of the developmental state (Johnson, *op. cit.*).

This discussion may seem esoteric but its effect is very real. In 2013, as this book was being written, debate raged in the UK about whether or not to invest in a new high-speed rail system from London to the north of England, to supplement the ageing Victorian trunk railway system. Those in favour (including politicians) tended to use empirical evidence (such as capacity shortages and the geographical impact of previous rail investment) and emphasized long-term transformational impacts on regional development and city regeneration, which could not be quantified. But the central technique used by consultants (and favoured by the British Treasury) was cost benefit analysis, and debate focused on whether the scheme was 'value for money' as measured by forecasts of demand and the aggregate time savings of passengers (converted into monetary values). The result was a slightly arcane disagreement about whether business travellers with laptop computers and mobile phones would actually save any time, rather than debates about potential long-term impacts on regional development, city regeneration or sustainable transport (Chen and Wray, 2011).

Planning, as defined by Self, exists not simply to anticipate the future but to actively shape it – and sometimes to change, rather than accommodate, current trends. Plans do not necessarily rest on the (sometimes doubtful) hard numbers of welfare economics but are the product of decisions made by powerful individuals often, but not exclusively, in a democratic political setting. Sometimes they do so for the better. As Self concludes: 'Economic techniques are not the only tools for proposing radical changes in society, although they would doubtless confirm the direction of such changes once in movement' (Self, *op. cit.*, 202)

A recent global research study (Omega Centre, 2012) provides much evidence to support Self's position, and helps to explore the difficulties inherent in identifying success. Led by Professor Harry Dimitriou at University College London, the Omega Centre studied thirty international case studies of mega transport projects to help establish what constitutes a successful twenty-first century project, in the light of increasing risks and uncertainties. The study looked at land based transport infrastructure investments connecting major urban areas, with a construction cost of over \$1 billion, which were seen as crucial to the success of urban, regional and sometimes national development.

These diverse projects ranged from the Oresund road and rail bridge, linking Malmo with Copenhagen, the Big Dig road project in Boston, USA, Hong Kong's airport rail links, the Millau viaduct in France, the UK's Channel Tunnel rail link, and Metro Rail in Perth, Australia. The research included in-depth interviews with key decision-makers, including politicians, officials, financiers, developers, consultants, contractors, the media and members of lobbying and community groups. Echoing Friend and Jessop over 40 years earlier, it recognized that the risks associated with these mega-projects are numerous; they lie within the project itself and in the external project environment.

Several important lessons were extracted from the interviews and data. These huge projects were often critical agents of change with multiple social, economic, environmental and other implications. Yet many of the projects were initially framed simply as transport projects, with little thought given to their implications for urban regeneration or spatial and economic change. Others were positioned as components of a wider strategy; yet these wider objectives were not always part of their initial *raison d'être*. Nonetheless all the projects had huge interdependency with their wider context and in seeking to adapt to this context the projects themselves could transmute. In other words they were rarely closed systems, but open systems, sometimes forced to change as a result of external community and political pressures. In a sense they were organic forms which went through an evolutionary process as the plans were developed.

And the lengthy gestation involved was not always a negative feature; rather it gave time for reflection and desirable adaptation. Happenstance – unforeseen circumstances – played its part; it proved impossible to control every aspect of project planning and delivery and crisis management was often necessary (and sometimes advantageous).

Making a judgment of project success or failure was complex and depended in part on the context which prevailed: 'they need to be understood as dynamic phenomena, to the extent that yesterday's failures can in some instances become tomorrow's successes (and vice versa)' (*ibid.*, p. 22). Half the case studies were successfully delivered at less than 10 per cent over budget. Half were delivered either on time or less than one year behind schedule. Only one-third achieved more than 75 per cent of their initial objectives, but where later emerging objectives were identified three-quarters of the projects achieved 100 per cent of their emergent objectives.

Different groups and individuals had different views of success or failure. These were often highly individual and based on one single aspect of a project. Post completion the perception of success could change – and sometimes dramatically. Thus the report argued for a wider, policy led, 'multi criteria analysis' for the appraisal of projects throughout their lifecycle (with distinct echoes here of Self's 'planning' rather than cost benefit approach). Again context was critical and determined by deep dimensions, including societal beliefs and values. All this made the Omega team rather doubtful of business case or 'iron triangle' considerations of project management (on time, on budget and within prescribed specifications) to judge the success of mega-projects. Inevitably these reduced the emphasis on 'non-business case' issues and achievements.

There were very different contexts for project expectations in countries that were characterized by strong or visionary government and planning traditions (with echoes of Johnson's developmental state). There was ebb and flow in context. Happenstance or serendipity might intervene, as unique opportunities could be seized during the gestation or implementation process. These could be triggered by major events such as political change, or a successful Olympic Games bid. In many countries there were huge advantages in sustained political support and the patronage of a specific political champion, helping to maintain both consensus and momentum. Japanese case studies (including the Kysushu Shinkansen high-speed rail line) enjoyed a long-term institutional framework, based on a rail related development strategy throughout the country.

All this led to serious doubts about the relevance of the so-called 'Iron Triangle' evaluation which undervalued the potential for transformational benefits and a more holistic world view. Instead it argued for the adoption of wider project framing, with greater clarity on the goals of these giant projects, and a policy led multi-criteria framework as the basis for decision-taking. Effectively the conclusions provide support for Self's scepticism and his 'planning' led approach to rational decision-making.

## Whiz Kids, Muddlers and Rationalists

We owe the technocratic planning style, which promised (and indeed delivered) so much, to the United States, and in large part to Robert McNamara and his team of wartime statisticians, popularly known as the 'Whiz Kids'. McNamara is perhaps the prime example of the 'sage technocrat' who ruled the world in the decades immediately after the Second World War. Educated at Berkeley in 1933, where he studied economics, McNamara was selected from Harvard Business School a few years later to join the American war machine as a civilian expert. His team introduced statistical methods into US bombing strategy and later was recruited *en masse* by Henry Ford II to apply wartime expertise to car production. At Ford, McNamara pursued efficient management controls and launched the Ford Falcon, his brainchild and a commercial triumph. McNamara became Ford president and put the company back at the forefront of world auto manufacturing.

Figure 1.4. *Robert McNmara (right) with President Lyndon Johnson and Dean Rusk, in 1968.* McNamara and his statistical 'whiz kids' pioneered technocratic planning during the Second World War; as US Defence Secretary during the Vietnam War, protests and failure caused his breakdown.

Attracting the attention of a new president, McNamara joined the Kennedy administration as Defense Secretary (Priestland, 2012). The question was whether the application of technocratic values would work in a wider setting and the testing ground came as McNamara applied the techniques developed in Ford to the Vietnam War. Kill ratios were estimated, new inputs (such as napalm) deployed, and body counts reported to press conferences. Vietnam however proved to be unwinnable. McNamara was deeply affected by the protests – especially in the universities – and in 1967 collapsed under the strain, moving on to become President of the World Bank. Those protests would reverberate through the late 1960s and early 1970s, as the entire technocratic planning model was called into question by a new generation.

Some had anticipated this rising tide of criticism. Charles Lindblom, a Yale University Professor of Economics, questioned the application of a rational and comprehensive approach to public policy in the late 1950s. In a celebrated paper called 'The Science of Muddling Through' he distinguished between 'rational comprehensive' and 'incremental' approaches. Rational comprehensive plans started from fundamentals each time and nothing was left out; they rested on comprehensive analysis, clarification of values or objectives, theory, and the application of means to ends. An incremental approach continually built out from the current situation, analysis and comparison of alternatives was limited, and means and ends were not distinct. Lindblom argued that the value of operations research related techniques were restricted to lower level problems; as complexity increased the rational approach was of diminishing relevance.

In reality administrators restricted their analyses to incremental or marginal differences in policies. Democracies in turn changed their policies almost entirely through incremental change: policy did not move in leaps and bounds. And every important interest had its watchdog, so that government agencies were always sensitive to pressures from interest groups. Thus policy is not made once and for all; it is made and re-made endlessly. Theory is of limited value; it is greedy for facts, can only be constructed on the basis of great collections of data, and is too imprecise for a policy process which moves in small changes (Lindblom, 1959).

Twenty years later Lindblom, argued for a 'disjointed incrementalism' as the sound basis for policy-making. Analysis would be restricted to familiar alternatives, attention should focus on problems to be solved rather than goals to be sought, and there should be a sequence of trials, errors and revised trials: 'Complex problems cannot be completely analysed and we therefore require strategies of skilful incompleteness' (Lindblom, 1979, p. 524). Thus disjointed incrementalism has distinct echoes of Popper's piecemeal social engineering and prefigures the critics of the rationalist and technocratic style, including Self and Taleb.

So we are left with a curious conclusion; that the technocratic style, for all its predictions, projections, cash flows, forecasts and numbers may not, after all, be the only or the best way to plan for the future. Perhaps there are other equally valid ways, based on a rather different set of outlooks and assumptions.

To sum up: broadly speaking there are two accepted methods of rational planning. The first is related to the setting of goals and objectives and is reflected in part in Self's definition of 'planning' as a decision-making style. Its critics take the position that the complexity of goal and objective setting cannot be pursued (and is not) pursued in the real world, where a rational planning of sorts is possible, though its incremental nature is inescapable. The second is more overtly scientific (at least in its pretensions). It is rooted in welfare economics and cost benefit analysis and is highly reliant on quantification and the numerical forecasting of costs, demand and time savings. Both approaches have their critics. Forecasting is decried by those who argue that the future cannot be known, that uncertainty is everywhere (not least in future social values) and that forecasts are largely spurious, either because of their innate unreliability, or because those using them have every incentive to bend the truth. The critics of rational planning, even of the less exuberant 'objective setting' style, suggest a more informal 'trial and error' approach, where the future is accepted as an unknown and to which incremental policy development is a perfectly reasonable response. The questions for us are whether great British plans will reflect either of these rational approaches, what style they will in fact adopt, and most important of all, why. With these thoughts in mind, it is time to re-consider the meaning of success and to briefly set out the narrative and the approach of the book as a whole.

## The Structure of Argument

The core of the book, in Part Two, is a series of case studies which review nine seminal British plans, spanning the years between 1700 and 2014, proceeding broadly in chronological order, investigating who was responsible for the plans, what decision-taking style and institution was involved, and why they were successfully implemented. Almost all the plans have a powerful innovative element, in their conceptual basis, their methods, or both. Most of the plans considered pre-date the arrival of welfare economics and reflect other styles of decision-making.

The selection of case studies reflects the following criteria of achievement:

◆ Significant impact on national infrastructure, the physical environment, or both;
◆ National or international impact;
◆ Full implementation;
◆ Innovation;
◆ Significant time lapse since initial implementation;
◆ Apparent success (at least as seen through a lack of commonplace negative criticism).

Table 1.1 sets out the case studies and their defining characteristics, and identifies the broad timescales. Identifying timescales is more difficult than it first appears, since some projects are still in progress, whilst the full story of others often greatly pre-dates a start on site.

Table 1.1. The case studies and their defining characteristics.

| Case Study | Dates | Defining Characteristics |
|---|---|---|
| London Roads and Squares | 1630– | The shaping and management of central London; its squares, roads and urban fabric |
| The Landscapes of Capability Brown | 1740–1783 | New rural landscapes and an internationally significant new landscape aesthetic |
| Birkenhead Park | 1847 | The world's first municipal park |
| Bletchley Park and 'Colossus' | 1938–1945 | The world's first electronic computer |
| Planning for Cambridge | 1948– | Planned restraint alongside phenomenal economic growth |
| The Motorway System | 1906– | Britain's motorways |
| Milton Keynes | 1967– | The construction of a new city and a new urban form |
| The Channel Tunnel Rail Link | 1998–2007 | Britain's first high speed rail line |
| The National Cycle Network | 1979– | Britain's first national cycle network and thus specific provision for cycling |

Arguing from case studies prompts the question of whether the plans selected for study have been chosen to support the author's predispositions. The accusation is difficult to disprove. The case studies do range widely in scale and time and almost all have the special characteristics of apparent success after a long timescale, and some degree, sometimes an important degree, of innovation. Many of the projects were firsts, either in Britain or internationally. Some have acquired that perverse indicator of widely accepted success – they have been officially listed as sites of great cultural or heritage value, and thus in need of conservation. Perhaps more will do so in time. Yet failure is much easier to demonstrate than success; a failed plan is one that has not been implemented or has not delivered the goods. As Olsen argues the passing of time is critical:

> A town plan cannot be judged a success until it has shown its ability to adapt itself to changing circumstances, changing technological and functional requirements, changing aesthetic values, changing kinds of life desired by its inhabitants. (Olsen, 1964, p. 200)

So it is best at this stage to emphasize achievement, rather than total success. Indeed it may be that achievement is as much as we can reasonably expect. As the Omega Centre research demonstrated, success is difficult to define and (as Friend and Jessop argued) can change over time as societal values transmute.

Later in the book we explore some of the mechanisms of the British state (including the civil service) and the history which has given rise to its institutions and its pluralistic tendencies. The clinching tests will be whether the more abstract and theoretical discussion supports and is supported by the evidence which is distilled from the case studies. If they do so, this will provide further support for the book's conclusions. But these are quite limited in scope.

The book is intended more as a journey of exploration, than a noisy and over assertive local guide.

## Introducing the Case Studies

The case studies open with the planning of London, and specifically with the successful evolution of Georgian London and its squares, and the two attempts to comprehensively re-plan the city's roads, first after the Great Fire, and much later in the 1960s. Why have the squares been such a conspicuous success and the roads such an abject failure?

The landscapes of Capability Brown (a gigantic physical achievement in their own right) helped to popularize and spread an entirely new approach to landscape planning. They owed much to a uniquely English appreciation of art and nature, a way of looking at and appreciating landscapes which was to spread widely to other cultures within the British Empire and beyond. They were indeed symbolic of the new political liberties which underlay them.

In Birkenhead Park we can see the first example of municipal as opposed to a private park, open to all and paid for at public expense. In design and concept, it is the direct forerunner of municipal parks across the world. Like the landscapes of Capability Brown – with which its design has more than a slight resemblance – the Park is with us today, functioning well after a recent restoration.

Without the code breakers of the Second World War Britain could have lost the Battle of the Atlantic and with it the Second World War, and the course of world history might have been very different. This was more than a victory for individual minds. At Bletchley (and Dollis Hill) the world's first electronic computer, Colossus, was invented and constructed; it was a triumph of information technology, as well as intellectual infrastructure. Who exactly laid the plans for Bletchley, brought the great and practical minds together, and orchestrated the plot?

In 1931 a Royal Commission on Transport set out its negative views on motorway building in Britain, using arguments which resurfaced in the 2000s as the Department for Transport sought to defuse demands for a national high-speed rail network. The initiative for building the motorways came from elsewhere; which explains why the Preston By-Pass, now part of the M6, became the first element in our national motorway system. How did the system get built; and what does this tell us about the role of local government and provincial initiative?

Milton Keynes is a new city on a largely green field site. Its construction was the culmination of a great post-war new town building programme. In its enthusiasm for growth, its decentralized layout and its car-based grid, Milton Keynes has been described as an English Los Angeles. What led to its creation? Who devised its plan and how successful has it proved?

Politically the Channel Tunnel was a French achievement. It was François

Mitterand who persuaded Margaret Thatcher to support the project. Yet for years high-speed trains left the tunnel on the English side only to join a congested Victorian railway network, trundling slowly towards their final destination. Official attempts to build a high-speed link foundered. It was only when an enterprising firm of English consulting engineers took up the cause that an achievable plan was set out, and the high-speed link to London constructed. It is still the UK's only stretch of high-speed railway.

Cambridge is a world centre for applied science, with a prodigious output of world beating small companies and ideas and a fast growing economy. Yet paradoxically, since 1948 Cambridge has been planned by its county council quite deliberately to stop and restrain growth. How has the circle been squared, and by whom?

Britain's National Cycle Network extends from Land's End to John O'Groats. After the motorways it is the most important new national transport network constructed in the twentieth century, extending to 14,700 miles (23,600 km) of safe cycling routes and traffic calmed minor roads. How exactly did we manage to create this new national asset, and what was the contribution of central government to the task?

In Part Three the book engages with both history and theory, returning to some of the wider themes first raised in this chapter. It draws out the main lessons from each plan and describes the common elements of planning style where these exist. It takes a look at the heart of the British government machine in the form of the civil service and the nature of the British state (an issue to which we have already made passing reference). It looks at how British history has contributed to the creation of the machinery which exists, the way in which power is distributed, the use of different 'institutional platforms', and the decisions (as well as the indecision) which have resulted. And it concludes by asking how British society and its institutions might best cope with the planning challenges which lie ahead.


## The Light Touch

Before we move to the case studies, perhaps a little more should be said about our opening engagement with the Royal Navy, and the improvisational style of some of its admirals. As the historian Paul Kennedy reminds us in his study of the Rise and Fall of British Naval Mastery, Britain's rise to globalism rested on its great maritime power, rather than land based or continental power (Kennedy, 1976). Before the days of radio, and sometimes even after that, naval captains would have taken their own initiative and their own decisions without recourse to higher authority. With a sea voyage lasting weeks or months there was simply no authority to appeal to. That inescapable reality must have shaped the culture and traditions of the Royal Navy, which in itself became a powerful institution in British life and British politics.

But the argument can be extended. A land-based power requires a large, land-based, standing army, and with that go the institutions and attitudes of absolute, centralized, indeed militarized, power. Much less central direction and control is needed by a naval power. In Kennedy's words: 'An empire based on sea power was usually more beneficial and less heavy handed than those based upon land power' (Kennedy, *op. cit.*, p.349). The light touch is a theme we will return to.

## Note

1.   Philip E. Tetlock is Leonore Annenberg University Professor of Psychology at the University of Pennsylvania and author of *Expert Political Judgement: How Good is It? How Can We Know?* (Princeton University Press, 2006).

## References

Acemoglu, D. and Robinson, J. (2012) *Why Nations Fail: The Origins of Power, Prosperity and Poverty.* London: Profile.

Altshuler, A. and Luberoff, D. (2003) *Mega Projects: The Changing Politics of Urban Public Investment.* Washington DC: The Brookings Institution.

Armitt, J. (2013) *The Armitt Review: An Independent Review of Long Term Infrastructure Planning Commissioned for Labour's Policy Review.* London: Labour Party.

Barnett, C. (1991) *Engage the Enemy More Closely: The Royal Navy in the Second World War.* London: W.W. Norton.

Flyvbjerg, B., Bruzelius, N. and Rothengatter, W. (2003) *Mega Projects and Risk: An Anatomy of Ambition.* Cambridge: Cambridge University Press.

Friend, J. and Jessop, W. (1969) *Local Government and Strategic Choice: An Operational Research Approach to the Processes of Public Planning.* London: Tavistock.

Chen, C.-L. and Wray, I. (2011) Can high speed rail save the regions? *Town and Country Planning,* **80**(3), pp. 119–127.

Hall, P. (1980) *Great Planning Disasters.* London: Weidenfeld and Nicolson.

Hollinger, P. (2015) Final approach for decision on airport expansion. *Financial Times,* 6 February 2015, p. 4.

Johnson, C. (1982) *MITI and the Japanese Miracle: The Growth of Industrial Policy, 1925–1975.* Stanford, CA: Stanford University Press.

Kay, J. (2011) *Obliquity: Why Our Goals Are Best Achieved Indirectly.* London: Profile.

Kennedy, P. (1976) *The Rise and Fall of British Naval Mastery.* Harmondsworth: Allen Lane.

King, A. and Crewe, C. (2013) *The Blunders of Our Governments.* London: Oneworld.

Knight, F. (1971) *Risk, Uncertainty and Profit.* Chicago, IL: University of Chicago Press (First published in 1921 by Houghton Mifflin Company).

Lindblom, C. (1959) The science of muddling through. *Public Administration Review,* **19**(2), pp. 79–88.

Lindblom, C. (1979) Still muddling, not yet through. *Public Administration Review,* **39**(6), pp. 517–525.

McCloughlin, J. (1969) *Urban and Regional Planning: A Systems Approach.* London: Faber.

Mathias, P. (1969) *The First Industrial Nation: The Economic History of Britain 1700–1914.* London: Routledge.

Olsen, D.J. (1964) *Town Planning in London.* New Haven, CT: Yale University Press.

Omega Centre (2012) *Mega Projects Executive Summary: Lessons for Decision Makers.* London: Omega Centre, Bartlett School of Planning, University College London.

Popper, K. (1960) *The Poverty of Historicism,* 2nd ed. London: Routledge and Kegan Paul.

Priestland, D. (2012) *Merchant, Soldier, Sage: A New History of Power.* Harmondsworth: Allen Lane.

Rodger, N. (2004) *The Command of the Ocean: A Naval History of Great Britain, 1649–1815.* Harmondsworth: Allen Lane.

Self, P. (1975) *Econocrats and the Policy Process: The Politics and Philosophy of Cost Benefit Analysis.* London: Macmillan.

Simmons, M. (2013) A new South East hub airport: issues and options. *Town and Country Planning*, **82**(7/8), pp. 338–343.

Taleb, N. (2007) *The Black Swan: The Impact of the Highly Improbable*. Harmondsworth: Penguin.

TCPA (Town and Country Planning Association (2012) *The Lie of the Land – England in the 21st Century, Summary*. London: TCPA. Available at: Reporthttp://www.tcpa.org.uk/data/files/Lie_of_the_Land_ExecSummary.pdf.

Part Two

# CASE STUDIES

# 2

# Landlords and Objectors
## London's Roads and Squares

*Practically everybody agrees that London today is the most civilized and agreeable of all the world's great cities. To have brought into existence the London we know, someone, sometime, must have done something right.*

Donald Olsen, 1979

On 2 September 1666 London was ablaze. The diarist and government official Samuel Pepys gave a celebrated account:

> … the wind great. So near the fire as we could for smoke; and all over the Thames, with one's face in the wind, you were almost burned with a shower of firedrops. This is very true; so as houses were burned by these drops and flakes of fire, three or four, nay, five or six houses… We staid till, it being darkish, we saw the fire as only one entire arch of fire from this to the other side the bridge, and in a bow up the hill for an arch of above a mile long: it made me weep to see it. The churches, houses, and all on fire and flaming at once; and a horrid noise the flames made, and the cracking of houses at their ruins. (Latham and Matthews, 1972, p. 271)

Pepys made his preparations to leave the city, but not before he had buried his wine and parmesan cheese in the garden. His confidence that, come what may, he would afterwards be allowed back to reclaim his land (and his cheese) is not without significance.

Starting as a small outbreak in Pudding Lane on 1 September 1666, the fire spread quickly and raged furiously, with little attempt at control. Only after it had burned for several days were parts of the city demolished and houses pulled down to create firebreaks. It ceased on 6 September, having destroyed much of the city: 13,200 houses were lost and 436 acres (176 ha) were laid waste, stretching from Castle Street, Holborn to Leadenhall Street, Fenchurch Street, Broad Street and near Cripplegate (Pevsner, 1957).

## The Great Fire Plans

On 10 September, with the fire smouldering, the King received Christopher Wren who handed him a plan for rebuilding the city. Three days later John Evelyn also presented a plan. On 20 and 21 September respectively, further plans were received from Valentine Knight and the mathematician Professor Robert Hooke.

Wren was only 34 years old but already a distinguished scientist, appointed as a professor of astronomy at the age of 24. In 1662 he had taken up architecture, acquiring his knowledge mostly through books. Doubtless his scientific skills were useful, but apart from a visit to Paris, where he had studied the new architecture at the Louvre, he had seen no buildings outside Britain (Summerson, 1993). Yet in his position as deputy surveyor of his majesty's works (and having recently prepared a plan for the restoration of St. Paul's Cathedral) he must have seen the rebuilding of London after the fire as a huge personal opportunity. His grand plan used the rond-point with radiating avenues as a motif, the current fashion for town planning in France (Pevsner, *op. cit.*). The entrances to the town were its gates and bridges. Houses should be rectangular and preferably all street corners the same. The Stock Exchange and St. Paul's Cathedral were given dominating positions; thus streets should radiate out from these dominant – one might accurately say iconic – structures. Thereafter the plan laid out a network of streets, wherever possible meeting at right angles. Wren had yet to discover the importance of the square in town planning and none were indicated in his plans.

As a wealthy educated noble, Evelyn had visited Holland, Belgium, France and Italy, and thus proposed a series of large and regular squares, with detailed recommendations for the width of streets (100 feet [30 m] wide for principal streets and no street to be narrower than 30 feet [9 m]). Evelyn's plan followed the French principles seen in Wren's, with the rond-points superimposed on his grid.

Robert Hooke's plan has been lost, but Knight's survives. It is driven, not by abstract street layouts, but by the practical need to divide the city into narrow blocks which could be developed without waste. Knight at least was thinking about implementation, the pragmatic process of moving from plan to reality. Yet despite the devastation which lay all around, not a single one of these plans was actually implemented. Indeed they did not even reach Parliament or the City Corporation for discussion (Rasmussen, 1982).

This was surprising, for the King had received Wren's plan positively on the

10 September. Charles II had inherited his father's interest in town planning, persuading Andre le Notre to visit London and enlarge St James Park before laying out Versailles for Louis XIV. Here surely was a fantastic opportunity to reshape and transform London. No more would it have to endure critics like Evelyn, who had compared London's poor nasty cottages with the splendours of the French capital.

The King's Private Secretary had written to the Lord Mayor immediately after the fire, commanding that no houses should be constructed on their old foundations, and that any unauthorized work would be demolished. Alas, it was the King's authority that was demolished, for only three days later he had given up on Wren's plan. This was not just because the plan was in itself impractical (which it probably was). It was because no mechanism existed for implementation, for buying out the multiple landowners, each of whom could point to the boundaries of his or her plot – and in at least one notable case to the site of his buried parmesan cheese. Slow progress was made with a land survey in the face of widespread non-cooperation and by November the survey had been abandoned. As Rasmussen observes: 'Wren's plan, finished in a few days, is a fine example of a certain type of town planning … it is the town planning of absolutism' (Rasmussen, *op. cit.*, p. 112). It might perhaps have worked in similar circumstances in a centralized state like France. It stood no chance of being implemented in Britain.

Although the survey failed, the King's Commissioners succeeded in their second task: to formulate methods of rebuilding (Summerson, 1993, *op. cit.*). Charles II's Act for the Rebuilding of the City of London in 1667 was essentially a form of building control, to guide a process of reconstruction left entirely to private initiative. It was a process of regulation, designed to help secure the rather limited objectives of 'uniformity and gracefulness'. Pevsner concludes that 'in the end the plan of the city remained narrow, confused and medieval' (Pevsner, *op. cit.*, p. 60). For all that, it proved, as we shall see, to be influential, speedy and effective.

## After the Blitz: A Second Failed Attempt

Almost 300 years would pass before there was a similar effort to re-plan London on a grand scale; and again the incentive and the catalyst was widespread fire and destruction. This time the cause was not a domestic accident but determined and massive attack, involving incendiaries and high explosives. London's Second World War blitz grew by accident out of Hitler's attempt to secure Britain's immediate surrender and continued in retaliation for British bombing of Germany. Hitler concentrated first on London, which was bombed every night from 7 September to 2 November 1940, before switching to more industrial targets: fifty-seven raids brought 13,561 tons of bombs. Physical damage inflicted by the blitz may have been overstated, certainly in relation to other cities. Later in the war the British dropped the same total of bombs on Germany in a week (Taylor, 1975). For all that, wide swathes of land were devastated, especially in the East End and in the districts around the City of London.

Most of all, the blitz and the war changed attitudes:

> Entire districts were demolished overnight. All traditional ideas of property became obsolete. A new thinking and a new planning was not only a possibility, it had suddenly become a new necessity. (Rasmussen, 1982, p. 427)

These new attitudes to planning coincided with a huge growth in the powers of government as the wartime machine was brought into life (Edgerton, 2011). Government had led development on a huge scale. Before and during the war compulsory purchase powers had been used to build ordnance factories and military airfields, while government had organized the clearance of bombsites as well as the repair of bomb damaged railways and roads (Hennessy, 1990).

Whilst German bombers did their worst, a small team of architects and planners led by Sir Patrick Abercrombie laid plans for recovery. Abercrombie was a particularly distinguished town planner. A former Professor of Civic Design at Liverpool University (the world's first planning course) he had practised as a regional planner and was the founding officer of the Council for the Preservation of Rural England. With help from J.H. Forshaw, Chief Architect of London County Council, and with a small team, he put together the London County Plan 1943, and the Greater London Plan 1944, documents designed as much to strengthen morale as to coordinate action. Planning for recovery became a propaganda symbol and quickly captured the public mood. The Royal Academy's exhibition 'London Replanned' in November 1942 was packed; as was County Hall when the County of London Plan was launched. Echoing the visions of Wren and Evelyn, a best-selling summary of the Greater London Plan promised to give the city order and efficiency with beauty and spaciousness (Hebbert, 1998).

Abercrombie's Greater London Plan had several key elements. There was to be a powerful containing green belt around the capital that would stop its sprawl once and for all. Beyond the green belt there were proposals for eight new towns, to provide a new and harmonious setting for industry and population, delivering for the first time the vision of Ebenezer Howard for new garden cities (see Chapter 8). Each new town would be a balanced and self-contained society. They would be constructed as state planned and state directed developments, built on land acquired by the state, if necessary with compulsory purchase.

Several rings of new highways would at last provide structure to the capital. There would be three inner rings, the so-called A, B and C ring roads running through the built up areas, with an outer D ring within the green belt. All these roads would be multi-lane motorways on the German model, rather than boulevards. Many would be set in wide parkways, extending the benefits of a

Figure 2.1. *Sir Patrick Abercrombie*. Abercrombie's wartime plan was only successful beyond London's built up area.

green way system, while stopping the risk of scattered frontage development which had so blighted the appearance of the pre-war by-passes. The highways and their parkways would help to define new community units, as cells within the wider organism of the city.

Set in this context, the prevailing mood was for a clean sweep of London's housing. Removal of old streets would secure the removal of private ownership. London County Council's development plan in 1945 made its commitment to the comprehensive redevelopment of areas considered obsolete. The stage was set for the architectural profession, especially within the County Council itself, to rebuild great tracts of the city in modernist architecture, realizing the urban visions of the French architect Le Corbusier. Since the Ministry of Housing and Local Government's usual cost sanctions did not apply to it, the Council's prestigious Architects Department was virtually given carte blanche (Hall, 1989).

The green belt and new towns were successfully delivered. Comprehensive development was implemented too, on a large scale, and there was a deliberate push for high-rise building solutions. It came from central government, reinforced by architectural fashion, industrial building, and the commitment to tight green belt policies. Yet few would now consider it a success. As Keith Joseph, the responsible Minister later regretted: 'I suppose that I was genuinely convinced that I had a new answer. It was prefabrication and, heaven help me, high blocks' (cited in Ward, 1994, p. 155). With the exception of the outer D ring (which became the M25 motorway) the ring roads were never built. It was a scale of retreat so great that the roads became an outstanding example of planning disasters (Hall, 1980).

Post 1945, in conditions of financial austerity, political priority was given to housing and health, not road building or infrastructure (Barnett, 1996). By the 1950s, with car ownership rising rapidly, traffic congestion was widely regarded as a problem needing solution. Yet it was only with the creation of the Greater London Council (GLC) in 1963 – a body in part specifically established in order to get new roads built – that a serious start was made. The Council's engineers set to work to implement the new network of ring roads and radial expressways, though the landscaped parkways were dropped.

Abercrombie had planned to achieve several objectives: better traffic flow; reduced environmental intrusion; new more homogeneous districts; and his landscape structure. The GLC engineers had a much simpler focus: new roads. They and their consultants were imbued with new scientific techniques imported from the USA, which centred on computer modelling of demand, and in particular demand for car travel. They adjusted their calculations to support the case; thus shopping trips were artificially inflated by an arbitrary factor of 25 per cent, since their computer forecasts did not reflect American experience. There was little development of public transport strategy, partly because the GLC was not responsible for public transport until 1970. And the plan for roads was accepted before full knowledge was available from the studies on which it was supposedly based (Hall, *op. cit.*). It was an early example of misrepresentation by professionals and consultants with vested interests at stake (Flyvbjerg *et al.*, 2003).

By 1967 the cost of the system had risen to £2 billion. The plans had been driven almost entirely by a political response to the problems of road traffic. But politics was moving against the scheme and well-informed and influential critics had emerged in two community groups, the London Motorway Action Group and the London Amenity and Transport Association. Both groups had professional experts on their side who set out to demolish the technical case on which the plans were built, advancing alternative solutions such as traffic restraint and investment in public transport. The public inquiry into the Greater London Development Plan heard 28,392 objections, most of them related to transport. Its Inquiry Panel sat for 63 days on strategic transport issues, and a further 67 on local transport issues. Though the Panel's conclusions tried to steer a middle course, events were moving rapidly against the roads:

> When the motorway plans were unveiled in 1965–7 both political parties, together with the media and a wide spectrum of public opinion were publicly and enthusiastically in favour. By the time they were abandoned in 1973, there was hardly a voice left in support. (Hall, *op. cit.*, p. 10)

In April 1973 Labour regained power at the GLC, and on the morning of their victory announced that the motorway plans would be abandoned. Apart from the M25, implemented entirely on green field sites by the Department of Transport, little remains of Abercrombie's roads, beyond a few scattered fragments like the Westway and the Blackwall tunnels, and sadly nothing at all of his landscaped parkways. Hall concluded: 'There was a profound shift of mood amongst thinking people in London and other cities, both about the problem and about its solution' (Hall, *op. cit.*, p. 85). London's second grand plan had failed.

Figure 2.2. *Westway and Harrow Road.* One small implemented fragment of the proposals for inner London roads.

## The City of Many Plans

It would be easy to conclude that planning for London has been a conspicuous failure; that the city is impervious to order, chaotically disorganized. And indeed there is a great deal of disorder in London. Compare the Google Earth images of London and Paris. Central London is an untidy palimpsest of streets and open spaces, without apparent method or system; central Paris is neatly dissected by its grand boulevards and civic rond-points. Equally there is duplication and disorder in London's social, cultural and economic life: 'In music, sport, religion, local government, hospital provision, and business London sails as a flotilla with two, three or four flagships' (Hebbert, *op. cit.*, p. 7). In truth both Paris and London are planned, but their plans differ in aims and character. London is a collection of autonomous 'villages', thoughtfully planned, but with little reference to each other. Paris grew up initially without a plan but was ordered and organized by Baron Haussmann's centrally imposed boulevards (Olsen, 1964).

The architectural critic Ian Nairn summarizes accurately:

> London as a single personality does not exist. It never has, at least from the moment that Edward the Confessor built his abbey on the marshes a couple of miles away from the original homogeneous commercial city. All the attributes of the capital pile onto this shallow basin of gravel, like rugby players in a scrum… London is indeed a thousand villages. (Nairn, 1966, p. 15)

Olsen takes a similar view:

> The visitor will search in vain for the great public buildings, the dramatic vistas, or the striking monuments of Rome, Paris or Washington … there is much in London that will please but little that will astonish… London rarely attempts to look like a great city, being content to be one. (Olsen, *op. cit.*, p. 3)

London does indeed seem to lack an organizing principle, a creative ordering. Yet such anarchic conclusions would mislead. It would be more accurate to say that London has multiple organizing foci. London may never have seen through a single grand plan or master plan, but it does not follow that it has not been successfully planned. It remains, in Olsen's words, more lovable mess than earthly paradise.

One after another London's squares and the elegant housing which surrounds them have been designated as listed buildings and conservation areas. They have rarely been abandoned or seriously run down in the classic sequence of urban growth and decline. London's experience shows that leasehold tenure does not necessarily lead to slums. Positive management on many estates has stopped slums from establishing themselves and maintained a high standard of repair and occupation in areas which were often less than fashionable (Olsen, *op. cit.*). These are amongst the most humane and successful examples of town planning in the world, and a central element in the very success and attraction of London as a twenty-first century city. Rasmussen makes this lyrical tribute to their appeal:

> On a summer day when the sun is shining you can walk for hours from one square to another under fresh green trees and see thousands of little circular spots cast by the sun on the green lawns. But in the dark seasons the squares are no less attractive. In the afternoon, when lights begin to appear in the houses, when tea is served … when London is being swallowed up in the moisture and fog of the same yellowish colour as the tea, the London square appears to be at the bottom of the sea, under branches whose indistinct outlines form a pattern like seaweed floating overhead. (Rasmussen, *op. cit.*, p. 200)

The truth is that London's successful plans are partial plans. They owe as much to regulation as initiative, standing on three foundations. First, the failure to get to grips with the opportunity presented by the Great Fire of London and the regulatory planning for which it acted as the catalyst; second, the organizing and land management skills of the great estates and the wisdom of their land owners; third, the initiative of private builders and speculators, who were influenced by example and directed by regulation.

Charles II's Act for the Rebuilding of the City of London was designed to regulate rather than lead redevelopment. It provided for the structural standardization of new houses in three types, all in brick and with specified floor heights and wall thicknesses. The roofs of types one to three were to be uniform, as were the heights of their storeys. Street widths were also defined, calling for a degree of intervention through compulsory purchase with compensation. The Act set out the legal basis which still applies today for the shared party walls of adjoining terraces. Under the control of three appointed surveyors – Robert Hooke, Peter Mills and John Oliver – the rebuilding of the city proceeded in conformity with the Act. There was no insurance or public compensation, apart from street improvements, and rebuilding was entirely the result of private enterprise and private wealth (Summerson, 1993, *op. cit.*). Implementation was successful; so much so that the Rebuilding Act was quoted in building agreements far outside London. Thus was individual initiative and architectural skill harnessed by the light touch of regulation.

In Lincoln's Inn Fields we have one of the earliest examples of town planning shaped by environmental objectors. When regular training in English law was

Figure 2.3. *Lincoln's Inn Fields.* Created in the early seventeenth century, this is perhaps the earliest example of open space secured by environmental objectors.

established for secular lawyers, its seat was between the City and Westminster, and students lived at the Inns of Court. The field west of Lincoln's Inn was a common walking and sports ground for clerks of the chancery, apprentices, students and common citizens. In 1613 the land was acquired by a would-be developer who petitioned the King for a licence to build houses. The Society of Lincoln's Inn immediately sent a protest to the Privy Council. The licence was refused and in 1617 gentlemen of the Inns of Court further petitioned the King that the fields might be converted into walks. In 1618 a Commission was granted to survey the fields and prepare plans for the walks (Longstaffe-Gowan, 2012). When William Newton acquired the lease of the fields to erect houses he considered it best to keep on good terms with the gentlemen and made the agreement to retain the walks as an open square. It remains today an area of extraordinary green tranquillity, surrounded by the quiet hum of legal discourse.

## The London Squares

Lincoln's Inn aside, the account of London and its squares begins in 1630 (shortly before the Great Fire) with Covent Garden. Covent Garden was formerly a convent garden, belonging to the Abbey of St Peter. Henry VIII confiscated the monastic estates during the Reformation and in 1552 Covent Garden was given to John Russell by the king, who made Russell the Earl of Bedford. In 1630, Francis, the Fourth Earl, decided to develop the site and Inigo Jones was brought in as architect. Jones proposed a large rectangular square, dominated by a monumental church, apparently influenced by the Place Royale, now Place des Vosges, in Paris. Today the square gives little impression of its appearance when built, but what is left remains notable, not least Inigo Jones's church. The buildings, which originally surrounded the square, were arcades, and the houses, of different depths and breadths behind the arcade, became fashionable places to live. Yet the square's gentility was not easily achieved as various factors contributed to the social decline of the briefly fashionable neighbourhood. The square itself was later filled with stalls and sheds, giving way to permanent market halls in the nineteenth century (*ibid.*).

Once Covent Garden became feasible, the London Square was recognized as a suitable form for town residences and many more squares were built. In 1635 Leicester Square was laid out in front of Leicester House. Bloomsbury Square was created by the Earl of Southampton in 1661. Its leasehold system set the pattern for all that was to follow. The Earl gave out plots to builders on 42-year leases at low ground rents, on condition that the builder constructed houses that would ultimately become the landlord's property. This system ensured that the owner of the land benefited from development and a regular income for the ground rent at minimal outlay, whilst retaining ownership for the long term. The builder developer benefited by acquiring a prime site and was often able to sublet. Most leases were fixed for 99 years. Bloomsbury Square also initiated a new arrangement where town houses were built in terraces around the squares with tradespeople or servants in side streets.

The Great Fire accelerated building in the West End and before the turn of the century more squares were added, including Soho Square in 1681, Grosvenor Square in 1695, Berkeley Square in 1698 and St. Jame's Square in 1684. The plans continued into the eighteenth century. At the end of the century the Duke of Bedford began to develop over 100 acres [40 ha] north of Oxford Street, first by laying out gardens for the use of his lessees. Buildings were grouped around the green areas and a whole sequence of squares laid out, Bedford Square being the first, where plots were leased out to speculative builders, their appearance having to conform to the uniform requirements of the lease. The whole estate was carefully managed through the leases, which were made to expire at different times, subverting plans for more radical change or sudden rent increases. Thus, despite its central location, there have been no great changes or decline and the estate has retained its appeal, attractiveness and value over a long period.

The London squares are modest in conception and do not rise to a great architectural climax. They are regular and uniform, linked together in any order. A French or German square would be expected to function as a monument to its absolutist rulers, 'whereas the English square on the contrary is merely a place where many people of the same class had their houses… These quarters are London's contribution to town planning in the eighteenth century' (Rasmussen, 1982, p. 199). They might be well described as monuments to pluralism.

Figure 2.4. *Bedford Square*. A town planning masterpiece, created in the eighteenth century by the Duke of Bedford's Estate.

Early nineteenth century speculative builders like Thomas Cubitt kept to the formula initiated after the Great Fire and perpetuated by the great estates. Cubitt built Belgravia, most of Eaton Square and Pimlico. He was well aware of the practical and aesthetic benefits of inserting garden squares into his new developments, starting with his first large development on the Bedford and Southampton Estates in Bloomsbury, and later with the Marquess of Westminster in Belgravia (Longstaffe-Gowan, *op. cit.*). The speculative estates were quickly successful and the builders, with their pattern book designs, moved on to Kennington, Stepney, Euston Road, Mile End and Stoke Newington. These relatively modest projects had gardens, wide streets and landscaped squares. The aim was to attract and retain good tenants over the long term, an objective which was supported by the system of leasing from ground landlords. As in the great estates, the ground landlords wanted long-term gains in property value alongside immediate rents, and this was secured by careful estate management and conservatism in style and layout. Thus much of Victorian London replicated its predecessor in Georgian London (Olsen, 1979).

A survey of surviving squares was carried out for the London County Council in 1905. It found that London had a grand total of 310 squares, covering 287 acres (116 ha) and in no less than 125 ownerships. British army officer and commentator on French life, Alexander Cavalié contrasted London favourably with Paris:

> How superior [London] is in public squares! The costly iron railings, the masterly statues that decorate some, and the pleasant shrubberies, smooth well-kept turf and well rolled walks which characterize most of them are nowhere to be seen in Paris. (Cavalie Mercer, quoted in Longstaffe-Gowan, *op. cit.*, p. 107)

## The Great Estates

The estates which brought so many squares into being are not remnants of history. They are living parts of the city and their policies remain largely intact. Any town planner would envy the power of the estates, which instead of selling their freehold interest or building on it themselves, chose to dispose of the land on long leases. The leaseholders erected buildings and kept them repaired, and when the leases expired the land and houses reverted to the landlord. From the seventeenth century to the nineteenth (and indeed beyond) the great estates combined the will to plan for the long term with the power and means to do so, controlling architecture, street plans, open space and zoning. Thus the estates prospered and remained intact as London itself prospered and expanded (Olsen, 1964).

In October 2013 the estates sponsored a revealing exhibition at the London Building Centre, celebrating their success, and raising their previously rather discreet profile. A map of the fifty-seven estates showed their remarkable concentration of ownership. In London's core area, bounded by Hyde Park, Euston Road, the Strand, and Grays Inn Road, more than 50 per cent of total site ownership appears to be in the hands of a small number of estates, notably Portman, Howard de Wald, Grosvenor, St. James, Regent Street, Bedford, the Foundling Hospital, Covent Garden, Soho and Conduit Mead. As the book which accompanied the exhibition drily noted: 'Where others come and go, the estates, with a commitment to long term success, are stewards of a great part of London' (Murray and Yates, 2013, p. 3).

The great estates fall into a number of categories. First and by far the most important are the old estates, which trace their origins back to the Reformation and the distribution of former church lands and properties to his friends by Henry VIII. The Crown Estate is older still. Its origins go back to 1066, when William the Conqueror assumed control of all the land in England in right of the Crown. Now managed under the terms of a 1961 Act the Crown Estate property portfolio is worth over £8bn. It has long-term ownership of properties around Regent's Park and is making a £1bn investment in Regent Street to cement its reputation as a world shopping centre. Since 2002 there has been 2 million square feet (185,600 m$^2$) of development behind the Regent Street façades and the frontages have attracted premium brands including Apple and Banana Republic, alongside English stalwarts like Burberry and Austin Reed. The investment has been carried out in partnership with Norway's sovereign wealth fund.

Almost as ancient are the landholdings of the City of London Corporation, where the post of City Surveyor, now with its thirty-fourth incumbent, stretches back to 1478. The Corporation owns 22 million square feet (2,043,900 m$^2$) of prime property, including the Barbican complex, which is a redevelopment of bomb damaged areas. Other ancient landowners' estates include the Duchy of Lancaster and the Duchy of Cornwall, the latter created in 1337 by the Black Prince Edward III to provide his heir with an independent source of income. It owns everything from office blocks to the Oval Cricket Ground. Of similar antiquity are the Mercers Company (1394), the Eton College Estate (1440), the Leathersellers Company (1444), the Skinners Company (1553), and the Portman Estate (1554).

Not all the estates are held for purely private gain and income; a good number channel their income into charitable causes, including Eton College, various naval charities, Dulwich School and Park, and biomedical research (the Welcome Foundation, which has purchased the Smith Charity Estate). But the larger estates are essentially commercial operations. The Bedford Estate, for example, has 200 buildings in Bloomsbury, where growing business income is anticipated given its proximity to King's Cross, the Eurostar terminal at St. Pancras, the Crossrail project, and potentially the High Speed Two terminal at Euston. Best known of the estates, and the one with the highest public profile, is the Grosvenor Estate, which is run on commercial lines and has extensive assets outside the capital, through the Grosvenor Group property company. The London landholdings are concentrated in Westminster, comprising a mix of office, residential and freehold residential properties in Mayfair and Belgravia. The long-term strategy is to manage these areas as high-quality places to live, work and visit, and Grosvenor has recognized the value of increased investment in the (privately owned) public realm.

Much less well known but of almost equal importance is the Howard de Walden estate, instrumental in the revitalization of Marylebone, where it owns 92 acres (37 ha). The estate was first acquired by the Duke of Newcastle in 1711 and has pioneered the art of place making, especially in its recent and adroit regeneration of Marylebone High Street. In 1995 a third of the High Street's shops were vacant or in temporary use. Management by the estate, post 1995, introduced a new range of retailers and 'anchor' tenants.

The great estates' historic run of success was not entirely unbroken. Things changed significantly in the early to mid twentieth century, when war, stagnant rents and high estate and death duties had an adverse impact. Some estates sold off tracts of land for development, or were subject to compulsory purchase for housing or education. From the 1960s onwards the Leasehold Reform Act gave residential tenants the right to buy freeholds. But this often prompted diversification and a more professional approach to management and development.

Figure 2.5. *Regent's Park*. A single exercise in urban design, with most of the façades around the park designed by John Nash; the park was the creation of the Crown Estate.

Royalty may never have re-planned London as a whole, but it did make one incomparable contribution to the city and to the wealth of the Crown Estate. In 1811 a large area of Marylebone Park reverted to the Crown. Here the Prince Regent and his civil servants John Fordyce and Sylvester Douglas saw an opportunity for change that would eclipse Napoleon, as well as the opportunity to maximize revenue for the Crown Estate at a time of royal extravagance and increased war expenditures. Both civil servants were engaged in the transformation of the Crown Estate into a modern government department. Fordyce sponsored the surveys which laid the groundwork for ultimate plans by architect John Nash (Longstaffe-Gowan, *op. cit.*). Work on Regent's Park started in 1811. Most of the façades around the Park were designed by Nash, so that the whole became a single exercise in urban design. Park Village was an extraordinary exercise in the picturesque, bringing villas and small cottages into what became the heart of the city. The terraces around the park were built with imposing frontages in the Palladian style (Sutcliffe, 2006).

In 1810 Nash presented his plans for Regent Street and a New Street Act was passed. Regent Street, an entirely new thoroughfare, was to be routed from the Palace to the Park, creating a sustained central spine for London. Yet even this project was not driven through the existing streets in the style of Haussmann's

Figure 2.6. *Langham Place.* It proved impossible to align the Crown Estate's plan for a new central spine for London; instead the street line was swung across and pieced together over the years.

Parisian boulevards. It follows the natural curve of division between Soho and Mayfair, seen by Nash as a natural division between areas occupied by the nobility and gentry and those of lesser status (Bell and Bell, 1972). Initial hopes of a straight-line route were abandoned; the cost proved too high. Instead the street was swung round at the southern end of Portland Street and in Regent Street itself and was pieced together in sections of different character over many years. Even here an absolutist writ did not run; yet that necessary twist in the road generates some masterly elements in subtle urban design.

## The New Great Estates

Alongside the historic great estates are the new estates, thirteen in number, ranging from Soho Estates through to Canary Wharf, Earls Court, Paddington Central and Broadgate. Many are owned by large property companies, such as British Land, Capital and Counties and Land Securities, and are the result of large-scale redevelopment. Some of this is still in progress on former brown field sites, released by the contraction of what Peter Hall referred to as London's 'goods handling' service sectors, especially former transport facilities. During the 1970s London lost 400,000 jobs in these economic sectors, as contraction occurred in the docks, in warehousing and in railway freight (Hall, 1989). Enormous tracts of land were released for redevelopment to cater for the needs of an expanding new 'information handling' economy.

The great estates legacy of high-quality residential environments has found recent application in the planning, redevelopment and management of large 'brown field' sites, such as King's Cross and the Queen Elizabeth Olympic Park. The same principles apply: managing the estate for the long term, not simply to provide short-term income; controlling the environment as a whole; focusing on a long-term master plan rather than on individual streets and buildings; creating an urban framework and sense of place; and providing holistic high-quality management. At King's Cross, for example, the developer Argent committed to long-term management, with stewardship at its core. At Broadgate, developer Stuart Lipton asked his architects to create a sense of place and the resulting open spaces like Broadgate Circle proved highly attractive to tenants.

King's Cross is one of the most interesting (and most recent) new estates, in large part constructed on disused railway yards. In the 1850s the Great Northern Railway built its London terminus at King's Cross. The area around it developed as an industrial district, later to become derelict as rail freight transport declined and then disappeared. A decision in 1996 to move the Channel Tunnel Rail Link terminus from Waterloo to St. Pancras, which lies adjacent to King's Cross (see Chapter 9), brought the landowners London and Continental Railways and Excel (now DHL) together. Argent was selected as the developer and the three organizations formed a joint venture, King's Cross Central Limited Partnership, which became the single landowner.

Figure 2.7. *King's Cross*. An entirely new district is being created by one of the 'new great estates' on a 67 acre (26 hectare) formerly disused site.

Across the 67 acre (26 ha) site, a new London district is being created, very much in the pattern of the older great estates, with 2000 homes, and 3.4 million square feet (315,900 m²) of work space. There will be 26 acres (10.5 ha) of public open space, and ten new public squares. Ten principles have been used to shape the master plan. Three are directly drawn from the historic approach of the great estates – creating a robust urban framework, committing to the long term, and making a lasting new place. An ownership structure is being created which will ensure that the development can be managed as a whole on the principles of good stewardship (King's Cross Central website).

Soho Estate has sometimes been described as the next great landed estate. It covers large parts of Soho's 87 acres (35 ha) and was created from the property acquisitions of the late Paul Raymond, a nightclub owner and entrepreneur. Raymond's Revuebar strip club opened in Soho in 1958 and he chose to invest his profits by buying up property within a five minute walk of his club. Acquired between the 1970s and the 1990s, at a time of relatively weak demand, the properties were bought from a wide variety of previous owners. On Raymond's death in 2008 the estate passed to his two granddaughters and in 2012 was valued in excess of £300 million.

Raymond bought properties purely to rent them out. He did not invest in the estate, concentrating his resources on further purchases. Most of the buildings date from between 1700 and 1850. There was substantial disrepair in the estate and the upper levels of many buildings were disused.

Figure 2.8. *Raymond Revue Bar Neon Sign*. The sign was reinstated by the late Paul Raymond's two granddaughters (pictured here), owners of Soho Estates, valued at £300 million in 2010.

Soho differs from other estates, and indeed many newer estates, in being founded on the acquisition of existing structures, rather than development land. The estate's strategy is now to enhance and add value to the building stock, through restoration and sometimes redevelopment. Keeping the 'edgy' character of Soho is a priority and the estate expects substantial increases in value from the construction of Crossrail. Recent projects have included major work to refurbish 76 Dean Street, a Georgian structure built in 1732 as the town house of the First Lord of the Fleet. In 2012 the estate acquired the old, and rabbit warren like, Foyles bookshop, which is to be redeveloped for a mix of uses, the bookselling relocated to a new building. It has plans for a £45 million project at Walkers Court, a narrow pedestrianized street, to include a restaurant, offices and the restoration of a theatre. Like the old estates Soho aims to manage its properties in a way which will secure a long-term future (Soho Estates website).

New and old estates have realized the importance of creating leisure destinations and attracting international brands, and of preserving and reusing historic and listed buildings, while bringing then up to modern standards of IT infrastructure. As the Great Estates exhibition book notes (slightly smugly perhaps):

The pressure to deliver quick results to the potential detriment of the longer term development of a company has become an entrenched feature of the UK business market ... the original estates provide a master class in corporate long termism and sustainability for the new estates. (Murray and Yates, *op. cit*, p. 14)

## Planning and Power

Government master planning for London has never been all powerful and rarely effective. Like Wren's proposals 300 years earlier, Abercrombie's road plans ran into the sand. They only succeeded outside London's urban area. Likewise his grand plans for creating parkway landscapes came to nothing. But his key regulatory proposal – the green belt – did work and it does today. The same is true of the building control system, which has its distant roots in the Great Fire Act. Initiative in creating green space and building environments which were valued came from beyond government; it came from the builders and the estates (including the Crown Estate of course).

Why was this so? Summerson has a simple explanation in his two foundation stones: taste and wealth. 'Taste', he says, 'reached London in 1615; taste that is in the exclusive, snobbish sense of the recognition of certain fixed values by certain people' (Summerson, 1988). It was a luxury import from Italy, received by a small number of noblemen and artists; people about the court had been to Italy and talked about the possibility of real Italian buildings being constructed in England. Inigo Jones became the architectural catalyst when he was appointed as Surveyor General to the King in 1615. It was Jones who initiated the London square at Covent Garden. All this, Summerson argues, was the foundation for two centuries of London taste. The basic principles prevailed and were understood before the great speculative building boom, and they shaped the activities of speculative builders such as the financier Nicholas Barbon. Thus received aristocratic taste, via the leasehold system, controlled wealth seeking and avarice.

Rasmussen has a more persuasive and historically sophisticated theory. Since the sixteenth century at least, power has never been absolutely centralized in Britain. In London it was divided between Parliament and the Crown, and powerful commercial elements in the City of London – the geographical separation of City and Westminster being hugely symbolic of this split. The merchant classes were made rich first by the wool trade, and later by banking. By the same token, Rasmussen argues, monarchs like Elizabeth I and Henry VIII never felt the urge or the need to assume absolute power. The Crown was happy to create new nobles, many of whom were recruited from the merchant classes. In the English Civil War it was the City which turned the scales in Cromwell's favour by financing the Parliamentary campaign. The British Empire was founded on the enterprise (as well as the slave trading, profiteering and piracy) of merchants and adventurers. Thus English government was less hierarchical and its rule less arbitrary, the course followed being influenced more by an association of merchants than governmental officials. The commercial City of London was the antithesis of Paris, the city of absolutism (Rasmussen, *op. cit.*).

It is a compelling argument, and one reflected by the facts, not least the evidence in bricks and mortar. The GLC's failure to drive through its motorways was foiled by a system of government which was less than absolute and arbitrary; the twentieth-century London motorway objectors had their parallels in the commercial interests who saw off Wren's grand designs and the private objectors who preserved the open spaces at Lincoln's Inn Fields. How strange to think that if Hitler's bombers had triumphed, and a successful invasion followed, Abercrombie's roads might have been implemented by a more disciplined and purposeful state machine. But this story has focused on London, Britain's capital and a unique case in so many respects. To what extent will we find its tale of failed government plans, clever improvisation, and dispersed initiative echoed in other places and other centuries?

## References

Barnett, C. (1996) *The Lost Victory: British Dreams, British Realities, 1945–1950*. Basingstoke: Macmillan.
Bell, C. and Bell. R. (1972) *City Fathers: The Early History of Town Planning in Britain*. London: Pelican.
Edgerton, D. (2011) *Britain's War Machine: Weapons, Resources and Experts in the Second World War*. Harmondsworth: Allen Lane.
Flyvbjerg, B., Bruzelius, N. and Rothengatter, W. (2003) *Mega Projects and Risk: An Anatomy of Ambition*. Cambridge: Cambridge University Press.
Hall, P. (1980) *Great Planning Disasters*. London: Weidenfeld and Nicolson.
Hall, P. (1989) *London 2001*. London: Routledge.
Hebbert, M. (1998) *London: More by Fortune than Design*. Chichester: Wiley.
Hennessy, P. (1990) *Whitehall*. London: Fontana.
King's Cross Central website (2013) http://www.kingscross.co.uk/.
Latham, R. and Matthews, W. (eds.) (1972) *The Dairy of Samuel Pepys*, Volume VII, 1666. London: George Bell.
Longstaffe-Gowan, T. (2012) *The London Square*. London: Yale University Press.
Murray, P. and Yates, S. (2013) *Great Estates: How London's Landowners Shape the City*. London: London New Architecture.
Nairn, I. (1966) *Nairn's London*. London: Penguin.
Olsen, D.J. (1964) *Town Planning in London: The Eighteenth and Nineteenth Centuries*. New Haven, CT: Yale University Press.
Olsen, D.J. (1979) *The Growth of Victorian London*. Harmondsworth: Penguin.
Pevsner, N. (1957) *The Buildings of England: London*, Volume 1. Harmondsworth: Penguin.
Rasmussen, S.E. (1982) *London: The Unique City*, revised edition. Cambridge, MA: MIT Press.
Soho Estates website (2013) http://www.sohoestates.co.uk/.
Summerson, J. (1988) *Georgian London*. London: Barrie and Jenkins.
Summerson, J. (1993) *Architecture in Britain 1530–1830*. New Haven, CT: Yale University Press.
Sutcliffe, A. (2006) *London: An Architectural History*. London: Yale University Press.
Taylor, A.J.P. (1975) *English History 1914–1945*. Harmondsworth: Penguin.
Ward, S. (1994) *Planning and Urban Change*. London: Paul Chapman Publishing.

# 3

# The Making of an English Landscape
## Capability Brown and the New Aesthetic

*The man of wealth and pride*
*Takes up a space that many poor supplied;*
*Space for his lake, his park's extended bounds,*
*Space for his horses, equipage and hounds;*
*The robe that wraps his limbs in silken cloth,*
*Has robbed the neighbouring fields of half their growth;*
*His seat, where solitary sports are seen,*
*Indignant spurns the cottage from the green.*

Oliver Goldsmith, *The Deserted Village*, 1770

Cutting a swathe from Birmingham to London through the heart of rural England and the Chiltern ridge, the M40 is one of the more recent British motorways. An observant traveller may be aware of the sensitivity with which it sits in the surrounding unspoiled landscape, so easily indeed that it almost feels as though the earthworks had been completed centuries before the road builders arrived. Long views from embankments or ridges are carefully preserved. There is no formal planting of individual trees or specimens, nor are there avenues. The trees are drawn from a small palette of native species, artfully arranged in small woodlands or clumps, and used to disguise bridges and intrusive structures. All is informal and naturalistic, so much so that the designer's skilful hand seems underplayed and deliberately understated. It is a tribute to the landscape architect's craft.

The skills and techniques on display here are part of Britain's unique contribution to landscape design, a contribution born of gradual evolution away from formal and symmetrical design towards a naturalistic and ideal landscape of trees, water and hill slopes. These concepts are recognized as: 'the one art that England has contributed to Europe since the Renaissance' (Dixon Hunt and Willis, 1975, p. xix) and 'England's greatest contribution to the visual arts' (Pevsner, quoted in Gregory *et al.*, 2013, p.1). They reached their climax in the energetic genius of British landscape designer Lancelot 'Capability' Brown, a man variously described as the Shakespeare of landscape design and 'a many sided genius not only in the practice of his art, but also in the management of men' (Hyams, 1971, p. 17).

Writing in the *Financial Times* in 2013, the landscape architect John Phibbs argued that the principles of landscape design practised by Brown, are visible, indeed ubiquitous, today. In Moscow the British consultants LDA Design, creators of London's Olympic Park, were brought in to lead on the £150 million restructuring of Gorky Park; here, Phibbs suggested, Brown's landscape style had acquired an unexpected and subversive political weight and its informality had become oddly attractive in today's Russia. 'There are no keep off the grass signs, no set places for walking, eating, music or riding in a Brown landscape' said Phibbs 'you may saunter over the grass or settle to have a picnic under the trees wherever and whenever you wish. In Brown's day this was a new freedom born of the English enlightenment, and with it came a certain humility. Brown's role was to tease out the capabilities of a place, rather than to impose his own ideas upon it' (Phibbs, 2013).

There is perhaps some element of adulation in this logic. Brown's landscapes were designed for his aristocratic clients and not the common herd. Yet there is truth in the argument too. These were not the imposed landscapes of a centralized state, but the creation of dispersed wealth, power and taste.

## Brown's Career and Contribution

Brown was born to humble origins in Northern England in 1716, the son of a Northumbrian farmer, and educated only until the age of sixteen. His career saw him reshaping and recontouring the English countryside on a colossal scale, with over 170 major commissions across the length and breadth of the country between 1751 and 1783 (Mowl, 2000). No less than 267 sites in England and Wales have been attributed to Brown (Gregory *et al.*, *op. cit.*). His personal connections developed steadily, achieving royal patronage, becoming a personal friend of King George III, and eventually arbitrating in political relationships.

Brown's formula was simple. He took a limited number of basic forms – the belt of trees on the estate perimeter, a semi natural series of clumps of forest trees, artfully disposed on wide expanses of turf, carefully graded slopes, and serpentine lakes. Though Brown planted huge numbers of indigenous trees, such as oak, elm and beech, he also made use of exotics, including American plane, cedar of Lebanon (his 'signature tree') and evergreen oak, as well as conifers such as Scots pine, spruce and larch (*ibid.*). Largely responsible for the widespread introduction of conifers into a British landscape (which had previously only had the yew as an evergreen species), Brown's same ideas were repeated on perhaps thousands of other estates by men he had trained, or by his many imitators (Mowl, *op. cit.*).

Brown's career as a landscape architect began with a stroke of luck. Having learned the basics of landscape gardening in his early career in northern England, he secured a job with Sir Richard Grenville of Wotton in Buckinghamshire. Grenville's son-in-law Lord Cobham needed someone to take charge of his kitchen garden and Brown got the job. In 1740, at the age of 24, he found himself working in Stowe (also in Buckinghamshire, and England's most famous garden) and for the greatest exponent of the new picturesque style of landscape gardening.

Successively Cobham had called in Charles Bridgeman, an early yet timid practitioner of the more informal landscape style, and William Kent, a leading exponent of picturesque and naturalistic landscapes. Kent's particular genius was

Figure 3.1. *Grecian Valley, Stowe, Buckinghamshire.* Brown used subtle planting to turn a slight undulation into the impression of an Arcadian Valley at Stowe, now a National Trust property.

to bring a painterly eye to garden design and to its integration with the natural landscape beyond. In a celebrated passage, Horace Walpole claimed that Kent was 'painter enough to taste the charms of the landscape, bold and opinionative enough to dare and dictate… He leaped the fence and saw that all nature was a garden' (Walpole, 1771, quoted in Dixon and Willis, 1975, p. 313). Brown learned at the feet of his master (of whom we shall hear more). Applying techniques learned from Kent, at Stowe Brown used subtle tree planting to brilliant effect to turn the slightest undulations in the landscape into the impression of an Arcadian valley.

Fortunately, Lord Cobham was a liberal employer and had no objection to Brown working for others. His first substantial commission came from the Duke of Grafton for his Wakefield estate, where Brown first used water in the manner learned from Kent. A long narrow lake was created in the valley and beyond it an expanse of lawns sweeping to the woods which surrounded the estate. Brown animated the landscape by improving the curves, bays and backwaters of the water body. At Wakefield he first adopted the 'wavy line of beauty'. Shores, woods and edges followed a serpentine line, and that line was extended into another dimension, as ground levels were subtly recontoured. Vistas too were carefully managed, and by the use of winding paths in woodlands Brown increased the apparent size of the estate. Unknowingly, Brown was reinventing the Chinese landscape style – an approach to landscape planning in which he was most unlikely to have had any previous experience. The Duke of Grafton was evidently a happy client, as further commissions followed from the Duke and others. Doubtless word of mouth recommendation circulated quickly in the House of Lords.

At Stowe and Wakefield, Brown made his first works of art. At Croome d'Abitot and Great Packington the mature forms emerged. Croome, laid out for the 6th Earl of Coventry, began as a more ornate 'Rococo' landscape but evolved into Brown's minimalist vision. Set low in a marshy valley with a low ridge to the north and limited vistas, Croome needed visual transformation. Brown heightened the low ridge with long belts of trees, including conifers. To draw the eye to this feature he demolished the existing church near the house and rebuilt it with a gothic tower up on the ridge. All the rest of Croome village was swept away in a clearance operation and the inhabitants rehoused in a new estate village (Brown was to make the social clearance for aesthetic purposes a common feature of his plans). To improve the west and north-west views, a long serpentine river was created to replace the marsh. At the northern tip it was expanded to form a lake. A gap to the north-west was filled with a clump of trees, followed in the 1760s by Robert Adam's Temple Greenhouse. Over the years an outer ring of vistas would be created.

At Great Packington in Warwickshire an original Rococo design was rejected in favour of Brown's concepts, extending the style developed at Croome. An existing pond was replaced by a long curling serpentine which effectively cut the park in half. At its eastern tip this disappeared from sight beyond a bridge, to suggest the continued existence of a broad river. Curving sweeps of woodland were introduced as belts around the northern edges of the park, almost all of the formal gardens of 1700 being destroyed. There was great potential for shooting, as enclosures had been skilfully created without the need for intrusive hedges. All was elegant, simple, naturalistic and uncluttered. Brown had seen his future; commissions in the same style followed at Kirtlington, Belhus, Burghley, Sherborne, Burton Constable, Longleat, Moor Park and Ragley.

Figure 3.2. *Croome Church, Worcestershire*. Brown heightened a low hill with belts of planting, demolishing the existing church and rebuilding a new tower on the ridge, the rest of the village being peremptorily cleared.

Figure 3.3. *Croome Landscape Park Lake*. Archetypal components of Brown's style: the serpentine lake and isolated Cedar.

It was the making (or remaking) of an English landscape, and would change the face of country estates, not to mention the appearance of botanic gardens and parklands, at home and abroad. None of Britain's many achievements in the visual arts is so original as the landscaped garden: 'Most of the styles which have affected British artists and architects had their origins elsewhere in Europe. But the landscaped garden was an entirely British invention' (Turner, 1985, p. 37). Brown's rules and methods were transmitted throughout the world, not least within the British Empire. They are seen reflected in the botanical gardens of Australia in Sydney and Melbourne, the Singapore Garden, the Kebun Reya in Java, Peradeniya near Kandy in Sri Lanka, in the gardens of the Villa Taranto in Italy, on the Huntington foundation in California, and in the Indian Botanic Garden at Howra on the Hooghly River (Hyams, *op. cit.*). Brown's influence is ubiquitous in the shapes of lakes, the slopes of grass and the placing of trees, and not just in Britain and its imperial possessions. The Russian Empress Catherine the Great wrote to Voltaire in 1772: 'I passionately love the English style, the curved lines, the gentle slopes, the ponds pretending to be lakes… I should say my Anglomania gets the better of planimetry' (quoted in Turner, *op. cit.*, p. 38).

Figure 3.4. *Peradeniya Royal Botanic Gardens, Sri Lanka*. Created by British colonialists, the lawns sweeping towards boundary woodlands and gently curving paths faithfully replicate Brown's formula.

William Cowper's poem, *The Task*, written in 1785 two years after Browns' death, captures the power and influence of Brown, the 'Omnipotent Magician', and his works:

He speaks. The lake in front becomes a lawn,
Woods vanish, hills subside, and valleys rise,
And streams, as if created for this use,
Pursue the track of his directing wand. (Cowper, quoted in Brown, 2011, p. 313)

## The Development of English Landscape Design

Brown may have been a genius, but he was no innovator. The concepts he employed came from others, now half-forgotten in the mists of landscape history. Brown was a populariser, a seller, an implementer of a new style of landscape and garden design which had emerged from earlier thinkers, artists, poets, eccentrics and designers, whose ideas simply came before their time. The new ideas of shaping places on a grand scale, integrating views and respecting the innate characteristics or *genius loci* of a place evolved slowly before they were accepted as conventional wisdom and implemented on a heroic scale.

In Tudor England the garden was simply an enclosed or self-contained area. Elaborate subdivisions of the square parterre gave rise to rectangular knot gardens defined by clipped box, lavender or other low evergreens. These design ideas – of nature controlled and contained – were ancient in origin and can be traced back to Moorish Spain and even Rome, where the garden was seen as a setting for social intercourse or solitary recreation, much like a sitting room, living room or reception room in a palace, villa or cottage (Hyams, *op. cit.*). The concepts were carried over into Elizabethan England, where garden design remained highly elaborate.

But an aesthetic counter attack was launched in the seventeenth century, the opening shots being fired by the philosopher Francis Bacon. In his essay 'On Gardens' Bacon decried Elizabethan knot gardens as 'toys' and recommended a more informal approach:

Whatsoever forme you cast it into; first it be not too busie and full of work. Wherein I, for my part, doe not like images cut out in juniper and other garden stuff; they be for children. (Bacon, 1625)

Bacon went on to devote one-third of his essay to the case for wilderness in garden design – an idea that lay on stony ground until the eighteenth century. Gardens, it seemed, remained rather treeless places. In England and France alike, topiary remained the main garden component. Le Notre had turned the use of topiary and the articulated shaping of garden materials into an art form, using green sculpture skilfully as punctuation rather than as ornament. Although in

France, the landscape architect Brenda Colvin noted: '... we do not hear of those huntsmen, hounds and horses cut out in box, nor of the sermon on the mount with Christ and the multitude in yew which adorned some English gardens of the period' (Colvin, 1948, p. 30).

Soon enough, the dictates of cold economics and pragmatic estate management would underpin the new philosophy of design. Fear of timber and fuel shortages had led, in 1544, to the first of several statutes aimed at preventing the felling of forest areas. Standard trees were to be left in each acre of land cleared. In Scotland the timber shortage had become acute earlier and Acts were passed in 1457 requiring tenants to plant trees. The Scots resisted this, and were it not for the later plantings by the government Forestry Commission Scotland would remain relatively treeless today (*ibid.*). And there was, of course, one crucial later influence: the development of new agricultural systems was more productive, profitable and flexible than the old strip farming system, generating the returns to individual landowners that would finance new landscapes of status and leisure. All would form the context for a new approach to landscape design and estate management amongst the land-owning aristocracy.

The case for planting trees was persuasively set out by the diarist, Cavalier courtier and melancholic son of the squire of Wotton in Surrey, John Evelyn. A four month visit to Holland in 1641 had left Evelyn with an admiration of the order of Dutch towns, and in particular their practice of planting rows of lime trees. In his book *Sylva, or A Discourse of Forest-Trees and the Propagation of Timber in His Majesty's Dominions*, Evelyn converted the English gentry from their love of flowers and topiary to a more profitable and utilitarian interest in planting trees. In so doing he began to change the face of England's great estates (Mowl, *op. cit.*). This essentially pragmatic and not untypical British interest in monetary returns would form a comfortable alliance with four aesthetic currents: the philosopher Francis Bacon; the poets John Milton and Alexander Pope; growing interest in Chinese landscape aesthetics; and the Mediterranean fantasy landscapes of the artists Claude and Nicolas Poussin.

Milton's conception of Eden or 'delicious paradise' took up Bacon's concept of wilderness:

> Of a steep wilderness; whose hairie sides
> With thicket overgrown, grottesque and wilde,
> Access deni'd: and over head upgrew
> Insuperable highth of loftiest shade,
> Cedar, and pine, and fir, and branching palm,
> A silvan scene, and as the ranks ascend
> Shade above shade – a woodie theatre. (Milton, 1667)

Pope's views were more vitriolic than lyrical. Keen gardener, poet, literary genius and celebrity of his time, he ridiculed the symmetrical and formal garden style in a celebrated essay in *The Guardian*[1] in 1713: 'We seem to make it our study to recede from nature … into the most regular and formal shapes … and are better pleased to have our trees in the most awkward figures of men and animals than in the most regular of their own' (Pope, 1713). His later 'Epistle to Lord Burlington' attacked symmetry and punctured the pride of landowners with previously fashionable terraces and formality:

> Grove nods at grove, each ally has a brother,
> And half the platform just reflects the other
> The suff'ring eye inverted nature sees,
> Tress cut to statues, statues thick as trees. (Pope, 1731)

The virtues in wilderness and informality espoused by Bacon and Milton, and Pope's utter dismissal of formality, found a strange echo in esoteric interest in Chinese landscape philosophy and a concept known as *sharawadgi*. Sir William Temple, philosopher and Whig politician, had learned, partly from intelligent observation of Chinese porcelain and lacquer work, but mainly from contemporary travel books, that the Chinese had a completely different aesthetic of landscape design from that practised in Europe.

In an essay published in 1692 Temple suggested that the Chinese scorned symmetry as the basis for aesthetic appeal. He argued that the Chinese had contrived a different landscape aesthetic 'where the beauty shall be great, and strike the eye, but without any order or disposition of the parts that shall be easily or commonly observed … where they find it hit their eye at first sight they say the *sharawadgi* is fine or admirable' (Temple, 1692). Joseph Addison, writing in 1712, echoed Temple's insight, attacking formal gardens and speaking of the desirable irregularity of Chinese gardens: the Chinese, he said, 'laugh at the plantations of our Europeans which are laid out by the rule and line' (Addison, 1712). Just as England was happily spared the absolutism of French politics, Addison believed its garden design should also be cleared of the orderly and prescriptive designs that mirrored this absolutism.

Little more was heard of Chinese gardens, and the word *sharawadgi* did not enter eighteenth century vocabulary. Hyams is doubtful about the impact of these ideas. He suggests that the early English love of nature simply reflects their climatically and topographically gentle land where nature was less the enemy of civilization and more its friend: 'In European culture the English were the first to conceive a love of nature… What was liked was nature's sweet disorder, and beneath that her very subtle order' (Hyams, *op. cit.*, p. 5).

The significance of Chinese aesthetics is open to debate. Yet one thing is certain: the way had been opened for painting to influence landscape design, for European landscape painters such as Claude and Poussin had (perhaps unknowingly) practised Chinese principles, and their influence on the aesthetic taste of landowners, partly through the grand tour, was to prove considerable.

## William Kent and the Arcadian Picturesque

Nowhere was the impact of landscape painting more significant than in the life and work of William Kent (later to be Brown's master) and his close friend and patron, Richard Boyle, 3rd Earl of Burlington and 4th Earl of Cork, Lord High Treasurer of Ireland and Lord Lieutenant of the West Riding of Yorkshire. Kent, ten years Burlington's senior, was his architect, designer, painter and gardener. The odd couple lived together in the same houses for almost thirty years, from 1719 to Kent's death in 1748, without it seems any hint of homosexual attachment. Burlington and his wife had three daughters; Kent left most of his money to the actress Elizabeth Butler and her children, who are reasonably believed to be his.

It was Kent who carried forward the innovations of Pope and Bridgeman, in creating the Arcadian picturesque. In 1716, when Burlington had started his work on the transformation of gardens at Chiswick, Kent was still studying to be a painter in Rome. There is little doubt his early career as a painter influenced his landscape concepts. After his death thirty landscape paintings were found in his studio, including works by Claude, Poussin, and Salvator Rosa. Colvin (*op. cit.*) suggests that Kent's studies in Italy had impressed him with the effects of light and shade created by trees in Italian gardens and this led him to see the potential of tall forest trees in an English setting. There is certainly an uncanny similarity between the templed Arcadian landscapes created by Kent and the paintings of Poussin.

Burlington had visited Rome on his grand tour in 1714–1715, and may have met Kent at this time. At any rate Burlington returned to England in 1715 with a strong drive to recreate the landscapes of antiquity in England, experimenting first at his home in Chiswick. On a second Italian visit Burlington had met Kent in Genoa, sending him on to Paris. Through the 1720s Kent still saw himself as a painter, whilst Burlington had begun to explore new themes in garden design in Chiswick, creating a heavily templed garden. When Kent took over its strategic direction in 1733 five acres was landscaped and four left as a virtually untouched wilderness. These five landscaped acres, a simple *Rus in Urbe* in the capital, made Kent's reputation. It was Kent, as we have seen, who played a central part in transforming Stowe, preparing the way for his follower Capability Brown to evolve a simpler style with fewer or no ornamental structures.

Thus in eighteenth century England a wholly new approach to landscape planning and landscape aesthetics (new, that is, to European minds) seems to have evolved and been accepted. The new tastes had a strange resonance with political ideas, individual liberties and freedom of thought. Innovation in design was acceptable and widespread. New ideas were not derided. The poets and writers who had helped to make the change referred to the delights of disorder. It was the antithesis to the rule of kings, which had disappeared in the Glorious Revolution of 1688. The wealth and power which funded the projects and led to the diffusion of new ideas, was dispersed amongst a coherent, yet individualistic, aristocracy.

## The Clients

Brown's clients were landowners whose wealth was increasing quickly as an agricultural and commercial revolution was taking shape. Some have suggested that national insecurity in the face of threats from abroad was a driving force for the creation of the English landscape style; the wealthy were driven to acquire, fence and beautify a patch of England in case the great world became too unbearable (Brown, *op. cit.*). Mowl (*op.cit.*) agrees that the landscape style was led by the aristocracy and especially by members of the House of Lords. British democracy, he argues, had been created over the 400 years since the dissolution of the monasteries by the long and skilful retreat of the House of Lords. For fifty years, from 1660 to 1710, the professional gardeners and designers ruled, expressing the political theory of the divine right of kings and an orderly authoritarian state by designs of regularity and axial unity. Yet by the second and third decades of the eighteenth century a reaction set in, and the result was the emergence of the English pastoral arcadia.

Turner (*op. cit.*) echoes these views. During Brown's lifetime Britain had enjoyed a period of stability and tranquillity not disturbed until the Napoleonic Wars. Socially and politically the country was dominated by a small aristocracy under whose power and patronage civil and personal liberties increased, toleration and wealth grew, and literature and the arts flourished. In Christopher Hussey's words: 'Where the seventeenth century had tried to impose autocratic patterns on an expanding world, the empirical English revolution found that the rational way to resolve the polarities confronting the Age lay in comprehending them' (Hussey, quoted in Turner, *op. cit.*, p. 13).

It was during this period that the office of Prime Minister was invented, as the role and powers of the monarchy shrivelled. Thus the great houses and estates of the aristocracy took over from the Court as dispersed centres of pleasure, politics, patronage and learning. The politics of toleration was central to the philosophy of John Locke, who believed that it was natural for men to live together peacefully, without the need or desire for an absolute ruler. Property was central to Locke's political philosophy and is the chief reason for the institution of civil government: 'The great and chief end of men uniting into commonwealths is the preservation of their property; to which in the state of nature there are many things wanting' (Locke, quoted in Russell, 1961, p. 604).

The landowners were important at local level and indeed at national level, where their influence was even stronger, through an overwhelming dominance of Parliament in the Commons, and in the House of Lords. About 400 families could be described as great landlords. Royal patronage and gift was no longer an easy route to power and land, as it had been in the past. For those without a landed inheritance the route to the top lay in outstanding achievement, either in commerce, the law or the military.

Political power, thought and influence is one thing. A parallel, simpler and perhaps more persuasive explanation is simply the scale of growing wealth, especially amongst the landowning classes. As the obstacles to enclosure were removed, the agricultural boom of the late seventeenth and the eighteenth century rebounded to the benefit of big landowners and capitalist farmers, not the peasant proprietors (Hill, 1969). The landscaped park was an indulgent, yet practical, status symbol. A modern scholar, Anne Bermingham, argues persuasively that as the enclosed agricultural landscape began to look increasingly artificial, like a garden, so the garden began to look increasingly natural: 'Thus a natural landscape became the prerogative of the estate, so that nature was the sign of property' (Bermingham, quoted in Gregory *et al*., *op. cit*., p. 24).

The great landowners had triumphed politically as well as economically. They could afford long-term planning and investment. Thomas Coke II of Holkham in Norfolk, for example, was able to raise the rents on his estate (landscaped by William Kent and possibly Capability Brown) from £2,220 in 1776 to £20,000 in 1816 (Turner, *op. cit*.). In the words of E.P. Thompson: 'The eighteenth century gentry made up a superbly successful and confident capitalist class. They combined in their style of living, features of an agrarian and urban culture'. Demonstrating a profoundly capitalist style of thought they were, 'zestfully acquisitive and meticulous in attention to accountancy … laissez faire emerged not as the ideology of some manufacturing lobby but in the great agricultural Corn Belt. Adam Smith's argument in the Wealth of Nations is derived very largely from agriculture' (Thompson, quoted in Hill, *op. cit*., p. 268). Profits from commerce also found their way into the land. Reflecting the peace and stability of the age, the English banking system grew steadily, creating new fortunes for bankers, such as Henry Hoare, who made his great landscaped estate at Stourhead in Wiltshire (Turner, *op. cit*.).

Capability Brown had the skills, managerial ability, good fortune and access to resources to implement the new ideas on a wide scale. His landscapes reflected wealth, and a distinctively English taste and intellectual outlook, little reflected in continental Europe. Dispersed private wealth proved conducive to originality, individualism, free thinking, and sometimes sheer eccentricity.

And there is a strange twist to the plot; for some of the new landscapes clearly had iconographic as well as aesthetic significance. Brown had learned his craft at Stowe and in many respects the landscape there, with its built and sculptural components, created by and for a family of eighteenth century Whigs, was intended to convey a specific political message. It has been described as a philosophic or political manifesto on the ground, and in this sense was not unlike the gardens created by the Emperor Hadrian at Tivoli (Bevington, 2011). Allegiance to the Hanoverian regime was demonstrated by a statue of King George I, followed by statues of the Prince and Princess of Wales.

Figure 3.5. *Temple of British Worthies, Stowe Landscape Park*. Landscape as iconography: the Temple of British Worthies included busts of Shakespeare, Milton, Newton, and Locke, being figures revered by the Whig establishment.

During the 1720s an eclectic combination of buildings was added; a Temple of Honour celebrating eight British Worthies; a Temple of Ancient Virtue; and statues of the seven Saxon Gods who gave their names to the days of the week. Appropriately perhaps the worthies were later relocated into part of the estate known as the Elysian Fields. By this stage, ideas that had been added piecemeal, without coherent thought, were being used as a key focus both for landscape design and iconography. When heroic figures were chosen for the Temple of Ancient Virtue, it was to Greece rather than Rome they turned, for the record of Roman rule recalled imperialism and tyranny, and thus French and Stuart despotism (Bevington, *op. cit.*). Thus the new English landscape both reflected and transmitted its underlying political values.

## Planning Style or Historical Vignette?

Were these great British plans? They seem to have very many of the required characteristics. The scale of intervention was simply enormous. Landscapes were reshaped, replanned and replanted, and communities relocated, often with brutal disregard to their wishes. There was innovation, improvisation and utter originality as a new style and aesthetic was born – one which would have lasting impact. Plans and decisions were not controlled by a centralized bureaucracy, a monarch or a despot, but dispersed amongst the great landlords, each with an independent power base and independent means. New ideas flowed through and developed within a network of enlightened patrons; they were not imposed from above.

During his lifetime Brown's work was eulogized by clients and critics alike. A decade after his death it came under attack from the 'Picturesque' theorists. His reputation was at a low ebb in the nineteenth century, as geometric features and tastes for a wilder nature came into fashion (Gregory *et al.*, *op. cit.*). Yet (as we learned in Chapter 1) tastes and values change from generation to generation. In 1950 Dorothy Stroud published a ground-breaking study on Brown, leading the re-evaluation of his work (Stroud, 1950). Today Brown's landscapes are respected if not revered and his approach is still regarded as a model for new landscapes, both private and municipal, in Britain and throughout the world. But all this happened so long ago, and under a distribution of power and client resources which seems part of a distant past. Is it truly characteristic of a British planning style – or simply a fascinating, yet ultimately esoteric, historical vignette? As this story unfolds an answer will be found.

## Note

1.   *The Guardian* was a short-lived newspaper published from 12 March to 1 October 1713.

## References

Addison, J. (1712) Paper in the Spectator, No. 414, 25 June 1712, quoted in Dixon Hunt, J. and Willis, P. (eds.) (1975) *The Genius of the Place: The English Landscape Garden 1620–1820*. London: Paul Elek, p. 142.

Bacon, F. (1625) Of Gardens, quoted in Dixon Hunt, J. and Willis, P. (eds.) (1975) *The Genius of the Place: The English Landscape Garden 1620–1820*. London: Paul Elek, p. 54.

Bevington, M. (2011) *Stowe: The People and the Place*. Swindon: The National Trust.

Brown, J. (2011) *The Omnipotent Magician: Lancelot 'Capability' Brown 1716–1783*. London: Chatto and Windus.

Colvin, B. (1948) *Land and Landscape*. London: John Murray.

Dixon Hunt, J. and Willis, P. (eds.) (1975) *The Genius of the Place: The English Landscape Garden 1620–1820*. London: Paul Elek.

Gregory, J., Spooner, S. and Williamson, T. (2013) *Lancelot 'Capability' Brown: A Research Impact Review* Prepared for English Heritage by the Landscape Group, University of East Anglia, Research Report Series no. 50-2013, London: English Heritage.

Hill, C. (1969) *Reformation to Industrial Revolution*. Harmondsworth: Penguin.

Hyams, E. (1971) *Capability Brown and Humphrey Repton*. London: Dent.

Milton, J. (1667) *Paradise Lost*, Book IV, quoted in Dixon Hunt, J. and Willis, P. (eds.) (1975) *The Genius of the Place: The English Landscape Garden 1620–1820*. London: Paul Elek, p. 79.

Mowl, T. (2000) *Gentlemen Gardeners: The Men Who Created the English Landscape Garden*. Stroud: The History Press.

Phibbs, J. (2013) Global Capability. *Financial Times*, 25/26 May 2013.

Pope, A. (1713) Essay from *The Guardian*, quoted in Dixon Hunt, J. and Willis, P. (eds.) (1975) *The Genius of the Place: The English Landscape Garden 1620–1820*. London: Paul Elek, p. 207.

Pope, A. (1731) An Epistle to Lord Burlington, quoted in Dixon Hunt, J. and Willis, P. (eds.) (1975) *The Genius of the Place: The English Landscape Garden 1620–1820*. London: Paul Elek, p. 213.

Russell, B. (1961) *A History of Western Philosophy*, 2nd ed. London: George, Allen & Unwin.

Stroud, D. (1950) *Capability Brown*. London: Faber.

Temple, W. (1692) Upon the Gardens of Epicurus; or, Of Gardening in the Year, 1685, quoted in Dixon Hunt, J. and Willis, P. (eds.) (1975) *The Genius of the Place: The English Landscape Garden 1620–1820*. London: Paul Elek, p. 99.

Turner, R. (1985) *Capability Brown and the Eighteenth-Century English Landscape*. New York: Rizzoli.

Walpole, H (1771) *The History of the Modern Taste in Gardening*, quoted in Dixon Hunt, J. and Willis, P. (eds.) (1975) *The Genius of the Place: The English Landscape Garden 1620–1820*. London: Paul Elek, p. 313.

# 4

# Urban Pastoral
## The Building of Birkenhead Park

*'It must be evident that it is the first importance to their health on their day of rest to enjoy the fresh air and to be able to walk out in decent comfort with their families; if deprived of any such resource it is probable that their only escape from the narrow courts and alleys will be those drinking shops where in short-lived excitement they may forget their toil, but where they waste the means of their families and too often destroy their health... Whether this neglect of what would appear to be a duty of government ... your Committee will not presume to determine'*

*Report from the Select Committee on Public Walks, 1833*

By common consent New York has one of the greatest parks in the world: 'a skinny streak of surrogate nature set into the rectilinear grid of Manhattan... It remains a paradigm' (Tate, 2001, p. 144). Begun in 1856, it is the first purpose built, publicly financed, landscaped public park in North America, setting the model in design and management for thousands of lesser American parks. Yet Central Park is more than a great example of landscape design. Like the Statue of Liberty, it is an icon of American cultural life. When the park opened in 1858, wealthy and middle-class New Yorkers flocked to its paths, concerts and skating lakes. It was (and remains) something of an elite park; poorer citizens preferred more commercial and less regulated pleasure gardens. The poet Walt Whitman noted the carriage parade of New York's wealthy in 1874, much as Woody Allen's metropolitan intelligentsia pondered the meaning of life here in 'Hannah and Her Sisters' (Rosenweig and Blackmar, 1992). In North America Central Park gave birth to the concept of public land, to the profession of landscape architecture and to 'American Pastoral' landscape style (Tate, *op. cit.*). American Pastoral in turn became the ironic title of Philip Roth's searing novel of a shattered American dream (1997).

## New York follows Birkenhead

The pressure to build the park came from New York's wealthiest men and women; their aim was to boost the city's international status and cosmopolitan image. Prominent landowners believed that a park would increase property values and the park's proposers claimed that it would serve the needs of New York's citizens as a whole. Thus, after a three year debate, the city authorities took possession of more than 800 acres (324 ha) of land. It was an extraordinary intervention in market economics, paving the way for future involvement in city planning and urban redevelopment.

Central Park's plan was selected from a design competition in October 1857. The Board of Commissioners for Central Park had offered prizes of four hundred to two thousand dollars for the four best proposals, with the winning design coming from the American designer Frederick Law Olmsted, and his much lesser known, yet equally important partner, the English architect Calvert Vaux. Everyone has heard about Central Park and many have heard of Olmsted. Few know that in concept, in design, and in principle, Central Park owes much to the plan for an almost unknown British predecessor, Birkenhead Park.

Figure 4.1. *Lake, Central Park New York*. Surrogate nature set in the rectilinear grid of Manhattan. (*Photo*: CC Ed Yourdon)

The echoes occur on so many levels. In design ethos Olmsted and Vaux's 'Greensward' plan for Central Park is heavily influenced by Paxton's plan for Birkenhead, a romantic and naturalistic vision which he in turn had absorbed from the English landscaped country estates (explored in Chapter 3). Most newspapers and politicians wanted European models; all agreed that Central Park should measure up to European standards to reflect the city's cosmopolitan progress. New York's elite evidently wanted an apparently boundless rural landscape, broad expansive and tranquil, rather than a formal pattern of planting – perhaps it resonated with New Yorkers of English descent. The Commissioners proposed inviting the superintendent of Birkenhead Park to advise the Board (in the event it was not taken up). Both Olmsted and Vaux were influenced by English landscape traditions and values. Vaux (who drew the prize-winning plan and provided the artists' impressions) supported the aesthetic values of well-balanced irregularity. Like Ruskin he believed that a skilled craft worker could express artistic inspiration. Olmsted had read Ruskin's *Modern Painters*, as well as literature on English landscape gardening, admiring the harmonious composition of English design (Rosenweig and Blackmar, *op. cit.*).

A walk around Central Park quickly reveals its debt to Birkenhead. Though the scale is so much bigger than Birkenhead, all the motifs are there: the curving paths, the mature trees set in grasslands, the sense of rurality deep in the city, the serpentine edges and lakes, the views through trees to water and the occasional urban intrusions from tall buildings (not so much in Birkenhead of course). The Swiss pagoda bridge and the boathouse in Birkenhead have more elegance than New York's Belvedere. But the exclusion of traffic by the short connecting tunnels, planted over bridges and underpasses is a triumph. A sponsored bench bears the inscription: 'Here nature is teacher'. There is indeed much 'relaxed

Figure 4.2. *Central Park Users*. Central Park's Literary Walk is a more formal element, found only on the edges of Birkenhead Park.

management', in Central Park (overgrown weeds and patches of undergrowth). But this is not nature, it is artifice.

Oddly, New York seems reticent to acknowledge its debt to Birkenhead, at least in public. A lavish book, written by the Park's official historian, includes no references to Paxton or Birkenhead. Misleadingly, Kenneth Jackson's preface claims: 'There were attractive parks in London and Paris and Copenhagen … but these open spaces had originally been assembled for monarchs and their invited guests. What made Central Park different was that it was the first grand public open space that had been intentionally set aside for the ordinary public in a prosperous and ambitious city' (Jackson, 2003, p. 6).

In truth, Olmsted had visited England, seen Birkenhead Park, and told a different story: 'Gardening here has reached a perfection which I have never before dreamed of … we came to an open field of clean bright green sward, closely mown, on which a large tent was pitched and a party of boys and a party of gentlemen in another part were playing cricket. Beyond this was a large meadow with rich groups of trees, under which a flock of sheep were reposing… Large valleys were made verdant, extensive drives arranged, plantations, clumps and avenues of trees formed'. Olmsted was equally, if not more, impressed by the park's wide and democratic appeal: 'There were some who were attended by servants … but a large proportion were of the common ranks and a few women with children or suffering from ill health were evidently the wives of very humble labourers… All this magnificent pleasure ground is entirely, unreservedly and forever the people's own' (Olmsted, quoted in McInness, 1984, p. 42).

Olmsted's sense of astonishment came not simply from the design, but from the mere fact of Birkenhead Park's existence. Here was the world's first public park, created for the public, and with public money. The plan was at once an urban, landscape, social, and political innovation of the first order, and would change the form of cities across the world and through the centuries. How had it come about? And why had Britain and Birkenhead led the way?

## Birkenhead's Astonishing Rise

Today Birkenhead is an undistinguished northern English town, forever in the shadow of its big and powerful neighbour Liverpool, just across the Mersey estuary. Yet in the nineteenth century it was a place to be reckoned with. By 1845 it was a booming wonder town; a sonnet in the *Illustrated London News* began:

> Another glory on the Mersey's side
> A town springs up as from a noble wand
> Behold these noble docks – the merchants' pride
> And the fair park extending o'er the strand.
> (Anon, quoted in Pevsner and Hubbard, 1971, p. 77)

Two years later Benjamin Disraeli, novelist and British Prime Minister could not contain the sweep of history:

> London is a modern Babylon; Paris has aped imperial Rome, and may share its catastrophe. But what do the sages say to Damascus? It had municipal rights in the days God conversed with Abraham… As yet the disciples of progress have not exactly been able to match this instance of Damascus, but it is said that they have great faith in the future of Birkenhead. (Disraeli, quoted in *ibid.*, p. 75)

The rise of Birkenhead was inseparably connected to the rise of Liverpool. Between 1801 and 1911 Liverpool's population grew at a phenomenal rate, from 89,100 to 1,150,600 (Lawton and Lee, 2002). Birkenhead, across the estuary, was at first insulated from the pressures of growth. The estuary was too wide to bridge and ferry services across its difficult tidal waters were unreliable and unpleasant, and it remained a rural hamlet with only 110 residents in 1801.

The new technology of steam-powered ferries, introduced in the 1820s, changed the town's fortunes. Money poured into Birkenhead, led by speculative investment by Richard Price (Lord of the Manor of Birkenhead) and then by William Laird, a Scot who had purchased land from Price and set up boiler works and a thriving shipbuilding yard. It was Laird who brought in James Gillespie Graham, an Edinburgh architect, to draw up a master plan for the town's expansion, based on his work laying out the lower new town of Edinburgh for the Scottish aristocracy. Graham's ambitious gridiron plan, based on long wide avenues, survives today, but with the solitary exception of Hamilton Square, the Georgian town houses never arrived. Birkenhead's street tramway system – the first in the world – opened in August 1860. It was the brainchild of George Francis Train, an American entrepreneur, whose colourful life had seen him announce his candidature for the US presidency, travel the world in 80 days (thus inspiring Jules Verne) and jailed for obscenity. Though Birkenhead's fortunes dipped in the 1860s, by 1901, underpinned by the trams, the steam ferries, and a new railway tunnel to Liverpool, its population stood at 110,915 (Brocklebank, 2003).

Growth on this scale was the essential crucible for innovation, for independent wealth and confidence, and for rapid urban change. The creation of Birkenhead Park must be seen in this context, and indeed in the context set by national reformers and the urban parks movement in Britain.

## Reforming the City of Dreadful Night

The explosive growth of Birkenhead and Liverpool was repeated throughout the nineteenth century in Britain. Between 1801 and 1881 Bristol grew from 61,000 to 307,000; Birmingham from 71,000 to 401,000; Manchester and Salford from 89,000 to 517,000; London from 1,008,000 to 3,881,000 (Conway, 1991). In their wake came great sources of new independent wealth – and initiative. Equally there came problems of air pollution, poor sanitation, risk of epidemics, social unrest and crime – problems which posed threats to the lives and health of the middle and upper classes as much as the lower orders. Describing the nineteenth-century slums as 'the city of dreadful night', Hall uses graphic contemporary accounts to underline his point. Working-class areas in the early Victorian city were often squalid, the morals and health of its inhabitants shocking, with the middle classes in constant fear of the mob (Hall, 1988). The response was a slow process of improvement, driven by social reformers, triggered by Parliamentary regulation and legislation, and taken forward by local government.

For parks and open spaces the reformer's Bible was the Report of the Select Committee on Public Walks (SCPW, 1833), which had emphasized the need for open space and the problem of working class recreation.

Until towns grew in size there was little need to provide space specifically for recreation. The marketplace, the churchyard and adjoining spaces like commons provided sufficient public space. But as population and urban areas grew, informal open space for recreation became correspondingly less accessible. Manchester's problem was well summarized in a letter to the Committee's Chairman from Dr John Kay, a leading reformer:

> Healthful exercise in the open air is seldom taken by the artisans of this town, and their health certainly suffers considerable depression from this deprivation. One reason for this state of the people is that all scenes of interest are remote from the town... I need not inform you how sad is our labouring population here. (SCPW, 1833, p. 5)

Part of the argument for creating parks was the belief that the labouring classes had easy access to the wrong sort of facilities, and that proper recreation should have an uplifting or improving tone, rather than an association with sexual licence, the consumption of alcohol and the misuse of animals. People should use their time in creative and productive ways. 'The cost of one singing master' said one ardent Christian reformer, 'will be a hundred fold compensated for by the means it will give the children of doing something better for amusement than pitch and toss, the roaring of obscene songs, and the torturing of little animals' (A. Lewis, 1871, quoted in Conway, *op. cit.*, p. 30).

The lower orders were not entirely without space for outdoor recreation. Pleasure gardens, where an entry fee was charged, first arose in London, Bath and Cheltenham, some evolving from tavern gardens. The most famous was London's Vauxhall Gardens, which by the 1830s included theatres, supper rooms, walks and gardens, a grand moving panorama (covering 7,000 square metres of canvas), a Battle of Waterloo spectacle, and Greek and Roman chariot races (*ibid.*). It sounded like fun, and for the reformers that was the whole problem: they saw it as a scene of disgraceful licentiousness, and a meeting place for drunks, prostitutes and criminals. The Committee was much taken by the experience of continental towns, concluding (perhaps on rather thin evidence) that people on the continent were healthier and more content than the English because of the existence of better parks.

There was no doubt that the Report had drawn Parliament's attention to the problem, but it was far from clear who might translate intentions into action. In Manchester, for example, no progress had been made by government in the provision of parks, and the task thus fell to the local community (Chadwick, 1966). John Claudius Loudon wrote in 1835: 'Public gardens are just beginning to be thought of in England; and, like most other great domestic improvements in our country, they have originated in the spirit of the people, rather than in that of government. On the continent the opposite has usually been the case...' (Loudon, quoted in Chadwick, *op. cit.*, p. 52). For much of the early nineteenth century local authorities were seriously inhibited by existing (and often restrictive) legislation. Even in 1860 legislation continued to emphasize the role of private benefactors as providers of parks. Post 1860 the authorities' position was strengthened, especially by the Public Improvements Act, which gave them the power to acquire, hold and manage open spaces out of the rates (Conway, *op. cit.*).

## Local Initiative

Thus the stage was set for municipal initiative, and it soon came in many towns and cities. Several places are contenders for the title of first public park; a good case might be made for the Derby Arboretum, for example. Yet the Derby Arboretum was created on land donated by a benefactor, its management remained with independent Trustees, and it was maintained by subscriptions. Birkenhead's development was authorized by Act of Parliament (Birkenhead's Second Improvement Act of 1843), its construction costs were met entirely from public funds, and it was designed explicitly for public use. When it was officially opened by Lord Morpeth on Easter Monday, 5 April 1847, Birkenhead Park became the first public park in the world (Lee, 2013).

The Park was first advocated in 1841 by Isaac Holmes, a Liverpool councillor who was a member of the Birkenhead Improvement Commission. A Bill was promoted in 1842 to enable the Commissioners to buy land for the recreation of inhabitants and for subsequent conveyances to individuals, who purchased plots around the park for the development of villas (Lee, *op. cit.*). The Commissioners purchased 91 hectares of swampy low-lying land for the park, of which 51 hectares was to be retained for public use. The land was not of good quality. Paxton wrote to his wife in 1843: 'It is not a very good situation for a park as the land is generally poor, but of course will rebound more to my credit and honour to make something handsome and good out of bad material' (Paxton, quoted in Tate, *op. cit.*, p. 74).

From the outset the park was seen as a form of municipal enterprise, and hopes were high that costs might be defrayed by profitable speculative development (not to mention the private gains realized by individuals who had the foresight to make speculative purchases of land). The park did indeed attract development, not as much as was anticipated in the master plan, but enough it seems to recoup the costs (Chadwick, *op. cit.*).

A key figure in the creation of the park was Sir William Jackson, Chairman of the Improvement Committee established after the 1843 Improvement Act. A successful Liverpool ironmonger, Jackson was the son of a Warrington doctor. Retiring in his mid-thirties to Italy because of overwork, he stayed for less than a year before returning to live in Birkenhead, soon to be elected to the Board of Commissioners. It was he who brought in Joseph Paxton as designer of the park; it was his personal enthusiasm for the project which had persuaded Paxton to overcome his initial scepticism and produce the first plan for the site (Thornton, undated). Subsequently Paxton brought in Edward Kemp as construction supervisor, and following completion Kemp became the park's long-term Superintendent.

## Joseph Paxton's Contribution

Paxton had begun his working life as an apprentice gardener, moving to the Duke of Devonshire's estate at Chatsworth in 1826. The parkland at the Chatsworth estate had seen contributions from several designers including George London and Henry Wise, and, perhaps most important, Lancelot 'Capability' Brown (of whom we learned in Chapter 3).

Paxton's involvement with Birkenhead Park ran from 1842 to 1846. He already had significant experience of park design and construction, applying the skills of parkland creation he had learned and developed in rural estates in an urban context. In 1842 Paxton had been commissioned by Richard Vaughan Yates, a prominent citizen of Liverpool, to design Princes Park, the design city's first (semi-public) park, on land bought from Lord Sefton in 1843. This was Paxton's first independent commission, covering 90 acres (36 ha) with residential development in and around it, and, as it turned out, the precursor to the much larger Birkenhead project. Similar ideas were incorporated in both parks: ornamental lakes, artificially mounded hills, curving paths, and subtly contrived views and vistas (Moscardini, 1978). In design concept (at Princes and Birkenhead Park alike) Paxton borrowed much from Humphry Repton, who in turn owed much to Brown. Brown's influence is clearly present in the serpentine line of lakes and paths and the naturalistic style, but the overall effect at Birkenhead is more suburban and less severe. To describe the style the term 'gardenesque' was coined in 1832 by John Claudius Loudon. In the gardenesque, pergolas, terraces, urns, exotic specimen trees and formal terraces, garden features in fact, joined the minimalist naturalistic style pioneered by Brown (Mowl, 2000).

Figure 4.3. *Birkenhead Park, Swiss Bridge*. One of several original architectural features repaired in the recent restoration.

Figure 4.4. *Cricket in Birkenhead Park*. Olmsted, Central Park's designer, noticed gentlemen playing cricket on his visit to the newly opened Birkenhead Park; and it is played today.

Chadwick argues that, consciously or not, Paxton was imitating Regent's Park in London. Birkenhead Park, he says: '… is an exceedingly competent essay in a style pioneered by Repton and Nash; an informal, gently picturesque landscape … ahead of anything else anywhere at the time' (Chadwick, *op. cit.*, p. 91). Pevsner and Hubbard also saw it as Paxton's most successful landscape design (Pevsner and Hubbard, *op. cit.*). The park displayed separate systems for through traffic (Ashville Road), for carriages inside the park (a circular drive) and for pedestrians; Olmsted built on these principles at Central Park, segregating through traffic completely by using a system of underpasses. The natural slope of the land facilitated the creation of rolling meadow-like parkland, whilst around the lakes irregular landscaped banks were created, accentuating the impact of the planted trees. The aim was to create picturesque pastoral meadows flanked by clumps of trees, many of which, such as holly, beech and silver pear, are still extant. Paxton was also responsible for the design of the lodges, which include Italian, Castellated, Gothic and Norman themed buildings, as well as the park railings (Tate, *op. cit.*).

## Why Birkenhead led the World

The national and international significance of Birkenhead Park cannot be doubted. The question is why it happened first in Birkenhead, and in large part the explanation must lie in Birkenhead's close relationship with the city of Liverpool. The town's explosive growth was, we have seen, closely related to the rise of its near neighbour, and in many respects Birkenhead was an early example of a commuter suburb, based on the ferries, its new tram system and later rail tunnel. The park's progenitors, Isaac Holmes and Sir William Jackson were both Liverpool men. Liverpool's immense seventeenth, eighteenth and nineteenth century wealth, as Britain's greatest imperial seaport (and it must be admitted profits from the slave trade) lay behind its role as a pioneer in urban development and design. It had built the world's first commercial enclosed wet dock (1715), the first inter-city passenger railway (1830), the first tram system (1860, in Birkenhead), and pioneered iron framed glass walled buildings (in Oriel Chambers (1864), and 16 Cook Street, (1866)). Its role as cultural and design innovator persisted into the twentieth century with Britain's first ring road (Queens Drive commenced 1903), the world's first town planning school (1909), one of the earliest examples of ferro-concrete construction (the Liver Building, 1911), and the longest underwater tunnel (the Mersey tunnel, linking Liverpool and Birkenhead, 1935), not to mention its role in 1960s popular music, led by the Beatles (Liverpool City Council, 2003).

The foundations for Liverpool's enterprise and innovation lay in its private and municipal wealth, in the platform provided by municipal government, echoed in the Birkenhead Improvement Commissioners, and in the drive and determination of its merchant classes to create a city which might rival Florence in the beauty and distinction of its architecture. During the nineteenth century, London apart, Liverpool produced more wealthy families than any other British city. At its peak, between 1880 and 1889, it produced as many millionaires as Greater Manchester, West Yorkshire, the West Midlands, Tyneside and East Anglia combined (Lane, 1997). Liverpool and Birkenhead were not alone in building municipal government in the nineteenth century (Hunt, 2004), but their elite wealth tended to set them apart from other contenders.

Government played no active role in the creation of Birkenhead Park, or in urban park projects elsewhere, beyond the creation of enabling and regulatory legislation in the form of the Second Improvement Act for Birkenhead. The seeds of Birkenhead's success and its world beating innovation lay in individual determination and private wealth, focused in local government through the Improvement Commissioners.

In 2007 a somewhat degraded Birkenhead Park was comprehensively restored, with the help of funds from Britain's national lottery. Once again personal initiative took the lead. The park's restoration was championed and the funds secured by a voluntary group, the Friends of Birkenhead Park, working in partnership with the local council. They remain actively involved in its management and maintenance.

## References

Brocklebank, R.T. (2003) *Birkenhead: An Illustrated History*. Derby: Breedon Books.

Chadwick, G.F. (1966) *The Park and the Town: Public Landscape in the 19th and 20th Centuries*. London: Architectural Press.

Conway, H. (1991) *People's Parks: The Design and Development of Victorian Parks in Britain*. Cambridge: Cambridge University Press.

Hall, P. (1988) *Cities of Tomorrow: An Intellectual History of Planning and Design in the Twentieth Century*. Oxford: Basil Blackwell.

Hunt, T. (2004) *Building Jerusalem: The Rise and Fall of the Victorian City*. London: Weidenfeld and Nicolson.

Jackson, K.T. (2003) Preface, in Miller, S., *Central Park: An American Masterpiece*. New York: Harry N. Abrams Inc. in association with Central Park Conservancy.

Lane, T. (1997) *Liverpool: City of the Sea*. Liverpool: Liverpool University Press.

Lawton, R. and Lee, R. (eds.) (2002) *Population and Society in West European Port Cities 1650–1939*. Liverpool: Liverpool University Press.

Lee, R. (2013) *The People's Garden: A History of Crime and Policing in Birkenhead Park*. Birkenhead: The Friends of Birkenhead Park.

Liverpool City Council (2003) *Nomination of Liverpool – Maritime Mercantile City for Inscription on the World Heritage List*, Liverpool, Liverpool City Council.

McInniss, J. (1984) *Birkenhead Park*. Birkenhead: Countyvise.

Moscardini, A. (1978) Princes Park, in *The Buildings of Liverpool*. Liverpool Heritage Bureau, Liverpool City Planning Department.

Mowl, T. (2000) *Gentlemen Gardeners: the Men who Created the English Landscaped Garden*. Stroud: The History Press.

Pevsner, N. and Hubbard, E. (1971) *The Buildings of England: Cheshire*. London: Penguin Books.

Rosenweig, R. and Blackmar, E. (1992) *The Park and the People: A History of Central Park*. Ithaca, NY: Cornell University Press.

Roth, P. (1997) *American Pastoral*. London: Jonathan Cape.

SCPW (Select Committee on Public Walks) (1833) *Report of the Select Committee on Public Walks*. Cmnd 448.

Tate, A. (2001) *Great City Parks*. London: Spon Press.

Thornton, E. (undated) *The People's Garden: A History of Birkenhead Park*. Wirral: Metropolitan Borough of Wirral, Department of Leisure Services and Tourism.

# 5

# The Uses of Disorder
## Bletchley Park and the World's First Computer

*As we were leaving the House [of Commons] that night [Churchill] called me into the Chamber to have a last look round. All was darkness except a faint ring of light around the gallery. We could dimly see the table but walls and roof were invisible. 'Look at this' he said. 'This little place is what makes the difference between us and Germany. It is in virtue of this that we shall muddle through to success and for lack of this Germany's brilliant efficiency leads her to final destruction. This little room is the shrine of the world's liberties'.*

From the diary of MacCallum Scott, March 1917

D-Day, the allied invasion of Western Europe, had been fixed for 5 June 1944. Loading had begun, and with Southern England enjoying a heat wave, the weather seemed perfect. Yet the meteorologists were concerned. There were anticyclones across Greenland and the Azores, and across the Atlantic an easterly depression was already bringing rain and heavy cloud. Meeting on 4 June, the forecasters predicted low cloud and a force six wind. With reluctance, General Eisenhower postponed the invasion to the 6 June.

By the evening of 4 June the winds were calmer, but the outlook was still poor. Eisenhower reassembled his commanders. Meteorologist John Stagg detected an improvement, with calmer winds for the next 48 hours. Reconvening at 4.00 am Stagg had good news: better weather was certain. Eisenhower thought for a few moments and took the decision, speaking quietly yet distinctively: 'OK, let's go' (Overy, 1995).

Figure 5.1. *General Eisenhower speaks to US paratroopers before D Day*. Eisenhower had just received a decoded message from Hitler to General Rommel, assuring Rommel that the invasion of Normandy was a feint.

## A 30-Year Secret

So much is common knowledge. Less well known is that in the final conference Eisenhower was handed another vital piece of information. It was delivered by courier from Bletchley Park, home of the British Government's code breaking operation. Bletchley Park had intercepted and decoded a radio transmission between Hitler and General Rommel. Hitler told Rommel that an invasion of Normandy was imminent, but that this would be a feint designed to move troops away from the channel ports where the real invasion would occur five days later. Rommel must not move any troops to Normandy. Eisenhower had all the information he needed – a break in the storms and a personal assurance from Hitler that he could start the invasion of Normandy knowing that he had five days without powerful opposition, giving him time to build up his bridgehead despite the indifferent weather. Eisenhower never revealed this information to any of his colleagues (Flowers, 2006).

At the end of the war Eisenhower wrote to the Bletchley Park staff to thank them for their contributions to the war effort: 'The intelligence which has emanated from you has been of priceless value to me... It has saved thousands of British and American lives' (Winterbotham, 1974, p. 2). Eisenhower later concluded that had it not been for the information supplied by the code-breakers, the war would have lasted at least two years longer than it did (Flowers, *op. cit.*).

For over thirty years the British government kept secret the success of the code breaking operations. The strictest security was maintained. All those involved were told: 'to ensure that nothing we do now should hinder the efforts of our successors… I cannot stress too strongly the need for the maintenance of security … at some future time we may be called upon to use the same methods'. Severe penalties would follow if anyone dared to publicise what they had done or seen. A trial with a complete ban on reporting would be followed by a long prison sentence (Gannon, 2007).

Hints that the German codes had been broken eventually emerged abroad, beyond the reach of the UK's Official Secrets Act. In 1974 the total ban was relaxed and Winterbotham's book *The Ultra Secret* was published. Yet the greatest secret remained. After 1 June 1944 the German messages (including Hitler's fateful D Day message to Rommel) had been decoded with the help of Colossus, the world's first electronic computer.

Bletchley Park's code breaking activities, assisted by Colossus, were in every sense a great British plan, in terms of organization, outcomes and the development of what is now known as IT infrastructure. The technology was an astonishing technological breakthrough and would underpin economic growth and technological innovation in the late twentieth and twenty-first centuries. How had it been achieved, how had it been planned, and who, or what, had brought it to fruition? To answer the questions we need to ask who established the Bletchley Park operation (and why), and how the electronic computer emerged, and was built. As we will see, although the technology proved to be wholly innovative, the plans had much that might best be described as traditional.

## Private and Personal Initiative

The last few months of 1938 saw an outbreak of activity in the old mansion house at Bletchley Park, on the edge of the quiet Buckinghamshire town of Bletchley. A rather unusual group of people, mainly middle aged 'professor types' accompanied by young women had arrived in August. Staying in local hotels they referred to themselves as 'Captain Ridley's shooting party'. Workmen were busy installing power cables and telephone lines. It appeared that an unknown agency had purchased the estate for £6,000. The story put about was that it was to be turned into an air training school.

In fact Bletchley Park had been purchased for the Secret Intelligence Service – now known as MI6 – to be used as a war station for various parts of this organization, evacuated from London and the threat of German bombs. Its location had been determined by its distance from London, proximity to the trunk GPO telephone cable which ran along the nearby A5, and no doubt the ease of rail access to London on the west coast main railway line. Its position midway between Oxford and Cambridge may well have been another bonus.

Was this an example of resourceful government preparation for the threat of war? It seems not. For Admiral Sir Hugh Sinclair, Head of the Secret Intelligence Service, had purchased the estate with personal funds. A former MI6 officer who later became the archivist for the service confirmed that, failing to get support from the War Office for a new site, Sinclair bought Bletchley Park himself (Smith, 2011). Sinclair's generosity did not stop at purchasing the property. He also recruited a top chef from a London restaurant to cook for the code breakers, complete with full waitress service. Sinclair left the estate to his sister Evelyn, which suggests that he was never paid. But Sinclair and his sister were both wealthy and did not need the money. Following his death in 1939, Evelyn signed the estate over to MI6.

Figure 5.2. *Bletchley Park*. Nerve centre of the British code breaking operations, Bletchley Park was purchased by Admiral Sir Hugh Sinclair, using personal funds, after the War Office turned the project down.

So establishing Bletchley Park was essentially an act of private philanthropy, rather than government action.

Sinclair was very much in the mould of British establishment eccentrics. A noted *bon viveur*, when director of naval intelligence, shortly after the First World War, he had located his department in London's fashionable Strand, close to the Savoy Grill, his favourite restaurant. For a short spell the code breakers had been moved to the Foreign Office, but when Sinclair was made Chief of Secret Intelligence in 1922, he brought them back into his control. Code breakers were recruited from a limited circle of people within the British establishment. There was little or no formal training and the structure of the office was disorganized. There were some fine scholar linguists, alongside mere passengers. The main targets were America, France, Japan and Russia. Perhaps that choice of targets explains why the activity remained so highly secretive, even after the Second World War.

At the end of the First World War Alistair Denniston, a former naval code breaker, was put in charge of the code breakers, known evasively as the Government Code and Cypher School. A main source of information was the international cable companies, who were required to hand over cables on request to the code breakers by a section in the 1920 Official Secrets Act.

As war with Germany grew closer Denniston realized shrewdly that his staff, dominated by elderly classicists, needed an injection of new skills. He spent the months before the war touring the universities looking for suitable mathematicians and linguists. Academics selected for a territorial training course by Denniston and his contacts were made to sign the Official Secrets Act and, on receipt of a telegram, told to report to Bletchley Park. Alongside the academics, an organization, staffed by bright young men from the London banks, was created to coordinate interception of messages.

The training course brought in a new class of code breaker: mathematicians with a particular interest in the problems of breaking codes. Amongst them was a brilliant, eccentric and homosexual Cambridge scholar called Alan Turing. Turing has been described as 'a great original, unmoved by authority, convention or bureaucracy' (Lavington, 2012a, p. 5). During the 1930s he had conceived of a theoretical machine capable of handling any mathematical algorithm or set of mathematical processes. By bringing mathematicians of Turing's stature into Bletchley Park, Denniston was, perhaps unwittingly, putting together a crucible of creative talent. Just as important, he was building an individualist culture where almost any eccentricity, background, or sexual orientation was tolerated.

There were other reasons for Bletchley Park's individualist culture, not least the management style of its most senior figure. Sinclair had been terminally ill with cancer through 1939, and following his death in November, he was replaced by his deputy Stewart Menzies.

Though he knew how to further his own ambitions, Menzies was no great thinker and had no idea how to manage the under resourced Bletchley Park. So the administration of the Secret Intelligence Service was chaotic and its headquarters in a state of upheaval throughout 1940 (Aldrich, 2010). Menzies regarded anything to do with personnel or administration as beneath him, and would go out of his way to avoid it. Sir Alexander Cadogan, Permanent Under Secretary at the Foreign Office, referred to a meeting with Menzies in his diary: 'A bad advocate on his own behalf. He babbles and wanders, and gives the impression he is putting up a smokescreen of words' (*ibid.*, p. 24).

## A Culture of Creative Chaos

Bletchley Park was chaotic, yet it was a creative and innovative chaos. People were allowed to go their own way. This informal style, mixing up individuals from three services with civilians, was unique and remarkable. Occasionally a visiting General would fulminate, seeing his staff dressed in bright pullovers, and demand a return to full uniform. Yet the code breakers continued to operate in a devolved and self-directed style. 'Tea parties' could be called by any cryptanalyst by writing an idea in the current research logbook and a note on the blackboard in the research room. The tea parties were completely informal meetings where many decisions were reached. But no tea was served (Good, 2006).

In Nazi Germany none of this would have been possible. Germany did not lack skilled scientists and engineers, but their skills could not be brought together by the centralized Nazi regime. Konrad Zuse had built an electromechanical computer. Helmut Schreyer produced a small electronic machine during the war. Yet his proposal for a machine with 1,500 valves was refused funding. Hitler's absolute and dictatorial style did not encourage individual initiative, whilst unified control of the armed services was undermined by separate fiefdoms in the Luftwaffe and the Navy. The Army and the Luftwaffe built parallel networks of landlines and wireless links. Six or seven different German cryptographic establishments fought each other with almost as much hatred as they reserved for the enemy (Aldrich, *op. cit.*). The organizational characteristics of the Nazi regime bred weaknesses that were fatal to collegiate and innovative behaviour, which demands a wide range of talent and experience, alongside a rather messy and organic sense of improvisation and freedom (Griffin *et al.*, 2012). Jews and misfits would by definition have been excluded. The Nazis discouraged dissenting and critical thinking in academia, encouraged conformity and obeisance, and killed many if not most of the country's Jewish, left wing or homosexual intellectuals and thinkers (who had not already fled abroad). Evidently, Nazi Germany was not the smoothly running automaton of popular belief.

At Bletchley Park individualism and eccentricity were evident in interception as well as code breaking. As the new recruits were absorbed, other branches of the intelligence services were expanding, not least for the interception of coded messages – the crucial feedstock for cryptanalysts. MI5, the internal branch of British security services, created a new body, the Radio Security Service (RSS), designed to intercept, locate and close down illicit wireless traffic from enemy agents in Britain. The task was given to Lord Sandhurst, managing director of Hatch Mansfield and Company, wine shippers. An enthusiastic radio amateur, his first act was to contact the president of the Radio Society of Great Britain, Arthur Watts. Watts swiftly volunteered the entire Radio Society of Great Britain Council; after a routine security check all were brought into the RSS.

The task of monitoring illicit radio transmissions fell largely to the RSS. In

1939 seven volunteers were monitoring hundreds of enemy stations. Unlike the Post Office and BBC, radio amateurs were used to working with weak transmissions and thus well suited to monitoring. They would return from work in the evening and listen for three or four hours to a predetermined wavelength. Soon the volunteers were intercepting large volumes of enemy point-to-point radio transmissions, between agents or their stations. Within three months 600 such transmitters had been identified, all of them on the other side of the English Channel. An enormous amount of raw material was generated, increasing the chances of breaking codes. It was, according to West, a classic example of British improvisation, with voluntary workers making considerable sacrifices to rescue an ill-prepared Whitehall (West, 1986).

Alongside Bletchley Park's mathematicians and academics, other individualists flourished. John Tiltman, one of the leading lights, knew nothing about electronics, statistics or algebra. Tiltman, it is said, could have walked off the pages of Edgar Allen Poe or Arthur Conan Doyle. He worked alone, standing at a specially constructed desk for days and weeks on end, following up guesses and hunches. He was an accidental cryptanalyst, with a brilliant knack for sensing patterns in coded text, in cross word puzzles, or a game of chess. Wounded in the First World War, he had been given a desk job to recuperate, landing by chance in Denniston's small interwar team of code breakers.

Tiltman's attitude to authority reflected the ethos of Bletchley Park. It was conveyed to a young private, assigned to him for duty. Approaching Tiltman's desk the private stamped his feet in drill fashion concluding with a crash of boots. Tiltman, it is recounted, looked up without a word, looked down at the private's feet, then back at his face. 'I say old boy,' he eventually responded, 'must you wear those damned boots' (Budiansky, 2006, p. 53).

## Dollis Hill: World Leader in Electronic Switching

The essential task of Bletchley Park was to decrypt messages which had been encoded by the German electromechanical 'enigma' machines, where a message could be scrambled by applying complex settings of rotating wheels inside the device. In the early years of the war the work was done by old school code breakers like Tiltman, working largely with hunches, pencil and paper. Their efforts were assisted by the so-called 'bombes', fast running electromechanical machines invented in the second half of 1939 by Alan Turing and built by the British Tabulating Machine Company in Letchworth. A bombe contained thirty rotating discs designed to replicate the discs in ten German coding machines – an electromechanical analogue of the enigma machines. It was designed to run through all the various possibilities of wheel settings at high speed, to see if a suspected or guessed piece of text (known as a 'crib') appeared in the message.

In 1940 German coding of teleprinter messages became more sophisticated and Bletchley Park began to receive messages in a code they could not recognize.

A new coding machine was in use which automatically encoded messages before transmission, and automatically decoded at the other end. There were no operators involved. The Germans used this system until the end of the war for their most secret messages, including Hitler's instructions to his generals. The Bletchley Park mathematicians deduced the characteristics of the coding machine and devised mathematical processes which could reveal the message when applied to the codes. But the processors required would need to work at speeds a hundred times faster than any machine available at the time. An entirely new approach was needed. The answer lay in a new technology which had been developed in the telephone industry just before the war, using electronic rather than electromechanical switches, and specifically in the use of thermionic valves.

Nowadays that process is undertaken by an electronic chip in a computer and digital electronics are commonplace in many household items. But in 1942 no one knew what lay ahead. The subject was known to very few people in very few places in the world and the possibilities it opened could only be guessed at. The Dollis Hill Communications Research Establishment of the British Post Office in suburban London was one of those places, and the post office engineer in charge of the research was Thomas Flowers. Born in 1905, Flowers was a working-class boy, the son of a bricklayer. His interest and aptitude for science and mathematics led to a place at a local technical college, a job as a trainee telephone engineer, and then a post in research. Flowers joined the Telephone Branch of the Post Office in 1926, after his apprenticeship at the Royal Arsenal in Woolwich. The Post Office was planning to install automatic switching gear into its telephone exchanges and needed to expand its engineering staff. A gifted and innovative engineer, he entered the research branch at Dollis Hill in 1930,

Figure 5.3. *Thomas Flowers.* Flowers and his team of post office engineers designed and constructed the world's first electronic computer, turning Alan Turing's concept into reality.

and was rapidly promoted (Copeland, 2006*b*). In the late 1930s Flowers started work on the use of electronics in communications control and switching.

A determined and driven individual, Flowers could upset others. Referring to an early project, he remarked of a colleague: 'The engineer working on the project wasn't getting anywhere, and that's because he wasn't any good'. Later Flowers came to blows with colleagues who did not share his opinion or insight. One colleague, Gordon Welchman tried to get Flowers reprimanded for high-handed behaviour: 'Mr. Flowers does not seem to mind how many valves he uses'. Welchman took a very serious view of 'the reckless use of valves' and argued that the Post Office could be seriously criticized. This seems to have had little impact on Flower's style, or on his results (Gannon, *op. cit.*, p. 253).

Flowers first came into contact with Bletchley Park in 1939 when Gordon Radley, director of the Research Establishment at Dollis Hill, asked him to help Alan Turing with an electromechanical machine for use with code breaking. It turned out that the machine Flowers worked on became redundant before it entered service. But Flowers made a good impression on Turing.

Flowers and his colleagues at Dollis Hill realized that the way ahead, indeed the only solution which would deliver the processing speeds required, lay in the use of electronic switching. Before the outbreak of war only a small number of engineers were familiar with the use of valves as high-speed switches. Thanks to his previous research he was possibly the only person in Britain who understood that valves could be used, and used reliably, for high-speed digital electronic computing. 'Before the war,' said Flowers, 'I had been working on thermionic valves instead of mechanical relays. I was convinced that we could get up to very high speeds and it would be very reliable. There was no one else in the world working on this technology, and that's what made it so difficult for me to explain to Bletchley Park, because they did not have any experience to guide them' (Gannon, *op. cit.*, p. 254). Flowers had first proposed the idea of a fully electronic machine in February 1943; it was 'received with incredulity at the Telecommunications Research Establishment and at Bletchley Park' (Copeland, *op. cit.*, p.74).

## Personal Initiative in the British Post Office

The machine proposed by Flowers would not itself decode messages. It would compare every possible combination of settings which might have been used on the German coding machines, leaving the cryptanalysts with the task of determining the correct settings. Flowers offered to build such a machine for Bletchley Park, but the offer was refused, apparently on the basis that a fully electronic machine would take a year or more to produce and get into service, although documents relating to these decisions either do not exist or have never been released (Gannon, *op. cit.*).

Backed by his manager Gordon Radley and his boss Sir Stanley Angwin, Flowers took the decision to design and make such a machine on his own initiative. A team of fifty Post Office staff was assembled, commandeering an old Post Office factory in Birmingham. They worked for twelve hours a day, often for six or six and a half days a week, producing the first prototype in 10 months. That machine contained 1,600 electronic valves and filled a room, but it was still not fast enough. So a second machine was produced, using 2,400 valves, working at a processing speed of 25,000 alphabetical characters per second.

Colossus Mark 1 performed its test run at Bletchley Park on a problem to which the answer was already known. It gave the correct answer with great speed. There was amazement from the Bletchley Park staff when the machine gave the same answer to the question on several repeat runs (Copeland *et al.*, 2006c). Colossus Mark 2 was delivered to enter service on 1 June 1944, just in time to help break the coded message sent by Hitler to Rommel, telling Rommel not to move troops from the Channel ports to Normandy.

In 1945 10 Colossus machines were in operation at Bletchley Park, supplying information up to the end of the war in Europe (Flowers, *op. cit.*). Most of the machines were quickly dismantled after the war and the documentation was burned (Budiansky, 2006). Churchill, it was said, had ordered the destruction of all the machines, leaving no part larger than a man's fist (Hayward, 2006). Flowers personally burned the plans, although another senior colleague, Alan Coombes, retained them (Gannon, *op. cit.*).

Some machines and documentation were officially yet secretly retained, ostensibly for training purposes, in Britain and in the United States (Gannon, *op. cit.*). Two machines were moved to Eastcote and then on to GCHQ at Cheltenham. One machine was dismantled in 1959 after 14 years' service; the other was dismantled in 1960 (Copeland, 2006d). Information on the use of the machines remains classified. Components were also shipped to the United States and reconstructed on the basis of plans being destroyed in Britain. Though information emerged on Bletchley Park's code breakers in the 1970s, even then it seems that there was deliberate effort to confuse the picture and keep Colossus secret (Gannon, *op. cit.*).

Was Colossus a computer? As Copeland admits, Colossus did not store programmes in its memory, and to set the machine up for a different job it was necessary to modify the wiring by hand, using switches and plugs (Copeland, 2006e). On the other hand, it included many individual architectural elements found in a modern PC, and stood on the brink of the fully programmable computer era. A technical metaphor for Colossus might be a modern microprocessor chip in an embedded application in a pace maker or calculator (Wells, 2006). Just as the embedded chip has the potential for wider applications, so the wartime Colossus, despite its focus on cryptanalytical objectives, had similar latent potential. Flower's electronic machine had created the technology which could turn Turing's conceptual thinking machine into a reality, and in so doing lay the foundations for the UK computer sector, and for IT infrastructure throughout the world.

Figure 5.4. *Colossus*. Flowers's thermionic valve based electronic computer, in operation during the Second World War, its existence kept secret for over half a century.

Was Colossus a success? In Chapter 1 some simple criteria were suggested by which to identify a successful plan: whether the plan was actually implemented; whether, after a suitable lapse of time, it is still widely regarded as successful; and whether it was innovative or transformational. There is little doubt that Colossus, with the 'Bombe', its crude electromechanical predecessor, passes the tests. Perhaps Eisenhower exaggerated the impact of Colossus code breaking on the length of the war. Yet breaking the German naval codes had changed the course of the Battle of the Atlantic, allowing the Admiralty to direct convoys away from concentrations of U boats, bringing down shipping losses to a bearable level. Signals intelligence contributed hugely to the outcome of the Battle of Britain (Aldrich, *op. cit.*). Though Colossus came later in the game its impact was just as significant.

## British Post War Computing

In terms of immediate outcomes Colossus was an undoubted achievement. Yet there is another strategic gain, which should not be overlooked. The development of this electronic, valve based, digital technology gave Britain a head start in the development of true computers - machines with a stored programme. Max Newman, the Cambridge mathematician who joined Bletchley Park in 1942, had specified the logical requirements of Colossus. He moved to Manchester University in 1945 taking with him two colleagues from Bletchley, David Rees and Jack Good. Turing moved to the National Physical

Laboratory, where he sketched out the design for a stored programme computer, named the Automatic Computing Engine by a colleague. Turing too moved to Manchester in 1948, where he took the lead in developing programming systems for Manchester University's Mark 1 computer. This was a development of the Manchester 'Baby' computer, the world's first universal stored-programme computer which first ran successfully in June 1948. It was followed by a fully engineered version at the end of 1949 – the Ferranti Mark 1 (Burton and Lavington, 2012). That project had an intriguing intellectual echo in the development of the UK's IT infrastructure; both the parents of Sir Tim Berners Lee, the inventor of the World Wide Web, worked on it.

In parallel the military secretly continued their own programme of computer development, at Borehamwood in Hampshire. By 1950 a team placed under the control of Elliott Brothers Ltd produced the first of a string of military computers, the Elliott 152. With the help of the National Research and Development Corporation, Borehamwood's computers were turned to civil applications. Thirty three Elliot machines were delivered between 1956 and 1962. By 1961 Elliot Automation made 50 per cent of the new computers sold in the UK. It was the high point of the British computer industry.

Yet the range of manufacturers, innovators and teams was too wide, and the production runs too small, to keep pace with the big American companies. By the 1960s IBM had 60 per cent of the world market (Paganamenta and Overy, 1984). Scientifically the British efforts had been world beating; eventually they were let down by commercial weakness in manufacturing. This cannot detract from the scale of the public sector achievement; in any event, as we shall see in the following chapter, in Cambridge, Britain's skills in software development and several converging technologies remain world leading.

## A Sort of Plan

What were the key characteristics of this plan? In a sense one could argue that it was not a plan at all. The creation of Bletchley Park is down in large part to personal and private initiative. There was indeed an aim and a purpose at Bletchley Park; but the response to the need to intercept Nazi communications was met by the inspirational genius of gifted individuals.

Sinclair bought the buildings with his own funds after the War Office turned him down. Denniston recruited on his own initiative using private and academic networks. There was no master plan in Whitehall. The culture of Bletchley Park was often rather disorderly. Those involved sometimes had limited inter personal skills and poor management ability. They were, often as not, difficult yet brilliant misfits. There was little competent planning under Menzies. Turing and Flowers found it difficult to work in teams and with others. Development occurred organically, depending on personal contact and personal networks. Individual initiative and improvisation were to the fore and in some ways the 'looseness' of public sector management was beneficial. Flowers and his colleagues at the Post Office Research Establishment were told that their electronic device could not be made, or not made in time at any rate. They proceeded on their own initiative nonetheless. The same air of informality and individualism appears to have been true of much post war computer development.

By now these have become familiar themes in this book. We saw them at work in earlier plans. They seem to reflect the essential characteristics of British society identified by Dahrendorf (1982) and in particular the autonomy of its institutions, which proceed at their own pace, with little or no regard to priorities set at the centre. Indeed, in this, as in so many of the examples we have encountered, the centre does not seem to set priorities at all. Rather it falls in behind plans and schemes driven hard by forceful and intelligent individuals working in what might be described as autonomous institutional platforms. It may not be the best way of making plans. But it is the one they used in the 1940s and, in its way, it did seem to work. Will the pattern persist in post war plans? The following chapters provide an answer.

## References

Aldrich, R.J. (2010) *GCHQ: The Uncensored Story of Britain's Most Secret Intelligence Agency*. London: Harper Press.
Budiansky, S. (2006) Colossus, codebreaking and the digital age, in Copeland, (2006*a*).
Burton C. and Lavington, S. (2012) The Manchester Machines, in Lavington (2012*a*).
Copeland, B.J. (ed.) (2006*a*) *Colossus: the Secrets of Bletchley Park's Codebreaking Computers*. Oxford: Oxford University Press.
Copeland, B.J. (2006*b*) Machine against machine, in Copeland (2006*a*).
Copeland, B.J. *et al*. (2006*c*) Dollis Hill at war, in Copeland (2006*a*).
Copeland, B.J. *et al*. (2006*d*) Mr Newman's Section, in Copeland (2006*a*).
Copeland, B.J. (2006*e*) Colossus and the rise of the modern computer, in Copeland (2006*a*).
Dahrendorf, R. (1982) *On Britain*. London: British Broadcasting Corporation.
Flowers, T.H. (2006) D Day at Bletchley Park, in Copeland, (2006*a*).
Gannon, P. (2007) *Colossus: Bletchley Park's Greatest Secret*. London: Atlantic Books.
Good, J. (2006) From Hut 8 to the Newmanry, in Copeland (2006*a*).
Griffin, A., Price, R. and Vojak, B. (2012) *Serial Innovators: How Individuals Create and Deliver Breakthrough Innovations in Mature Firms*. Stanford, CA: Stanford University Press.
Hayward, G. (2006) The British Tunny Machine, in Copeland, (2006*a*).
Hennessy, P. (1996) *Muddling Through: Power, Politics and the Quality of Government in Postwar Britain*. London: Victor Gollancz.
Lavington, S. (ed.) (2012*a*) *Alan Turing and his Contemporaries: Building the World's First Computers*. Swindon: British Informatics Society.
Lavington, S. (2012*b*) The ideas men, in Lavington, (2012*a*).
MacCallum Scott (1917) MacCallum Scott Mss, Glasgow University Library.
Overy, R. (1995) *How the Allies Won*. London: Pimlico.
Paganamenta, P. and Overy, R, (1984) *All Our Working Lives*. London: British Broadcasting Corporation.
Smith, M. (2011) *The Secrets of Station X*. London: Biteback Publishing.
Wells, B. (2006) The PC users guide to Colossus, in Copeland, (2006*a*).
West, N. (1986) *GCHQ: The Secret Wireless War 1900–1986*. London: Weidenfeld and Nicholson.
Winterbotham, F.W. (1974) *The Ultra Secret*. London: Weidenfeld and Nicholson.

# The Cambridge Paradox
## Phenomenal Growth; Planned Restraint

*Creative scientific thinking ... will require plenty of encouragement and careful handling, but probably as little direct management as possible.*
John Butterfield, Vice Chancellor, Cambridge University, 1985

William Holford was the outstanding British planner of his generation. Professor of Civic Design at Liverpool University in 1935 (at the age of 29), and Professor of Town Planning at University College London in 1948, Holford was a member of the small yet influential reconstruction group serving Lord Reith at the Ministry of Works in 1941. In 1943, when a separate Ministry of Town and Country Planning was established, Holford became its principal advisor, laying the foundations for British post-war planning. Here he directed an extraordinary range of talent, including men like Hugh Casson, Colin Buchanan, and Myles Wright. Holford's team drafted the technical content of the 1947 Town and Country Planning Act; Myles Wright personally wrote the crucial ministry handbook *The Redevelopment of Central Areas*. In 1946 Holford was appointed planning consultant to the City of London, setting out his proposals for redeveloping areas around St. Pauls Cathedral in 1956. He became a long term consultant to the Central Electricity Generating Board and member of the Royal Fine Arts Commission, and was made a life peer in 1965, the first architect or town planner to be so honoured (Miller, 2004).

As brilliant as he was eminent, Holford had a gift for rapid comprehension and synthesis. Myles Wright recounts how a complex problem with multiple elements could be put to him and a solution suggested, only for Holford to 'look at the ceiling for 30 seconds or so' and suggest a completely different and much better approach (Wright, 1982, p. 185).

With Myles Wright as his assistant, Holford was appointed in 1948 as consultant to Cambridgeshire County Council, to prepare a plan for Cambridge. His principal recommendation, although buried in the text, was simple enough: Cambridge should not grow. Its population should be capped at 100,000 and new manufacturing development should not be permitted (Holford and Wright, 1950). Yet by the mid-1980s Holford's restrictive strategy seemed to be unravelling. Advanced technology companies were growing at a phenomenal rate in Cambridge – indeed the title of a seminal research report alluded to a 'Cambridge Phenomenon' (Segal Quince Wicksteed, 1985). Starting in the early 1960s, and accelerating in the late 1970s and early 1980s, 260 small high technology companies had been created – a growth rate which stood comparison with California's San Francisco peninsula. A further study in 2012 estimated that 4,000 high technology companies had been created since the 1960s, with 1,400 companies then employing 48,000 people (Kirk and Cotton, 2012).

It was an astonishing success story and an extraordinary paradox. Was the Holford plan a failure? Was it as irrelevant as it appeared? Was the emergence of the new companies entirely down to chance (or 'unplanned') as some argue? If not, what were the crucial strategic decisions and how did they reflect the British planning style? We will find the answers to these questions buried in a long history of powerful institutions, and in the behaviour of critical individuals within them.


## A University Shapes its City

To understand Cambridge and the story of its economic success, you need first to understand the University, for Cambridge is a University that has shaped its small city, rather than the opposite. Oxford and Cambridge are ancient universities, dating back to the twelfth and early thirteenth centuries. The precise origins of Cambridge are hazy, but a key event was a migration of Oxford students to the city in 1209. Both Oxford and Cambridge had been essentially clerical institutions, evolving after the Reformation and Dissolution of the Monasteries in the 1530s (see Chapter 13), with the growth of individual colleges enriched by individual private endowments. Post-Reformation they began to educate increasing numbers of sons of the gentry, as a sort of finishing school. But their main interest remained ecclesiastical.

With the Restoration of the Monarchy in 1660 (see Chapter 13), the Church of England's dominance of the universities was re-established; fellows and heads removed by the Puritans were reinstated, and post-1688 both universities entered a long and uneventful sleep. Higher education in England generally languished in the eighteenth-century (Hill, 1969). In Oxford and Cambridge the number of undergraduates fell sharply, degree courses were dull and outmoded, and professors ceased to lecture at all (Green, 1969). It was in the northern Dissenters Academies that new intellectual life flourished, closely tied to the dynamism of emerging industrial society. Excluded from the old universities, where classics based courses had scarcely changed since the Reformation, many religious Nonconformists (or Dissenters) went to continental Europe or to Scotland, returning to work in the Dissenters Academies. These positively welcomed new subjects, teaching modern politics and history, mathematics, modern languages and, above all, science – then known as natural philosophy (Uglow, 2002). The chemist Joseph Priestley, for example (credited with the discovery of oxygen), taught in 1761 at an Academy in Warrington, where the atmosphere was lively and progressive, the school patronized by local iron masters, glass makers, weavers and merchants.

By the nineteenth century a reaction had set in. English society was rapidly urbanizing and a new wealthy capitalist class was emerging. Industrialization went hand in hand with colonialism, and this created demand for an educated class of administrators, especially overseas. Yet as late as the early nineteenth century Oxford and Cambridge remained as training schools for the Anglican Church. Between 1831 and 1840, 413 of the 1,239 matriculating Cambridge graduates were to be ordained as Ministers. Only a few colleges had an entrance examination, and the suggestion that this was required was seen as impertinent interference in the rights of the colleges.

Before they could take on a new role as suppliers of the administrative and professional classes, major change was needed, the initial impetus being provided by the reforms of the early 1830s. Incapable of self-reform, their statutes and constitutions were altered by a succession of nineteenth-century Royal Commissions (Rothblatt, 1968). These reforms compelled the universities to provide new professorships, lecture rooms, laboratories and libraries, not least to take on the challenge from the Dissenters Academies and the newly emerging redbrick universities in London, Liverpool, Manchester and other industrial cities, often funded by merchants and industrialists to promote the development of useful technical skills and knowledge. By the 1880s the pattern of modern Oxford and Cambridge had been set, their objectives being the supply of civil servants, schoolmasters, administrators, and professionals (Green, *op. cit.*). Yet they retained a Church of England bias and a distinct aversion to the needs of trade and industry, fed by an overriding belief in liberal, non-vocational education – an aversion that was to remain well into the late twentieth century. According to one critic, the Dons assessed 'the worth of an academic subject by its usefulness to industry and commerce. In their view almost no subject which could be turned to the benefit of business deserved university recognition' (Rothblatt, *op cit.*, p. 252).

Mid-nineteenth-century Cambridge was still very poorly equipped to provide the education needed by manufacturing. Religion was part of the problem. Dissenters were not allowed to graduate from Cambridge until 1856.

Celibacy and the need for teachers to be in Holy Orders restricted the pool of teaching skills and deterred young lecturers, and the cost of fees was high. There was tension between the rich colleges and the relatively poor university. Teaching the arts was relatively cheap. Developing science would require large-scale investment in facilities – and who was able to pay?

## The Emergence of Scientific Excellence

A crucial distinction developed between Oxford and Cambridge. Oxford offered no scholarships in the physical sciences, whereas Cambridge offered scholarships and received good applicants. The scientific tradition, especially in mathematics, was strong in Cambridge, where mathematics became the backbone of later developments in mathematical philosophy, engineering, economics and physics. The first Lucasian Professor of Mathematics was appointed in 1663; Sir Isaac Newton was appointed to the Lucasian Chair in 1669, though the impetus established by Newton and his school was not sustained in the eighteenth century. Recovering from its eighteenth-century torpor, Cambridge introduced a Natural Science Tripos in 1848. Crucially the Cavendish Laboratory was constructed in the early 1870s, and investment in physics, engineering and

Figure 6.1. *Sir Isaac Newton.* Appointed to the Lucasian Chair in Mathematics in 1669, the scientific impetus from Newton's school was not sustained into the eighteenth century.

chemistry followed (Sanderson, 1972). The Cavendish was neither funded by government nor the University. It was built and equipped with a personal gift from the University's Chancellor, the Duke of Devonshire, with Clerk Maxwell appointed first Cavendish professor of experimental physics in 1873 (Green, *op. cit.*). Shortly the Oxford and Cambridge Act would oblige colleges at both universities to support science.

The Cavendish laboratory rose to a position of unparalleled excellence in British science, winning three Nobel prizes, in 1904, 1906 and 1908, respectively for Rayleigh, Thomson and Rutherford. But like the mathematical

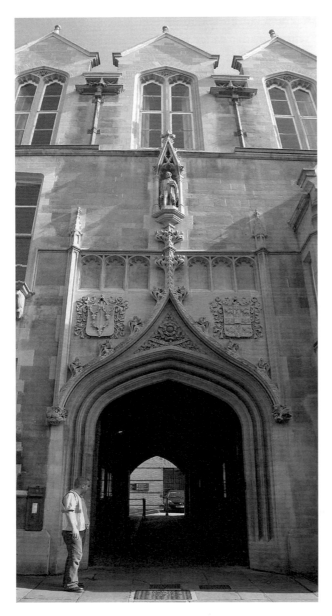

Figure 6.2. *Entrance to Original Cavendish Laboratory.* Crucial to the growth of scientific excellence in Cambridge, the Laboratory owes its existence to an act of personal philanthropy.

tradition which preceded it, the research seemed detached from worldly needs. Rutherford's research into radioactivity and the analysis of radiation was a case in point, focusing on the fundamental nature of matter (Sanderson, *op. cit.*). Like the abstract tradition in Cambridge mathematics, this was mandarin or 'blue sky' science, with little apparent useful application (*ibid.*). It was only in the rising department of engineering that stronger links were built between research and commercial application.

Nevertheless the scientific performance of Cambridge was vastly superior to Oxford. As late as 1900, Oxford produced only thirty-seven science graduates, whereas Cambridge graduated 136 natural scientists, plus a further eighteen mechanical scientists. By 1914 Cambridge graduated 152 natural scientists, and forty-three mechanical scientists – as well as 112 mathematicians (Edgerton, 1996). The basis for a leading world role in science had been established; and this would be hugely amplified by the impact of the Second World War, as a war of applied physics, in atomic weapons, radar and wireless. Research at the Cavendish, which had once seemed abstract, became hugely relevant to the war effort, and to the new technologies spawned later, especially in electronics, computers and nuclear energy. The Cavendish played a leading role in the British atomic bomb project, and, with government's Bawdsey Research Station, in the development of radar (Barnett, 1986). Thus Cambridge became the premier scientific university in Britain and, in several critical fields, one of the leading centres in the world. Sanderson concludes: 'Much of this depended on the fortune of personalities. Cambridge had Stokes, Clerk Maxwell, Thomson and Rutherford, Ewing and Dear' (*ibid.*, p. 59). He might perhaps have added the Duke of Devonshire to his list. Thanks to his philanthropic act, allied with the minds of brilliant academics, by the 1960s Cambridge was equipped with much of the knowledge needed to underpin late-twentieth- and twenty-first-century innovation. It was primed for growth. Yet critics still doubted whether that could lead technological change, since 'the disdain for *homo oeconomicus* in Cambridge was altogether too complete' (Rothblatt, *op. cit.*, p. 273).

## The Holford Plan

It is time to put the Holford plan under scrutiny. By 1951 the population of Cambridge had reached nearly 90,000, with a further 19,000 in an inner ring of nearby villages. Some 20 per cent of the total population had been migrants in the previous two decades. This level of growth, and especially the industrialization which accompanied it, was not welcomed. We have already noted the aversion to commerce and industry in the University. More widely, people feared that the character of Cambridge as an ancient university town with a significant architectural heritage might be lost. Lewis Silkin, who had been appointed as the first Minister of Town and Country Planning in the post-war Labour government, took a personal interest. He was keen to protect and conserve the town and its setting, and this was one reason why planning powers for Cambridge were given to Cambridgeshire County Council, rather than the City Council. These were the concerns that led the authorities to establish a special team under Holford to prepare an advisory plan for Cambridge. The team was largely financed by the County Council and accommodated in the county's new planning department (Segal Quince Wicksteed, *op. cit.*). Thus the relationship between the work of the team and the County Council's own planners was close. This would not be an imposed plan.

Holford's report was published in 1950. The report said that Cambridge could be expected to grow quickly unless active measures were taken to stop this. It identified several potential sources of growth: modern 'scientific industries' (although it cited the motor industry in Oxford as an example); new manufacturing firms moving in; commuting, including commuting to London; university expansion; development as a regional centre for government and others in East Anglia; and non-university research functions, especially government research. Most people, the report argued, would want to retain the essential qualities of Cambridge: the University, the college buildings and their setting, the central open spaces, short commuting, good housing, and the distinctive market town character. Presciently, the report added that 'far-sighted people' might favour expansion of the University and 'some expansion of research and prototype work closely connected with the scientific work of the university' (Holford and Wright, *op. cit.*, p. 49).

At most an additional 10,000 people might be tolerated, but a general growth of population was undesirable. Cambridge was big enough to retain most large town services, but small enough for a short commute by cycle. The proximity of countryside and green spaces within the city were real assets. Growth would hinder the work of the University, which would need larger and more complex facilities in the future. It would damage social life within the University and especially the nearness of buildings to each other. There would be pressure to build on green spaces, and more competition for building land in general.

The report concluded that the rate at which Cambridge was growing should be reduced, reaching a stable population not much in excess of current figures: 'We suggest 100,000 as the ultimate ceiling … to be reached as slowly as possible' (Holford and Wright, *op. cit.*, p. 50). The borough's population in 1948 was estimated at 86,000 with an additional 17,600 outside the borough boundaries, and population had increased by 24 per cent between 1931 and 1948. So this was an ambitious target.

Essentially the argument was that Cambridge should remain as a university town. Government clearly wanted to expand university provision, especially in the sciences, and the work of the University would be hampered by rapid growth. New employment especially in mass production was the least justifiable form of growth, but the expansion of existing industries in Cambridge might be acceptable if this involved research and prototype work and did not require production in quantity in Cambridge. Mass production should be discouraged, by moving firms elsewhere in the UK, or by relocating them to towns 14 to 18 miles (23 to 29 km) distant from Cambridge.

Holford believed that Central Cambridge, at its present size, had great attractions. The town's character should be retained even at the expense of new roads, and the pre-eminence of the college buildings should be retained in longer views. This was an early statement of conservation principles at a time when comprehensive redevelopment often had the upper hand (although the plan was not exactly short on road proposals). The collegiate plan of central Cambridge, involving domestic and community buildings from the twelfth and thirteenth centuries onward, should be preserved, not just in its own right, but in order to promote convenience, economy and compactness. There was a strong argument for keeping new university buildings in the centre of town. Short distances between rooms and teaching accommodation would encourage acquaintance between students of different disciplines. There should nonetheless be a large reserve of land for future university expansion.

The Holford report was in the spirit of the times. It followed the principles of the Barlow Report, which had recommended the relocation of industrial employment to areas of need, and the Abercrombie plan for London, essentially an exercise in containment and relocation to the proposed ring of new towns (see Chapters 2 and 8). But Holford's report was nuanced: it foresaw a specialized role for Cambridge as a world leading university and realized that research, prototypes, and small batch production might have a role in the town's

Figure 6.3. *Clare College*. The Holford plan protected the collegiate buildings and their setting to promote conservation, compactness and personal interaction.

future. It was opposed to large-scale production facilities and the growth of other non-essential functions. It was strong on conservation, wanting to preserve the character of ancient and sensitive townscapes as well as green spaces. It was in favour of walking and cycling, and short commuter trips, when conventional wisdom was moving rapidly to favour the car. It had even realized the importance of planning to encourage chance personal interaction, across the disciplines.

Holford's report is sometimes portrayed as a huge strategic error, something that got in the way of growth. Perhaps it is more accurate to say that in opposing the wrong sort of (essentially nineteenth century) growth it had helped to lay the foundations for a very different form of twenty first century growth. John Butterfield, University Vice Chancellor in 1984 made the point succinctly. Amongst the many factors which had shaped Cambridge's success in high-technology business should be counted its relative isolation, and 'its sequestration from industrial society as it has evolved in Britain's cities since the last century' (Butterfield, 1985).

## The Cambridge Phenomenon

How much growth has occurred in Cambridge and what were the immediate causes? The key sources of evidence are a report prepared by Segal Quince Wicksteed (*op. cit.*) for a mixture of mainly local private and public agencies, and a book prepared for Cambridge Phenomenon Limited (Kirk and Cotton, *op. cit.*) which provides a very detailed account of developments since 1985. The following account borrows freely from these sources.

The Segal Quince Wicksteed research charted the growth of 261 firms from 1960 to 1983. It found that, while there was some growth of firms in the late 1960s, rapid growth of firms took place in the early to middle 1970s. The sheer number of firms was striking, as was their youth, most being established after 1978, with 190 set up between 1974 and 1984. No less than 88 per cent remained independent, with only 4 per cent being acquired by or merged with other firms. Total employment in 1984 was estimated at 13,700, accounting for aggregate output of £870 million. Although there was some representation of chemicals and biotechnology, the dominant sectors were related to electronics, computing and instrument engineering – especially computer software and electronics capital goods. Key individuals moved repeatedly from one company to another, bringing a direct transfer of knowledge from business to business. The University was central to the process of firm creation. Although only 17 per cent of new firm formation could be attributed to individuals coming directly from the University, or starting within it, indirectly the University was the origin of virtually all the companies tracked in the survey.

Later research by the same consultancy found a further seventy-one companies. The process of firm generation appeared to be speeding up as 75 per cent of the firms had been started between 1980 and 1984. During the 1990s numerous additional companies were born, as Cambridge-based companies reached $1 billion stock market valuations. The growth rate slowed down in the 2000s with high-technology companies stabilizing at around 1,400–1,500 businesses. Significant new businesses born in the later stages of process included microcontroller technology, mobile phone processors, advanced 'Bluetooth' chips, 3G mobility technology, wireless email technology, accurate powder delivery, hardware security technology, iPod docks, cell network products, networking and modem software, video search technology, database software development, antibody biotechnology, and advanced pharmaceuticals (Kirk and Cotton, *op. cit.*).

Biotechnology played second fiddle to electronic and computing technologies in the early days. The Segal Quince Wicksteed survey found only four biotechnology companies, as against twenty-two electronic capital goods companies, twenty-three software companies and seventeen instrument engineering companies. Yet by the 2000s biotechnology was emerging as a vital part of the high-technology cluster, caused in part by the development of human genome research, as well as engagement with big pharmaceutical companies. Cambridge Antibody Technology, for example, went into alliance with UK pharmaceutical giant Astra Zeneca. Astra Zeneca's new £330 million R& D site will open on the Cambridge biomedical campus in 2016, employing 2,000 people and building relationships with other research, academic and healthcare organizations in the city. The company is closing its in-house R&D facility in Cheshire as well as its London HQ (BBC, 2013).

## Clusters and Convergence

Kirk and Cotton (*op. cit.*) identified six separate clusters in Cambridge high technology: electronics, engineering, health care and bioscience, software, technology consultancy and telecommunications.

Instrument engineering formed the basis for the earliest technology companies in the engineering sector. The catalyst for the emergence of the first instrumentation companies was the establishment of the natural science Tripos in the 1860s. Studying the natural sciences required new instruments and companies were established to meet that demand. Horace Darwin arrived from Kent with an apprenticeship in engineering to set up the Cambridge Scientific Instrument Company. Another early company, Pye, was established in 1896 by William Pye, after he left his job as a technician in the Cavendish Laboratory. Marshall, a Cambridge company, which dates back to 1909, was expert in the production of high-value low to medium volume products. These three companies proved crucial in supporting the newly emergent technology sector, not least as a source of skilled technical labour. More recent examples in the engineering sector include companies with expertise in mass spectrometry, spectrophotometry, cryo preservation freezers, fluid processing, undersea power cables, and solar energy – the last being a specialism of Eight19, spun out of the University's Department of Physics in 2010. Eight19 includes three Cambridge professors on its advisory board, and is working on printed plastic photovoltaic cells. Initially developed at the University, the cells are flexible, robust, and lightweight, and benefit from high-speed manufacturing and low fabrication costs. With a fraction of the embedded energy of conventional solar modules, they are well suited to consumer and off-grid applications (Eight19 website).

Electronics was the base for the first wave of Cambridge innovators. It led from radio to semiconductors, and then into inkjet printing and computing technologies. The Pye Company was at the heart of the process. Although Pye's Cambridge operation was closed down after acquisition by Philips, it had brought skilled people to Cambridge who later formed the bedrock for many other ventures in electronics.

Sinclair Radionics, a success story in the 1970s with its electronic calculator, was an innovator in personal computer technology. Acorn Computers was similarly successful, producing the BBC Micro, a spin-off from the BBC's government backed computer literacy project, commissioned specifically for the TV programme. It was designed and produced by Acorn Computers of Cambridge and sold 1.5 million units before being replaced by Sinclair's ZX Spectrum. Acorn and Sinclair are no more. Indeed there are no longer any personal computer manufacturers in Cambridge, yet the legacy of Acorn is of worldwide significance. The chip technology developed by ARM, a descendant of Acorn, has become globally dominant. By 2014 20 billion ARM processors had been manufactured and 95 per cent of mobile phones across the world contain

Figure 6.4. *Apple/ARM A5 Chip in iPad Mini*. ARM is a descendant of Cambridge's Acorn Computers: 95% per cent of mobile phones across the world contain at least one ARM chip.

at least one ARM designed chip (Arm.com, 2014). Like so many Cambridge companies ARM's business model centred on research and intellectual patents, rather than volume manufacturing (exactly as anticipated by Holford in 1950).

Computing in Cambridge can trace its history back to Alan Turing (see Chapter 5), who conceived of his 'Turing Machine' in Cambridge in 1937. A digital stored program computer was developed in Cambridge in 1949 in the Computer Laboratory, originally established in 1937 to provide computing services to the University's radio astronomers, meteorologists and geneticists. Roger Needham took over as director of the Laboratory in 1980, making connections which led Microsoft to set up its first research operation outside the USA in Cambridge in 1995. On retirement Needham became the first director of Microsoft Cambridge.

Software development was a natural partner for computer hardware, ranging from data search, security, and risk management, to computer games. The software sector was first stimulated by the early Sinclair and Acorn microcomputers. Several founders of recent companies cut their computing teeth by learning to programme these cheap machines. Visiting the USA in the early 1960s, Maurice Wilkes, the Head of the University Mathematical Laboratory (now the Computer Laboratory), met Charles Lang, who was working on early computer graphics in MIT's CAD (Computer Assisted Design) research group. Wilkes persuaded Lang to move to Cambridge and set up a CAD group in the mathematical laboratory, arriving in 1965.

Figure 6.5. *Maurice Wilkes.* As Head of the University's Mathematical Laboratory, Wilkes persuaded Charles Lang to move from MIT's Computer Assisted Design (CAD) team, establishing a new CAD centre in Cambridge.

Two years later, in 1967, Harold Wilson's Ministry of Technology funded a CAD Centre in Cambridge. Mintech, as it was known, was the most tangible and successful element of the Labour government's commitment to the 'white heat' of technology (see Chapter 12), controlling government scientific and industrial research, and absorbing the functions of the Department for Scientific and Industrial Research and the National Research and Development Corporation, alongside government aviation and nuclear research (Coopey, 1993). The CAD Centre proved to be the crucial stimulus for software development. The University's policy of short-term contracts for researchers meant that individuals who wanted to stay in Cambridge had to look for other ways of making a living and in turn this stimulated the emergence of a commercial CAD sector. Dick Newell, for example, left the CAD Centre in 1977 to form Cambridge Interactive Systems, which was sold to Computer Vision in 1989. Newell then set up Smallworld, a geographic information systems company which grew to have bases in forty countries. It was sold to General Electric in 1999. CAD Centre became a private company in 1983 – an early Thatcher government privatization – and was bought by ICL which was subsequently acquired by Fujitsu. But a successful management buyout was secured in 1994 and after its flotation CAD Centre expanded globally. Renamed as AVEVA it had offices in thirty-nine countries and was valued at £1 billion in 2012.

Telecommunications was a logical partner to the computer hardware sector, driven by powerful market demand and development in wireless and smart-phone technology. Expertise in smartphones dates back to the first of the Pye companies in the 1920s. Pye produced military and domestic radios, televisions and broadcasting equipment, including early versions of the mobile phone. A spin off from the Physics Department, Cambridge Positioning Systems was a pioneer in geolocation, becoming a supplier of chip designs for Bluetooth, GPS and Wi-Fi. As we noted, Cambridge research became critical to smartphone technology. Several Cambridge companies have been acquired by multinational partners, but as in the bioscience sector, many have seen the logic in retaining Cambridge as a base for R&D.

Electronics and instrumentation was at the heart of the first wave of innovation in Cambridge through the 1970s and 1980s. Biotechnology and telecommunications grew fast in the 1990s. Energy, nanotechnology and medical technology may be amongst the future stars. But these technologies are converging and few other places in the world have so many clusters of science and high technology, cross-fertilizing and feeding off one another. In health care, for example, it is quite possible that a new form of contact lens could transmit information on blood sugar levels, allowing continuous clinical monitoring of diabetes. Such a device, suggested by Professor Chris Lowe, Director of the University's Institute of Biotechnology in 2010, would bring together bioscience, materials and information technologies.

The growth of bioscience rested on an institutional research base in and outside the University, including the Babraham Institute, the Wellcome Trust Genome Centre, the University's Institute of Biotechnology, and the Medical Research Council's Laboratory of Molecular Biology (LMB). Established by the Medical Research Council in 1947, the LMB began life in the Cavendish Laboratory, like so many other organizations. Early work focused on protein structure, but the addition of DNA and virus research induced Francis Crick and James Watson to move to the Laboratory. Crick and Watson announced their discovery of the structure of DNA in Cambridge in 1953. Aside from its contribution to pure science, their discovery would be a crucial foundation for the growth of bioscience and healthcare in Cambridge.

Figure 6.6. *Laboratory of Molecular Biology*. Funded by the Medical Research Council, the Laboratory is a critical element in the Cambridge research base, moving into this new £200m facility in 2012.

In 1962 the LMB moved to new premises at Addenbrooke's Hospital. Monoclonal antibodies, which can be used to identify cancerous cells and determine molecular targets for drugs, were invented at the LMB in 1975. Several companies emerged from the LMB, including Cambridge Antibody Technology, Ribotargets (acquired by Glaxo Smith Kline in 2006 for £230m), Celltech, and Biogen. In 2012 LMB moved into a new £200m development on the Addenbrooke site, which also houses the Cancer Research UK Cambridge Research Institute, the Hutchinson Medical Research Council Research Centre, and the Glaxo Smith Kline Clinical Unit. This concentration of research facilities opens the door to knowledge transfer between start-up companies, research institutes, and big pharmaceutical companies. It was doubtless a key factor in Astra Zeneca's decision to relocate to Cambridge.

## Explaining the Process

No one can doubt that the growth of high technology in Cambridge is a national success story, on an unparalleled scale. The process has unfurled over around 50 years, a relatively short time span for the development of an economic cluster. Future growth potential looks enormous, especially if the scale of activity is accelerated by the arrival of more corporate research centres and by the convergence of technology and application across different sectors. It is quite possible that Cambridge and its region will emerge over the next 50 years as one of the world's most important concentrations of high-technology innovation and development. What is more, as manufacturing processes become increasingly automated and robotized, this cluster of innovation may yet be reunited with volume manufacturing (Brynjolfsson and McAfee, 2014) and indeed with the development of advanced machine intelligence (Bostrom, 2014). The question which arises is whether what has happened is sheer good luck, the random unplanned workings of the market place, or the result of a sequence of critical strategic decisions.

There are three levels of explanation for the Cambridge Phenomenon. First is an immediate explanation: what we now see is the result of a self-sustaining process of business innovation and development. Second is a set of proximate causes, set in the events of the last 50 or 60 years in Cambridge, involving decisions taken by government, local government and especially by the University itself. Third are the deeper long-term causes, which have some parallel with the conception of French historian Fernand Braudel for the *longue duree*, the inter-acting relationship of human society driven by underlying forces, physical constraints and social customs over a long time span (Murray, 2002).

Segal Quince Wicksteed (*op. cit.*) dissected the proximate causes. They were sceptical about the impact of the Cambridge Science Park and doubted whether the Holford Plan's restriction of industrial development had a negative effect. Indeed the latter might well have had positive benefits in protecting what were in effect infant industries, and retaining a non-industrial character in a relatively small place with flexible and non-unionized working practices, where it was easy for people to know what was going on. Retaining the attractiveness of Cambridge as a place to live as well as work had helped to develop many interlocking and informal networks of talented individuals. During the 1960s IBM had proposed bringing its European research HQ to Cambridge, a development which was turned down by the planning system. Segal Quince Wicksteed wonder whether its arrival might have had a damaging impact: 'If IBM had been allowed to establish in Cambridge in the 1960s this might unintentionally have had an inhibiting effect on the development of the local computing industry and on new company formation' (Segal Quince Wicksteed, *op. cit.*, p. 63).

One absolutely crucial factor lay in demand, rather than supply. Demand for CAD technology took off in the 1970s. New market opportunities emerged and

Cambridge-based companies played a central role. The development of Pye and Cambridge Instruments was fostered by specialized demands in the University. In Acorn's case a major individual client – in this case the BBC – provided strong and stable demand which enabled the supplier companies to grow. Massive falls in electronic hardware costs made it easy for small firms to enter the market. The costs of entry were low. Small businesses in the software sector could start in a garage or shed (where they were often hidden from the planners). Yet if markets had not been expanding so strongly, the latent supply capacity in Cambridge would have been much less significant.

What of the deeper issues? The dynamic processes still evolving in Cambridge have all the characteristics of the theory of agglomeration economies set out by the great neoclassical economist Alfred Marshall, and periodically rediscovered by later thinkers:

> When an industry has chosen a location for itself, it is likely to stay there long: so great are the advantages which people following the same skilled trade get from near neighbourhood to one another. The mysteries of the trade become no mysteries, but are as it were in the air… Good work is rightly appreciated; inventions and improvements in machinery, in process, in the general organization of the business have their merits promptly discussed: if one man starts an idea it is promptly taken up by others and combined with suggestions of their own; and thus it becomes the source of further new ideas. (Marshall, quoted in Hall, 1998, p. 303)

Published in 1920, Marshall's theory was informed by what he had seen and learned of nineteenth-century manufacturing industry. But he might just as easily be describing the processes of interaction and innovation at work in Cambridge today. It supplies one level of explanation – in a buoyant business cluster, impetus, innovation and growth simply becomes self-sustaining. But what creates the cluster?

Reviewing Marshall's insights (and more recent contributions from Putnam, Krugman and Porter) Hall concluded that breakthroughs occur in certain types of regions, characterized by a set of social and cultural structures favourable to conceptual advances. There are strong but often informal structures for the exchange of knowledge and ideas, and a high rate of in migration, particularly amongst young people, who are often experimental and untraditional in outlook. Barriers to innovation are so low as to be almost non-existent and there is a constant search for new ideas and approaches. Levels of synergy are high, not just between like-minded individuals, but between seemingly disparate social groups, in an archetypal open society (Hall, *op. cit.*). It is almost a description of events in Cambridge.

## Values and Attitudes within the University

Let us turn to some of the deeper causes. In a memorandum submitted to the House of Commons Select Committee on Science and Technology in 1999 the

University set out its ethos on innovation. Trust and professional autonomy, said the University, underpinned the liberal policy towards innovative activity by its staff. The University was non-bureaucratic and largely self-governing. Academics have considerable autonomy, but an informal system of checks and balances ensured close attention to teaching, research and administrative duties. In the engineering department, for example, which has the highest number of University spin-out enterprises, teaching performance and student assessments were closely monitored and professors heavily involved in undergraduate teaching. There was a strong research culture and incentives to maintain research performance. Assessment was based on output and there have been minimal bureaucratic obstacles to staff engaging in innovative activities. The approach to intellectual property was part of this liberal ethos. Unlike almost all other universities, Cambridge did not claim title to the intellectual property created by its employees in the course of their duties. In practice, research in the University was largely funded by the Research Councils, charities and industry. All of these external sponsors required the University to manage the intellectual property output of their funding to the benefit of the inventors and the University. As a result the prevailing ethos was one in which the inventors were motivated to exploit their research. The University was able to work with them in a facilitating way rather than compelling them to work with a potentially heavy-handed bureaucracy, driving activities underground or stifling initiative (Cambridge University, 1999).

Cambridge had a distinct, and arguably exclusive, style - a confidence and assurance based on a long history, which perhaps encouraged people to think long term and not be deflected by the pressure of immediate events. According to Segal Quince Wicksteed this bred an ethos of independence, individualism and self-confidence amongst dons and students. But perhaps there is another overlooked factor: wealth. Cambridge has long been a wealthy and powerful elite institution, attracting wealthy, confident and intelligent individuals (and their families).

Reflecting its ethos on innovation, the University had interesting contractual practices – and in some senses these were ahead of their time. Even in the 1980s a high proportion of teaching and research staff were on short fixed term contracts, with no expectation of tenure, reflecting the University's wish not to build up large overheads, and recognition that in making appointments the University was always in a strong position. When their contracts expired those wishing to stay in Cambridge had every incentive to look for employment in local businesses (or establish their own). For those in University employment on the other hand, the contractual arrangements were extraordinarily flexible and loose. Academics were expected to devote themselves to their subject to promote the University and to educate their students. Beyond this they had enormous freedom, especially in relation to the commercial exploitation of research. The University's policy was to leave it to staff members to decide how to engage in outside work and in the applied sciences the presumption was that staff would be involved in consultancy. The attitude towards intellectual property rights was similarly relaxed. These were vested in individual academics rather than the University unless a specific research contract stated otherwise. Thus an environment was created in which all kinds of commercial activity were allowed without regulation, sanction or bureaucracy (Segal Quince Wicksteed, *op. cit.*).

## Whose Plan?

Thus the proximate causes of growth in Cambridge are set in a series of strategic decisions over a long period, rooted as much in social custom (and sometimes prejudice) as in economic logic. These start with the establishment of Cambridge as a seat of learning, the decisions to develop and sustain its role as a centre for scientific thinking and research as far back as the establishment of the Lucasian Chair in Physics in 1663, the re-ignition of scientific excellence in the nineteenth-century reforms, the philanthropic funding and establishment of the Cavendish centre, the brilliance of late nineteenth and early twentieth century research and the utilization and acceleration of that research in the Second World War. These are the essential foundations for all that came after the War.

The strategic decisions rested firmly within the University as an institution, although on two occasions – the nineteenth-century reforms and the Second World War projects – the state intervened, pushing developments in a particular direction. In a faint echo of war time socialism the state intervened again in the 1960s with the creation of the Ministry of Technology.

Was the Cambridge Phenomenon unplanned? It depends what you mean by planning. Certainly it was not planned by the state, nor was a precise outcome established through some sort of rational process; but neither did events emerge randomly. Most of the key decisions that led to recent outcomes were taken, not through pure market processes, but within a single, powerful, and long lived institution with a distinct and deep-seated culture: the University. Within that context and upon that institutional platform (and sometimes in response to external pressures, threats or opportunities) individuals played a central role, initiating, innovating and improvising, in an environment where a great deal of freedom was on offer. This was an open society at work, and if you like, a process of orderly disorder. There was indeed plenty of encouragement and careful handling, but little direct management, and very little state direction. If it was not a great British plan, then it has to be said that it shares many of the characteristics of one.

Was the Cambridge experience a national success story? Here the answer has to be somewhat equivocal. On one level the answer is clearly positive: Cambridge has had extraordinary success in generating new firms and innovation at the cutting edge of technology and science, and its potential for the future looks undiminished. The Holford plan did not cause damage and arguably was one of the conditions for post-war growth. But set against this some very difficult questions remain to be answered. Has the very high rate of young company acquisitions, by foreign (often US) predators been of net long term benefit to the UK economy? (Garnsey and Mohr, 2011). Has the remoteness of Cambridge based science research and innovation within the UK deprived manufacturing in other regions of the opportunity for new ideas which have so readily entered the world market? That issue was put into sharp focus for the Massachusetts economy by Professor Michael Best of the Lowell Centre for Industrial Competitiveness: 'We run the risk of turning into Cambridge, England: we'll have isolated clusters of the very best University research and a number of small R&D firms but not the downstream production, service and support jobs that make a vibrant economy. We'll create all the new ideas – but others will get too much of the benefit' (Best, quoted in Minshall and Gregory, 2013). The judgement of success, as we have already seen, is very far from simple.

## References

Arm.com (2014) Website. Available at: http://www.arm.com/about/company-profile/index.php.

Barnett, C. (1986) *The Audit of War: The Illusion and Reality of Britain as a Great Nation*. London: Macmillan.

BBC Cambridgeshire News (2013) Astra Zeneca Staff to Make Cambridge Move Before New HQ is Built. Available at: http://www.bbc.co.uk/news/uk-england-cambridgeshire-25003507.

Bostrom, N. (2014) *Superintelligence: Paths, Dangers, Strategies*. Oxford: Oxford University Press.

Brynjolfsson, E. and McAfee, A. (2014) *The Second Machine Age: Work, Progress and Prosperity in a Time of Brilliant Technologies*. New York: WW Norton.

Butterfield, J. (1985) *Foreword* in Segal Quince Wicksteed, *The Cambridge Phenomenon: The Growth of High Technology Industry in a University Town*. Cambridge: Segal Quince Wicksteed.

Cambridge University (1999) Memorandum Submitted to the House of Commons Select Committee on Science and Technology, 17 January 1999, Cambridge.

Coopey, R. (1993) Industrial policy in the white heat of the scientific revolution, in Coopey, R., Fielding, S. and Tiratsoo, N. (eds.) *The Wilson Governments 1964–1970*. London: Pinter.

Edgerton, D. (1996) *Science, Technology and the British Industrial 'Decline', 1870–1970*. Cambridge: Cambridge University Press.

Eight19 website. Available at: http://www.eight19.com/company-overview/company-overview.

Garnsey, E. and Mohr, V. (2011) Who Owns the Cambridge Phenomenon? Institute of Manufacturing, University of Cambridge. Available at: http://www.clarehall.cam.ac.uk/fileadmin/template/images/6.0_lifemembers/E-Bulletin/Elizabeth_Garnsey_Article.pdf.

Green, V. (1969) *The Universities*. Harmondsworth: Pelican.

Hall, P. (1998) *Cities and Civilization: Culture, Innovation and the Urban Order*. London: Weidenfeld and Nicolson.

Hill, C. (1969) *Reformation to Industrial Revolution: The Pelican Economic History of Britain, Volume 2, 1530–1780*. Harmondsworth: Pelican.

Holford, W. and Wright, M. (1950) *Cambridge Planning Proposals: A Report to the Cambridgeshire County Council*. Cambridge: Cambridge University Press.

Kirk, K. and Cotton, C. (2012) *The Cambridge Phenomenon: 50 Years of Innovation and Enterprise*. London: Third Millennium.

Miller, M. (2004) Holford, William Graham, Baron Holford. Oxford: The Oxford Dictionary of National Biography. Available at: http://www.oxforddnb.com/view/printable/31245.

Minshall, T. and Gregory, M. (2013) Evolutions of the Cambridge Phenomenon, Institute for Manufacturing, University of Cambridge. Presentation given at the Delhi Innovation Roundtable.

Murray, O. (2012) Introduction, in Braudel, F. *The Mediterranean and the Ancient World*. Harmondsworth: Penguin.

Rothblatt, S. (1968) *The Revolution of the Dons: Cambridge and Society in Victorian England*. London: Faber and Faber.

Sanderson, M. (1972) *The Universities and British Industry 1850–1970*. London: Routledge and Kegan Paul.

Segal Quince Wicksteed (1985) *The Cambridge Phenomenon: The Growth of High Technology Industry in a University Town*. Cambridge: Segal Quince Wicksteed.

Uglow, J. (2002) *The Lunar Men: The Friends Who Made the Future, 1730–1810*. London: Faber and Faber.

Wright, M. (1982) *Lord Leverhulme's Unknown Venture: The Lever Chair and the Beginnings of Town and Regional Planning 1908–1948*. London: Hutchinson.

# 7

## Driving Ambitions
## Engineering the British Motorways

*Who built the UK's motorways?… What I observe first is the complexity of the task when seen as a whole, and the scarcity of certainties in it… What was ordered was a system. But it was not ordered as a whole. Successive parts of it were ordered, with degrees of uncertainty about detail at the time of announcement, and uncertainty about what would be ordered next and when, if at all.*
Sir Peter Baldwin, former Permanent Secretary, Department for Transport, 2004

Half hidden behind plastic litterbins, there lies at Charnock Richard motorway service station in Lancashire a remarkable little concrete monument, in the shape of single standing car wheel. It records the construction of the M6 motorway, a fact now evidently taken for granted by its users, yet a feat of British planning and engineering almost without parallel. For the M6 motorway is where Britain's post-war motorway building project began, specifically in an 8 mile (13 km) long project called the Preston By-Pass, opened by Conservative Prime Minister Harold Macmillan in 1958. It is hardly an exaggeration to say that the building of these motorways was the first government funded transport plan since the departure of the Roman legions in AD 410. For Britain's railways and canals had been built at private initiative, and its early toll roads, like its ports, were not built by government.

There is no doubting the credentials of this infrastructure programme as a significant British plan. Yet why did the project start in Lancashire, an old industrial region far from London and many of the UK's other big cities and with a modest scheme to by-pass a modest town? Who was responsible for

# DRIVING AMBITIONS: ENGINEERING THE BRITISH MOTORWAYS • 105

Figure 7.1. *Monument recording the construction of the M6 Motorway, Charnock Richard Service Area, Lancashire.* A forlorn totem, hidden away behind signs and waste bins, records the first stages in the greatest public works programme since the departure of the Roman Legions.

driving the whole project onto the political agenda and turning the plans into reality? What caused government and the civil service to lend support? These are the central questions in this chapter; answering them turns out to be quite a long story.

## The First Proposals

Writing at the turn of the century, H.G. Wells had anticipated the need for motorways with customary prescience: 'Through the varied country the new roads will run, here cutting through a crest and there running like some colossal aqueduct across a valley, swarming with a multitudinous traffic of bright, swift (and not necessarily ugly) mechanisms' (Wells, 2008, p. 63). In 1901 the future Prime Minister Arthur Balfour wondered whether, in addition to railways and tramways, great highways might be constructed solely for use by motor traffic (Morrison and Minnis, 2012). The first Parliamentary Bill for motorway construction, a private members bill for a new road between London and Brighton, dates back to 1906. It was promoted by John Douglas-Scott-Montagu, the 2nd Baron Montagu of Beaulieu. Restricted to mechanically propelled vehicles, Montagu's proposal would have been a dual carriageway, with slip road access and without a speed limit. It was withdrawn after opposition from the railway lobby, which saw it (correctly) as a great threat to their business.

Another private members bill, introduced in 1923, sought powers for the construction of a 226 mile (364 km) Northern and Western Motorway, linking London with Liverpool. This was to be a toll motorway and was supported by local authorities along the route. Though revived again in 1929 the project found no support from government (Charlesworth, 1984). Whitehall's only positive contribution to road building came in 1909 with the creation of a Road Board, under the Development and Road Improvement Funds Act, by Chancellor David Lloyd George. The aim of the Board was to create fast roads explicitly for motor traffic; but in practice these roads never came about, thwarted by disagreements with local authorities and highway agencies, and by their cost. Instead of motorways, plans were made for a new set of arterial roads to serve London. Set out in the report of the London Traffic Branch of the Board of Trade in 1910 (Morrison and Minnis, *op. cit.*), these included proposals for a new Great West Road, Western Avenue, Eastern Avenue and New Cambridge Road. Government was thinking small. None of these schemes were 'grade separated' roads on the motorway model. Instead there were modest proposals to relieve bottlenecks by building bypasses, such as those at Kingston upon Thames and Croydon. Although priority was given to the Great West Road, progress was delayed by the First World War (when all funds were diverted to war work) and the first scheme implemented was a modest Croydon bypass. In 1919 the Road Board's powers passed to the new Ministry of Transport, which began work on a major programme of road improvement, but did nothing to advance the cause of motorways (*ibid.*). Thus the overall condition of British roads deteriorated.

## Dictators and Autocrats

It was a different story on the continent, where Italy and Germany led the way. Doubtless the construction of motorways was an attractive project for the dictators. With authoritarian control of government and politics, they were easy to achieve and as positive demonstration projects they showed the Fascists' determination to build a strong state and tackle unemployment. With Mussolini in support, Italy led the way in building roads solely for motor traffic. In 1923, as Britain began its programme of patch and mend improvements and bypasses, Italy created state subsidized companies to construct and operate toll roads which subsequently reverted to state control. The *autostrada* consisted only of a single carriageway, but unlike the British trunk roads they were entirely separated from adjoining land and development. On the motorway model, traffic could only enter and leave at defined points. Mussolini began his *autostrada* programme in 1924, and over the next 10 years 300 miles (483 km) were completed; by 1935 the system stretched across northern Italy from coast to coast (Drake *et al.*, 1969).

Motorways were no less attractive to Hitler, but were engineered to a much higher standard than the *autostrada*. Their construction was an important part of the Nazis pre-war public works programmes, designed to reduce unemployment and build an efficient economic infrastructure. Yet the *autobahnen* were also concrete and highly visible symbols of the new Germany and soon became a focus for propaganda at home and abroad. In 1938 Fritz Todt, Hitler's General Inspector of Roads, described the new roads as 'the most vivid example of the unity of the Reich' (Todt, quoted in Merriman, 2007, p. 31). Whilst there remains debate about the military purpose of the new roads, there can be little doubt that they had military utility, as a means of supporting logistics and swiftly moving troops and vehicles. Whatever their purpose, the scale of construction was impressive. Historically, responsibility for German roads had been shared by twenty-six provincial and 600 township authorities. In 1934 the Nazis passed a law delegating all responsibility to the Reichsautobahnen, a subsidiary of German state railways with a capital of 50 million marks. In 1933 work started on a national network of 4,300 miles (6,900 km) of *autobahnen* (*ibid.*). By the end of 1939 over 2,300 miles (3,700 km) of *autobahnen* had been opened to traffic, all with a quality road surface, easy gradients and sweeping curves. Reporting directly to Hitler, Todt was given sweeping powers and authority to get the roads built (Drake *et al.*, *op. cit.*). It is difficult to imagine that he had any problems with objectors.

The dictators did not have a monopoly on public works and inter-war road building. In the United States a controlled access parkway road, the Bronx River Parkway in New York City, was completed in 1925. During the early 1930s the Long Island State Park Commission under its autocratic and determined chairman, Robert Moses, was developing another new road system on Long Island. In 1934, Moses, by then Construction Coordinator for New York City, began work on the construction of a system of expressways and parkways (the latter reserved solely for cars) for the whole of New York. By 1939 164 miles (264 km) of four- and six-lane highways, all grade separated from the rest of the road system, had been completed (*ibid.*).

Yet it was the *autobahnen* which caught the imagination of British engineers and politicians, not least because the Germans were so keen to promote their achievements. In September 1937 a group known as the German Roads Delegation, including more than 200 representatives from the British Parliament, local authorities, engineers and vehicle operators, visited Germany to inspect the new system. The delegates saw over 500 miles (800 km) of the new roads – also finding time to visit the Munich Oktoberfest, Leipzig Opera House, Heidelberg Castle, the Berlin Olympics Stadium, and an event featuring appearances by both Hitler and Mussolini. A report prepared for the County Surveyors Society extolled the qualities of the new road network, which was helping to reduce road accidents, and had cost less to build than widening existing roads. But not everyone found the German motorways to their taste. An editorial in the 1938 *Geographical Magazine* thought that, while dictators might be happy to express themselves in grand public works, democratic governments like the British were always subject to critical opposition and could not afford to burden their Exchequer from motives of self-advertisement (Merriman, *op. cit.*). This would become a familiar objection, chiming well with the orthodox Treasury and civil service view of national road investment.

## Government Opposition

Throughout the 1920s the Ministry of Transport continued to hold the line that piecemeal improvement to existing routes, rather than big projects, should have priority. Grants were offered to local authorities, especially the county councils, to take forward this work. But the 1930s economic crisis caused even this limited programme to be cut back, so that by 1935 only 500 miles (800 km) of bypass had been completed, less than half that planned, and in sharp contrast to the achievements of the dictators. In 1931 a Royal Commission on Transport set out its views on new roads, concluding that taking into account this (rather limited) achievement and the work planned, it could not support any scheme involving large-scale additional expenditure on roads. In relation to motorways the conclusion was dismissive: 'We feel that roads of this type are not required'. Motorways built as toll roads came in for particular criticism: 'We are strongly opposed to any suggestion of this nature' (quoted in Charlesworth, *op. cit.*, p. 9). It was an official view repeated by Frederick Cook, the Chief Engineer at the Ministry of Transport, in 1939: 'In a densely roaded country such as ours, conditions would not permit the construction of a system of motorways' (quoted in Charlesworth, *op. cit.*, p. 16). Cook was merely repeating the line taken by the Transport Minister Hore Belisha, responding to a parliamentary question on motorways in 1936:

> I have often given consideration to this matter, but, in a thickly populated and thickly roaded country such as ours, I am not prepared to recommend embarking on the construction of an entirely new road system. I think our task is to improve the system we now have. (Quoted in Cook, 2004, p. 112)

So the official conclusions were unshakeable: motorways were not required in Britain; and in any event they could not be built. It is an extraordinary fact that the Eddington transport report, produced for Tony Blair's government in 2006, deployed the same arguments and took almost exactly the same line in opposing high-speed railways (HM Treasury, 2006).

Oddly, it was in the provinces, especially in North West England, and specifically in Lancashire, that most progress was made with new roads before the war. The Liverpool–East Lancashire Road, built between 1929 and 1933, was one of the most important new routes in Britain. Although all its junctions were still at grade, the road was close to motorway standards, its 28 mile (45 km) length constructed almost entirely as dual carriageway on new alignments. Within Liverpool the Corporation had pioneered the provision of dual carriageways, such as Queens Drive and Broad Green Road, built essentially as suburban avenues and boulevards rather than long-distance roads. Queens Drive was the most important new road scheme started before the First World War, being one of the earliest dual carriageways and the first British ring road. Designed by James Brodie, the council's dynamic city engineer (also the inventor of nets for football goals) the scheme passed through farmland on the edge of the fast expanding city. Work began in 1903 and was competed in the 1920s, the road conceived as a linear park resembling the broad single carriageways being used by Parker and Unwin in Letchworth Garden City, and echoing the parkway concept which was to emerge later in the United States. It was partly financed by a charge levied on developers of new houses fronting onto the road (Morrison and Minnis, *op. cit.*).

Brodie designed several more boulevards in Liverpool as radial routes with tramways in the central reservation, but his ambitions were not restricted to roads. With Sir Basil Mott and Sir Maurice Fitzmaurice, he was responsible for the greatest engineering feat of the 1930s, the two mile (3 km) long Mersey tunnel. Connecting Liverpool and Birkenhead, it was the longest underwater tunnel in the world, a giant sinuous single 44 ft (13 m) diameter bore, with provision for two lanes of traffic in each direction. Originally lined with a Vitrolite black glass dado, framed in stainless steel, and with six monumental ventilation shafts by the architect Herbert Rowse, this was a supremely confident and glamorous expression of municipal power and ability (Liverpool City Council, 2003). Thus, as Whitehall continued to doubt the case for brand new roads (a transport system which could have proved invaluable in the Second World War), industrial Lancashire and Liverpool powered ahead, setting a trend which was to continue.

## Lancashire Leads the Way

The German road plans may not have impressed Whitehall's officials; but they had an enormous impact on the local authority engineers who had joined the 1937 German Road Delegation (including James Drake, a young civil engineer). These municipal engineers had seen the future, and it worked. In October 1937 the County Surveyors Society held a meeting to review their members' experiences in Germany, concluding that entirely new roads were a necessity, new alignments would be much less costly than improving existing routes, accidents would be substantially reduced, well designed new roads would cause less environmental damage than widening old roads (and could in time even be seen as positive features), and that a coordinated national network was essential. The Society promptly established a committee for national motorways, and in May 1938 set out its plan for a 1,000 mile (1,600 km) system of motorways, linking all the main centres of population and industry (Charlesworth, *op. cit.*).

Although it was a more realistic plan than the earlier call from the Institute of Highway Engineers in 1936 for a 2,800 mile (4,500 km) national network (Baldwin, 2004), none of this found favour with the Minister. Yet the long-term impact of the County Surveyors' plan and their subsequent lobbying activity would be profound.

The Second World War was pivotal. On every front, wartime planning accelerated social and economic change. The state machine grew in power and ability, not just in the military sphere but in construction and development too, using powers of compulsory purchase and state direction on a large scale. In Whitehall professionals entered the ranks of the civil service: 'Wartime Whitehall was a success story, a crucial factor in producing what became the most thoroughly mobilised society' (Hennessy, 1989, p. 88). The airfield construction programme used massive construction and machinery, and led to a new understanding of civil engineering techniques. In 1939 RAF Bomber Command had only twenty-seven grass-covered airfields; in 1944 it had 128 airfields, of which only two were grass (Edgerton, 2011). By the end of the war government had also seen at first hand the quality of the German *autobahnen* (Baldwin, *op. cit.*).

On planning for post-war motorways the initiative still rested with professional bodies, rather than officials and the Ministry remained characteristically unconvinced. Philip Noel Baker, Joint Parliamentary Secretary at the Ministry of War Transport, said that the government did not see a justification for a widespread system of motorways, despite a consulting engineers' report showing that it would be no more costly to build a length of motorway than improve an existing road, and that trucks would travel faster and at lower running cost on a motorway. Thus the 1945 Labour government carried forward an austerely low programme of investment in roads, at only 75 per cent of the pre-war level. Its 1946 Ten Year Plan (which again gave priority to completing conventional road schemes instead of motorways) was pared back still further by the Transport Ministry in its programme for 1948–1952 (Barnett, 1995).

Local government in Lancashire remained purposeful. In 1938, shortly before the outbreak of war, the County Council had persuaded Leslie Burgin, Minister of Transport, to support their proposal for an experimental motorway running for 60 miles (97 km) north–south from Warrington to Carnforth, on the line of the present M6 (Charlesworth, *op. cit.*). The war stopped the scheme, but did not dent Lancashire's resolve. Led by its energetic and ambitious engineer, James Drake, newly appointed in 1945 as County Surveyor and Bridgemaster, the County prepared a remarkable 'Road Plan for Lancashire' in 1949, with road building seen as a central component of its strategy for economic development. Drake's plan included twelve new express routes, totalling 217 miles (349 km), of which 94 miles (151 km) were to be motorways, 190 miles (306 km) of dual carriageways, and 280 miles (450 km) of linking roads (Lancashire County Council, 1949).

Over the next 50 years a very substantial part of Drake's plan was to be

Figure 7.2. *Sir James Drake, County Surveyor and Bridgemaster, Lancashire County Council.* Intelligent, forceful and assertive, civil servants in the Ministry of Transport warned each other when Drake was in the building.

implemented. Armed with its plan Lancashire continued to press government for motorway construction. Drake realized that, with little public funding available, the best chance of building a continuous system was in breaking the project up into smaller schemes, which could ultimately be knitted together to create a network. He kept his staff busy designing schemes for the shelf, so that they were ready to go as soon as government finance became available (Drake *et al.*, *op. cit.*). When the mood changed in Whitehall in the early 1950s Drake was ready to build: schemes for the Preston Bypass and Lancaster Bypass were confirmed by the Minister in 1955 and work started on the Preston scheme in 1956. In 1956 the Council submitted a third scheme for the Stretford Bypass (now part of the M60 Manchester ring road) and, following confirmation by the Minister, work started on site in 1957. By all accounts Drake was assertive almost to the point of belligerence in pressing his case for motorway investment on civil servants. His deputy, Harry Yeadon, recalled that on Drake's visits to the Ministry of Transport in London, word swiftly went round the civil servants: 'Drake's in the building' (cbrd, 2014).

## Government Finally Persuaded

Lancashire was blazing a trail in motorway construction, but it could not have done so without support from government itself – not least as its schemes were financed with the help of 75 per cent government grants. What had led to the change of mood? In truth it had been a long slow process, beginning in the war, when the government machine had acquired the capability to act (through the massive airfield construction programme and the clearance and repair of war damaged cities) and shown the first real evidence of a change in attitude. By 1942 even Frederick Cook had accepted the potential benefits of motorways, although his advice to government remained equivocal (Cook, *op. cit.*). By 1943, alongside the County Surveyors Society, the Institute of Highway Engineers and British Road Federation were lobbying vigorously. In 1944, Cook, by now Sir Frederick, had been replaced at the Ministry of War Transport by A.J. Lyddon, who swiftly recommended a national motorway plan; his successor Major Aldington in 1945 showed a similar level of commitment. In 1946 the Labour Transport Minister, Alfred Barnes finally announced the government's Ten Year Trunk Road Plan, including 800 miles (1,290 km) of motorways (Edbrooke, 1971).

Yet the post-war Labour government continued to pursue a policy of piecemeal improvements to existing roads. Money was short and the government's priorities were focused on health and housing, rather than the provision of basic economic infrastructure. The historian Corelli Barnett is scathing in his condemnation of wartime and immediate post-war government policy:

> The wartime coalition government failed across the whole field of industrial and educational policy to evolve coherent medium or long term strategies capable of transforming Britain's obsolete industrial culture... Instead all the boldness of vision ... all the lavishing of resources had gone towards the working of the social miracle of New Jerusalem. (Barnett, 1986, p. 304)

On roads the Treasury view prevailed. Interviewed in 1953 by the House of Commons Select Committee on Roads, a Treasury official patiently explained that the Transport Ministry had first to bid for resources from the Investment Programmes Committee. The Committee's decision would then be referred to the Treasury whose sole objective was to squeeze the Ministry's estimate simply in order to save money and reduce the scale of investment (Charlesworth, *op. cit.*).

Though they were not to spend for several years, government did at least provide the regulatory framework for motorways in the 1949 Special Roads Act. According to Sir Peter Baldwin, Frederick Cook's work on specifications, alongside data freshly gathered from the German roads, provided the basis for the Act. It gave highway authorities the power to acquire land after a scheme had been confirmed by the Minister (Baldwin, *op. cit.*). Thus local authorities, rather than government, remained the agents for action – quite unlike the state powers used by the pre-war dictators. Building motorways was now a government commitment, but economic conditions would need to improve before action could be taken. The necessary shift in attitudes took place in the early 1950s with a Conservative administration in power. With an improving economic situation, pressure mounted from local authorities and commercial interests, whilst rising car ownership led to a broad based demand for better roads. In the United States, President Eisenhower had supported the creation of an interstate highway system – 37,000 miles (59,590 km) of motorway standard limited access roads –

both for economic reasons and to assist in the evacuation of cities in the event of nuclear attack (Charlesworth, *op. cit.*).

The Preston bypass, built as a four lane road with grass verges and wide bridges to accommodate future growth, began life as a disjointed fragment of a motorway project that took 16 years to complete. Priority was at last given to the 55 mile (89 km) London to Birmingham motorway, the M1, with consultants commissioned in 1951 to study the route. Again the County Councils were used as agents for construction. Work began on the M1 in 1958 and Ernest Marples, Transport Minister, opened the motorway in 1959. Yet only in the 1960s did Government truly pick up the gauntlet; in 1962 Marples announced a commitment to build 1,000 miles (1,600 km) of motorways by the early 1970s. Amazingly, the County Surveyors Society pre-war target had become official government policy. The Surveyors promptly responded, upping the ante by making proposals for an additional 1,700 miles (2,740 km) of motorway.

Figure 7.3. *The Prime Minister's Convoy on the Preston By Pass, 1958*. More than 50 years after the first Private Members Bill for construction of a motorway style road, the first section of British motorway is opened.

Motorways had entered the mainstream of government policy, with the county councils and their engineers firmly in charge of delivery, and a simple form of cost benefit analysis, based on time savings and accident reductions, used to justify the schemes (Drake *et al.*, *op. cit.*). Local government remained in charge until the mid-1960s, when the Labour Transport Minister, Barbara Castle, displaced the county councils by creating the government's own regional Road Construction Units. The cost of building the network was huge, and though Ministers considered imposing road tolls this was never seen to be practicable.

Figure 7.4. *Newly constructed M6 motorway near Salmesbury.* Not built to relieve congestion, the motorway plans were essentially visionary.

By 1961, 150 miles (240 km) of motorway were in use, rising to 400 (640 km) by 1966, and 1,000 (1,600 km) in 1972. Thus a complete national system was created, including the M1 from London to Doncaster (completed in 1972), the M2 from London to Faversham (completed in 1965), the M3 from Lightwater to Popham (completed in 1971), the M5 from Avonmouth to Birmingham (completed in 1971), the M6 from Rugby to Carlisle (completed in 1972), and the M62 across the Pennines from Lancashire to Yorkshire (completed in 1971), a project which proved to be a considerable test of skills and endurance for the engineers and their contractors (Motorway Archive website and Morrison and Minnis, *op. cit.*). The 1946 Ministry plan bore an extraordinary resemblance to the County Surveyors Society 1938 proposal, the completed motorway network in 2010 picking up all the remaining routes identified by the Surveyors, as well as many others.

## Opponents and Protestors

By the early 1970s the wind had changed, as the first environmental protests against road building began to emerge. Partly, the new mood had an economic explanation. In the 1973 oil crisis, the main producers quadrupled their oil prices, triggering an energy crisis and an economic collapse (Cairncross and Macrae, 1975). Government introduced speed limits to reduce energy consumption, and there was some evidence of a decline in traffic volumes (although this did not last long).

In parallel a sea change was occurring in the public mood amongst a rising generation, and especially amongst a small group of young and well organized protestors. By the 1970s they had become expert objectors, questioning the forecasts and assumptions of officials with growing skill and conviction (as we saw in the case of London's failed motorway plans in Chapter 2). Books like Ed Mishan's *The Costs of Economic Growth* (Mishan, 1967), E.F. Shumacher's *Small is Beautiful: A Study of Economics as if People Mattered* (Schumacher, 1973) and not least Jane Jacobs's *The Death and Life of Great American Cities* (Jacobs, 1962) challenged the *status quo*. They had a resonance with the young, helping to shape a new set of values and attitudes, critical of headlong economic growth, technocratic planning, and its adverse impacts. The new values were to permeate all Western societies. In the United States, Altshuler and Luberoff characterized the period between the mid-1960s and early 1970s as an 'era of transition' in the provision of transport mega projects. Adverse impacts on communities and the environment led to intense protests, driven by growing citizen activism, a call for environmental protection, as well as the Civil Rights Movement (Altshuler and Luberoff, 2003). Historian David Priestland sees 1968 as the pivotal year, a year when the post-war settlement began to crack, technocratic planning (epitomized by the US Defence Secretary Robert McNamara), was called into question, and the ethics of the flower power generation were on the rise (Priestland, 2012).

Not only did protestors dispute the officials and their plans, they also began to use disruptive tactics. An individual called John Tyme, a lecturer at Sheffield Polytechnic, became a notorious exponent of disruptive tactics at public inquiries. Tyme took the view that the motorway building programme was an evil, and that more road building simply generated more traffic, making certain the decline of other methods of transport. The road lobby and the Transport Department (which Tyme referred to as the Department of Highways) were involved in a technocratic conspiracy to which Parliamentary approval had never been given, thus Gandhi-like civil disobedience was a legitimate response (Tyme, 1978).

Tyme's views might have seemed extreme, but they proved to be highly influential. By the 1970s the protestors realized that government officials were little influenced by their arguments and were turning to direct action. The route of the M40, for example, involved a controversial cutting through the Chilterns. When this route was confirmed by the Minister following a public inquiry, protesters believed their views had been ignored by officialdom. Similarly the extension of the M40, between Oxford and Birmingham, was strongly opposed. New and sometimes ingenious tactics were deployed. When the Ministry decided to route the M40 through Otmoor against the recommendations of a planning inspector, objectors divided up a field on the route into over 3,500 tiny plots, selling each to an individual objector. The route was changed to avoid this clever legal obstacle and veered away from Otmoor (Morrison and Minnis, *op. cit.*).

Perhaps the most important example of protest and direct action came at the environmentally sensitive Twyford Down near Winchester, designated as a Site of Special Scientific Interest within an Area of Outstanding Natural Beauty and containing several Scheduled Ancient Monuments. In 1990 it had nonetheless been determined as the route of the M3, following several inquiries. Campaigners argued for a tunnel, taking their objection to the European Community, without success. It was the arrival of the so-called 'Dongas Tribe' which turned Twyford into an environmental *cause celebre*. The Dongas, a group of fifteen travellers, claimed a spiritual connection with the land and formed an unlikely alliance with local middle-class protestors. Their eviction in 1993 served only to increase the numbers of protestors, yet without effect at Twyford as the engineering works were well advanced and the road completed in 1994. But a new trend had been set and the protestors moved on to occupy tree houses on the Newbury Bypass, to build tunnels under the A30 at Newmill in Devon, and to declare 'independent republics' along the route of the M11. Policing costs at Twyford Down alone were £2m and the protestors were making life increasingly difficult for politicians (*ibid.*).

It was the end of a golden age for motorway building, which was cut back in the late 1980s and 1990s. During Edward Heath's 3 years in office (1970–1973) 475 miles (765 km) of motorway were constructed; during Mrs Thatcher's 10 years in office (1979–1989) only 385 miles (620 km) were constructed (Baldwin, *op. cit.*). Of course the falling rate of construction was not simply a reflection of the level of protest; the fact was that the national network had been substantially completed. The emphasis of transport policy would begin to shift from building more roads to the more intensive use and management of the assets which had been created, and (to an extent) the needs of pedestrians, cyclists and public transport users. Yet a great task had been completed and a great plan implemented.

## Was It a National Plan?

In some ways this story has slightly odd and surprising features. Surely this was a critical national investment plan? Surely it would have been led decisively by central government or some nationally appointed agency? But the evidence suggests otherwise. Government was consistently indifferent, if not actively hostile, to motorways for the best part of four decades. It took 50 years to get from the first Private Members Bill promoting a motorway style scheme to a start on site. Unlike the Roman roads, the British motorway builders were not led by the dictates of some imperial regime.

Indeed, as Sir Peter Baldwin hinted in the slightly cryptic quote which opened this chapter, there was little drive or direction from the centre. He was certainly in a position to know, having moved in the highest levels of government for 25 years. After classics at Corpus Christi College, Oxford, Baldwin moved to Whitehall and the Treasury and, from 1966 to 1967, was principal private secretary to the Chancellor of the Exchequer, James Callaghan, during Harold

Wilson's administration. His final post was as Permanent Secretary in the Department of Transport from 1976 to 1982. There he detached transport from Prime Minister Edward Heath's Department of the Environment, and became a powerful advocate and champion for motorway building (*Guardian*, 2010).

The truth, hinted at by Baldwin, was that central government played a remarkably limited positive role in the whole process. Unpaid volunteers in a professional society produced the master plan for the national network in 1938. Having endorsed the principle, the objective and most of the plan in 1946, almost a decade later, government was still confining its activities to research, and an essentially regulatory piece of legislation in the Special Roads Act. The real drive for investment came from local government in the county councils (especially in Lancashire) where capable individuals skilfully prepared the ground for a tussle with Whitehall for scarce resources. In a sense government simply fell in behind their plans, against a background of lobbying from the private sector and an emerging popular demand for better roads. For over a decade – until Barbara Castle created her Road Construction Units in the mid-1960s – local government was, almost literally, in the driving seat, designing the schemes, letting the contracts, and doubtless lobbying the government for yet more finance.

For a critical national programme these proceedings had an almost decentralized air; and yet somehow it had all worked. Indeed the reader might be forgiven for detecting in the account faint echoes of Bletchley Park and its code breakers: brilliant minds (Drake had a first in civil engineering from Manchester, Baldwin, a first in classics from Oxford); original thinking, passionate energy and enthusiasm; leadership exercised outside government, with perhaps an air of improvisation. Perhaps that is not too far-fetched a comparison, for the mild mannered Sir Peter would have been no stranger to cryptic messages and improvised activity. During the war he had been one of the Bletchley Park code breakers. With his colleagues in Room 25, Hut 4, he had broken the Japanese diplomatic ciphers, thus giving uninterrupted access to all their secret messages until the fall of Hitler.

## References

Altshuler, A. and Luberoff, D. (2003) *Mega Projects: The Changing Politics of Urban Public Investment*. Washington DC: Brookings Institution Press.

Baldwin, P. and Baldwin, R. (eds.) (2004) *The Motorway Achievement*, Volume 1. London: Thomas Telford.

Baldwin, P. (2004) The circumstances of formation of official policy towards motorways and the execution of the motorway programme, in Baldwin, P. and Baldwin, R. (eds.) (2004) *The Motorway Achievement*, Volume 1. London: Thomas Telford.

Barnett, C. (1995) *The Lost Victory: British Dreams, British Realities 1945-1950*. London: Pan Books.

Barnett, C. (1986) *The Audit of War: The Illusion and Reality of Britain as a Great Power*. London: Macmillan.

Cairncross, F. and Macrae, H. (1975) *The Second Great Crash*. London: Methuen.

cbrd website (2014) *Sir James Drake*. Available at: http://www.cbrd.co.uk/people/james-drake/.

Charlesworth, G. (1984) *A History of British Motorways*. London: Thomas Telford.

Cook, F. (2004) Post war planning and motorways, in Baldwin, P. and Baldwin, R. (eds.) *The Motorway Achievement*, Volume 1. London: Thomas Telford.

Drake, J., Yeadon, H. and Evans. D. (1969) *Motorways*. London: Faber and Faber.

Edbrooke, B.F. (1971) Motorway Planning, in *Motorways in Britain: Today and Tomorrow*. London: Institution of Civil Engineers.

Edgerton, D. (2011) *Britain's War Machine: Weapons, Resources and Experts in the Second World War*. Harmondsworth: Allen Lane.

*Guardian* (2010) Obituary: Sir Peter Baldwin. 8 June 2010. Available at: http://www.theguardian.com/politics/2010/jun/08/sir-peter-baldwin-obituary.

Hennessy, P. (1989) *Whitehall*. London: Martin Secker and Warburg.

HM Treasury/Department for Transport (2006) *The Eddington Transport Study: The Case for Action: Sir Rod Eddington's Advice to Government*. London: The Stationery Office.

Jacobs, J. (1962) *The Death and Life of Great American Cities*. London: Jonathan Cape.

Lancashire County Council (1947) *The Lancashire Roads Plan*. Preston: Lancashire County Council.

Liverpool City Council (2003) *Nomination of Liverpool – Maritime Mercantile City for Inscription on the World Heritage List*. Liverpool: The City Council.

Merriman, P. (2007) *Driving Spaces: A Cultural-Historical Geography of England's M1 Motorway*. Oxford: Blackwell.

Mishan, E. (1969) *The Costs of Economic Growth*. London: Penguin.

Morrison, K. and Minnis, J. (2012) *Carscapes: The Motor Car, Architecture and Landscape in England*. New Haven, CT: Yale University Press.

Motorway Archive website http://www.ciht.org.uk/motorway/m62bounpole.htm. Downloaded February 2015.

Priestland, D. (2012) *Merchant, Soldier, Sage: A New History of Power*. Harmondsworth: Allen Lane.

Schumacher, E.F. (1973) *Small is Beautiful: A Study of Economics As If People Mattered*. London: Blond and Briggs.

Tyme, J. (1978) *Motorways Versus Democracy*. London: Macmillan.

Wells, H.G. (2008) *Anticipations of the Reaction of Mechanical and Scientific Progress upon Human Life and Thought*. London: The Floating Press (reprint of 1902 edition).

# The City as Chessboard
## Constructing the New City of Milton Keynes

*For some minutes Alice stood without speaking, looking out in all directions over the country – and a most curious country it was. There were a number of tiny brooks running straight across it from side to side, and the ground between them was divided into squares by a number of green little hedges, that reached from brook to brook. 'I declare it's marked out just like a large chessboard!' Alice said at last.*

Lewis Carroll, *Alice Through the Looking Glass*

Geographically, Milton Keynes sits in the gentle English countryside of rural Buckinghamshire. Conceptually, it rests forever in the optimistic sunshine of 1960s California, and in particular in the visionary thoughts of Melvin Webber, Professor of Planning at the University of California, Berkeley. Webber had come to the university from the consultants Parsons, Brinckerhoff, Hall and Macdonald where he worked on the San Francisco Bay Area Rapid Transit Study. But while others decried urban sprawl, calling for higher densities and better public transport, Webber had fallen in love with the American suburb and the motor car, as the twin apostles of a new form of urban life, which he christened as 'order in diversity: community without propinquity' (Webber, 1963).

### The Non-Place Urban Realm

The car, said Webber, offered huge advantages over public transport – it gave a door to door, no wait, no transfer, private and flexible route service – and the new highway systems then under construction would offer the traveller unprecedented freedom and flexibility. Decision-makers would have easy access to each other wherever their offices happened to be located. Communication would be easier and costs would fall; thus the high-density city would be increasingly unnecessary and unattractive. Never before had people been able to communicate with each other so easily over long distances; never before had intimacy been so independent of geographical proximity. Rising educational standards were giving access to books, music and the media to more and more people; thus new communities of shared interest would emerge, displacing communities of place.

When Webber was writing, the internet, email, social media, home working and video conferencing had not been dreamed of (though his surname was weirdly appropriate). Yet he clearly foresaw the potential of emerging electronic technologies. New electronic data processing equipment, he said, could operate quite efficiently from a distant location, far removed from the executive offices it served. All of this opened the door to new patterns of living, with communities dispersed, decentralized and linked together with a 'web of communications'. Settlements and patterns of land use: 'are likely to be as pluralistic and diverse as society itself ... our spatial plans, then, will be plans for diversity' (Webber, *op. cit.*, p. 51). In a later essay Webber coined the slightly cumbersome phrase for which, amongst the planning fraternity, he would be best known: 'the non-place urban realm' (Webber, 1964). Lewis Carroll might have appreciated its surreal quality. But his central point was important: the practice of planning should be less about creating idealized communities, and more about enabling a flexible process of change and development.

Webber's breathless optimism, the reality of the Californian dream, and its appeal to a 'do your own thing' generation, were as far sighted as they were seductive. And the remarkable plan for Milton Keynes fitted Webber's concept of economic and social planning frameworks, rooted in diversity and ease of communication. Flexibility and choice underlay the strategy, and arguably the built forms. Derek Walker was Chief Architect and Planner to Milton Keynes Development Corporation from 1970 to 1974, and subsequently Chief Executive of Central Milton Keynes. He described Webber as 'the father of Milton Keynes', acknowledging that his ideas had powerfully influenced the master planners.

In conceptual terms Walker was correct. Yet in terms of design British master planners were already thinking along similar lines. In developing their master plan for Washington New Town, the planners had explored the use of a half mile (0.8 km) grid of roads, which bore an uncanny resemblance to later proposals for Milton Keynes. The fine mesh grid proved unacceptable to traffic engineers, and a more conventional arrangement with motorway style interchanges was substituted. The Washington planners also questioned the relevance of traditional neighbourhood planning, as new levels of mobility meant that people could belong to a whole range of different 'neighbourhoods' (Llewellyn Davies, Weeks and Partners, 1966).

## Llewelyn Davies Leads His Team

Webber visited the new city in its early years and attended Monday evening seminars with the staff. He had spoken to Board Members at an informal seminar in December 1967 on the urban society of the future; earlier new towns, he argued, were products of the middle industrial era, whereas Milton Keynes would be part of the post-industrial era characterized by the 'knowledge industries of education, research and development, decision making, information handling and systems analysis' (Webber, quoted in Bendixson and Platt, 1992, p. 47). Webber had close links with the Centre for Environmental Studies (CES) in London, where Llewellyn Davies was Chairman of Trustees (Jeffery, 2012). Indeed both Llewellyn Davies and Richard Crossman, the Labour Minister for Housing and Local Government, had been highly active in creating CES, seeking funding from the philanthropic Ford Foundation, based in New York. The British new towns had been an important factor in the bid for American funding, for here, it seemed, was something that the Americans could learn from. Crossman drafted the terms of the request to the Ford Foundation, and when finances were secured, steered Llewellyn Davies deftly into the Chairman's job (Clapson, 2004).

Led by Llewelyn Davies, a small group of architects, planners and social scientists, based in London's Bloomsbury, where Llewellyn Davies held the chair in town planning at University College London, were to lead the creation of the new city. Llewellyn Davies worked extremely closely with Lord Campbell, the Milton Keynes Chairman. Jointly they drove the planning process, deciding at the outset on the basic layout (Shostak, 2015). Though some strategic elements were fixed – like the road grid and the drainage network – there was a high level of intrinsic flexibility. As Lee Shostak, former Milton Keynes planner puts it: 'You could flip a grid square from housing to employment without destroying the integrity of the plan' (*ibid.*). Thus the plan combines strategic direction with elements of non-prescriptive (or non-absolutist) style. In that sense it has a resonance with the loose and sometimes vaguely anarchic British planning style we have encountered before. As specified by consultants Llewellyn Davies, the plan sets out its goals for the new city: opportunity and freedom of choice; easy movement and access; balance and variety; an attractive city; public awareness and participation; and efficient and imaginative use of resources (MKDC, 1970). The plan's fixed elements would allow the greatest possible scope for freedom and change as developments unfurled. Like a mantra, freedom of choice is referred to repeatedly in the plan. In his introduction the Chairman emphasized the concept of flexibility, and the fact that Milton Keynes was amongst the first new towns designated with the objective of securing 50 per cent owner-occupied housing and 50 per cent of its investment from the private sector.

Perhaps it was the plan's ethos that won over Steen Eiler Rasmussen, that great admirer of London and its essentially associational, and pluralistic planning style (see Chapter 2). He would surely have supported Webber's endorsement of pluralism and diversity. 'Milton Keynes' said Rasmussen, 'represents a reaction to a number of the conventional principles of the new town ... but it is nevertheless a true child of that movement. It is only – like any normal child – critical of its parents... Milton Keynes is, in my opinion, an utterly English phenomenon' (Rasmussen, 1982, p. 408).

## The Nature of Milton Keynes

Emphasizing choice and populism made the plan very different from its new town predecessors. The key design element was the 1-kilometre grid of dual carriageways, rather than a concentric city plan. It was an open new town; anyone could move there by choice, rather than nomination by local authorities in an 'overspill housing' arrangement. Densities were low, there were extensive public open spaces, and employment and retail uses were decentralized across the city. This was an optimum arrangement for car users as it spread traffic and reduced central area congestion, but a difficult arrangement for public transport operators, because demand for travel was diffused, rather than concentrated along corridors (Jeffery, *op. cit.*).

The physical parallels between Milton Keynes and American cities seem obvious enough. Writing in the Architects Journal, Tim Mars famously described it as a 'Little Los Angeles in Buckinghamshire' (Mars, 1992). Yet American comparisons can be overdone. Milton Keynes is not Los Angeles, a city where new roads were retrofitted to existing suburbs, nor is it the creation of market forces pure and simple. On the contrary, so many elements and details have been carefully and thoughtfully planned and controlled, from the sewers and roads to the trees and park benches (the Milton Keynes bench, designed by a Development Corporation architect in 1974, became a widely sold commercial success). Development was driven, not by private developers, but by an enterprising, autocratic, and frequently evangelistic, bureaucracy. When the Corporation was condemned for ignoring cyclists and pedestrians, it made amends, creating the 'redway' (cycleway) network – one of the most extensive networks of cycle routes and footpaths of any city in Britain, connecting housing, schools, shopping and employment.

Tim Mars invented the Los Angeles tag, but was doubtful about architectural and urban design parallels. He saw Milton Keynes as a scaled-down English version of South California, and a 'rationalized' Los Angeles. In design terms, he said, Chief Architect, Derek Walker, had built 'the sort of city – urban, visual and monumental – that Webber had shown to be obsolete and irrelevant' (Mars, *op. cit.*, p. 23). These criticisms echoed Walter Bor, one of the original consultant planners, who claimed that 'arrogant master planners had turned the plan inside out' (Bor, quoted in Bishop, 1986, p. 94). The Corporation had become home to a group of young architects known as 'the undertakers' because of their penchant

Figure 8.1. *Dansteed Way, Milton Keynes.* By turning the back of development onto the main road grid, behind lavish landscaping, a remarkable garden city appearance is conjured, as too is the realisation of Melvin Webber's 'non place urban realm'.

for black suits. Each architect was given a grid square to design, and this they did, starting from a blank sheet of paper as though nothing else had existed. Thus each square became highly individualistic (Bishop, *op. cit.*). Rather than relating to the road network, the grid squares were turned in on themselves, with shops and other centres unrelated to the main road grid (Shostak, *op. cit.*). Wide open reservations alongside the roads were retained. Lavishly landscaped, they created a garden city feel, but also contributed to the lack of local identity, a 'non place' in Webber's parlance.

Mars argued that Milton Keynes was not a city at all, but a form of urban countryside: its parks offered environments for pedestrians and cyclists without parallel, and this was hardly a hallmark of Los Angeles. Indeed, English landscape concepts permeated the city's design. Landscape architect Peter Youngman influenced the final form of the road layout. His colleagues were intent on an American style geometric grid. Youngman walked the site with them, and persuaded the planners to abandon an American style rigid grid for a traditionally British curvaceous design, responding to gentle undulations in the landscape (*Guardian*, 2005), whether consciously or not, in the spirit of Capability Brown, Paxton and the English landscape school. Youngman prescribed a landscape palette, comprising one dominant forest tree, small tree and shrub, for each city zone, comprising several grid squares. The roads avoided underpasses and flyovers by an essentially British device – the traffic roundabout.

## The Proposal Emerges

Indeed, the entire Milton Keynes project had emerged from a thoroughly British planning process. Local rather than central government first mooted the idea of a new town in Buckinghamshire. In the early 1950s Bletchley's determined Labour councillors were frequently in Westminster, making the case for their town's growth under the Town Development Act (Bendixson and Platt, *op. cit.*). By 1962 Fred Pooley, Buckinghamshire's County Planning Officer, anticipating the growing pressure for housing development, argued that planned development in northern Buckinghamshire would help to preserve the green belt in the south of the county. Yet Pooley's vision for what became Milton Keynes was a far cry from Webber's. Influenced by the thinking of architect Le Corbusier, he foresaw a high-density city of apartments and houses linked by a monorail system. Within the County Council Pooley's idea had a good deal of support, and was warmly welcomed by the influential journalist and arch critic of suburbia, Ian Nairn (Clapson, *op. cit.*)

Pooley's proposal had sown the seed, but it needed much wider support. This came in the mid-1960s from two sources: in the deathless prose of fellow planners; and the political drive of a new Labour government, focused on modernity and change. In the words of Prime Minister Harold Wilson's celebrated speech to his 1963 party conference, a new Britain was to be forged in

Figure 8.2. *Prime Minister Harold Wilson.* Wilson embraced modernity and the use of state planning; the passing of the second New Towns Act in 1965 paved the way for the creation of Milton Keynes.

the white heat of scientific revolution. Wilsons's theme was uncompromisingly dirigiste. Labour would use state power to modernize industry and plan the economy. He concluded: 'We must use all the resources of democratic planning, all the latent and underdeveloped energies and skills of our people to ensure Britain's standing in the world' (Wilson, quoted in Pimlott, 1992). Support for positive planning was duly cemented by passing a second New Towns Act in 1965.

The regional planners had been at work before Labour's arrival in power in 1964. The need for more new towns in the south was flagged in the South East Regional Study in 1964, which highlighted forecasts of natural increase of 2.5 million people in the South East and a further 1 million in migration. It proposed major new cities for Bletchley in Buckinghamshire, as well as locations in South Hampshire, Berkshire, Essex and Kent, alongside several large expansions of existing towns (Ward, 1994). Initially the new Labour ministers were sceptical of the case for massive investment in the south of England. Their priority was growth and investment in the north. But population forecasts gave the South East Study an inescapable credibility. By 1964 Britain's population was growing as it had not done for decades. The Milton Keynes public inquiry heard from the Ministry that by 2000 population was expected to grow by 20 million (Bendixson and Platt, *op. cit.*). A coalition between two key Whitehall Departments, the Ministry of Housing and Local Government, and Wilson's newly created Department of Economic Affairs, led respectively by the formidable figures of Richard Crossman and George Brown, won the day against the doubts of other Ministers. Thus Bletchley new town, renamed Milton Keynes after a small village on the site, was designated in 1967 (Ward, *op. cit.*).

About 45 miles (72 km) distant from central London and 25 miles (40 km) from the edge of London's built up area, it was thought that Milton Keynes would be sufficiently large and sufficiently distant from London to act as counter-magnet to the capital. The Minister proposed to designate 10,210 hectares for new town development, reduced to 7,530 hectares following a public inquiry. Civil servants were forceful in rejecting the inspector's call for further size reductions; they were determined that the huge development they had in mind should not be strangled by lack of space (Bendixson and Platt, *op. cit.*).

## Implementation

With Milton Keynes designated, Lord Campbell of Eskan became Chairman in April 1967. He was to remain Chairman for over 15 years, until 1983, a powerful and persuasive guiding presence, and equally a powerful source of continuity, in vision and direction. Campbell was a successful businessman and high-minded socialist, first introduced to the Milton Keynes project over lunch by Sir David Stevenson, the Ministry's permanent secretary. Did he know anyone who might be interested in taking on the chairmanship of the biggest new town in Europe?

Campbell immediately volunteered himself, but to his surprise the offer was not immediately taken up. Not long afterwards, lunching with the new Minister, Antony Greenwood, Campbell was once more introduced to the Milton Keynes idea. His appointment came shortly afterwards (Bendixson and Platt, *op. cit.*).

The Board's brief to four teams of consultants emphasized the need for a plan flexible enough to accommodate future changes in living and working. Campbell had already had long discussions with Llewellyn Davies about the issue. A master plan was duly commissioned from consultants Llewellyn Davies, Weeks, Forestier-Walker and Bor (MKDC, 1970). Their interim report was presented to the newly created Development Corporation in December 1968, and a final report submitted to government in March 1970 (Osborn and Whittick, 1977). Crucial decisions were taken at a two-day Board Meeting in the autumn of 1968. The most important of these was to be the distribution of new employment sites. Should these be concentrated so that they could be easily served by a grid of public transport, or dispersed, reducing congestion but increasing reliance on car commuting? Eventually the Board backed a dispersed option, with profound implications for the form and appearance of the new city – and for the viability of different modes of transport. It remains a controversial issue. In 2010 only 4 per cent of Milton Keynes commuters used the bus and only 7 per cent walked; whereas 71 per cent used their car, against a national average of 61 per cent (Milton Keynes Council, 2010).

Implementation followed a tried and tested route. The Development Corporation used the powers of the New Towns Act to purchase all the land needed within its designated area, where necessary using compulsory purchase (or its threat) near to existing (i.e. essentially agricultural) use value. Thus, as development took place, all the growth in land values brought about by new infrastructure, development, landscaping and marketing would be returned to government. Many of the grid roads were built in advance of development in order to lay down basic infrastructure, and to commit the delivery of the project while government was still positive and funds still flowing. The same was true of sewerage. The Board authorized a huge single plant, fed by massive tunnels, draining the entire site. It was a deliberately and inherently inflexible solution, designed to commit the project as a whole. Yorkshire miners were brought in to dig the deep tunnels (Lock, 2014). This defensive posture was not surprising. In 1966 new national population forecasts were produced. These showed that birth rates were falling, not rising, and that the South East's population was now expected to grow by only 2.6 million, rather than 3.5 million.

Initially progress was slow, partly because of uncertainty about the site proposed for a third London airport. Two of the sites considered by the Roskill Commission (appointed by government in 1968 and reporting in 1970) were very near to the designated areas – Cublington, only 6 miles (10 km) from the boundary, and Thurleigh, just 24 miles (39 km) distant. If either site was chosen there would be serious noise and economic impacts on the new town. The

Roskill Commission eventually chose Cublington, but only four months later the government announced its preference for Foulness near the Thames Estuary. In the event neither Foulness nor Cublington was built (Hall, 1980). The way was clear for the new town to grow unimpeded and by 1976 development was well under way. Almost 14,000 houses had been completed, nearly 10,000 by the public sector and the remainder by private builders (Osborn and Whittick, *op. cit.*).

## Suburbanism Displaces Modernism

Jeff Bishop, an academic commissioned by the Development Corporation, divided its housing into an early 'rationalist' phase and a later 'vernacular' phase. The rationalist phase, financed largely by the public sector, used materials like steel, glass and plastic. It had a coherent modernist design ethos in the collective new town tradition. Chairman Jock Campbell was sympathetic. He had told Richard Crossman that he wanted a properly planned publicly owned new town, and not one, as the Treasury preferred, in which volume house builders would create half the houses. And it was an entirely pragmatic position: in the early days there were national brick shortages, and in any event the volume house builders were simply not confident that demand could be created (Shostak, *op. cit.*). Chief Architect Derek Walker delivered the vision, first in Netherfield, where long modernist terraces ran across the ground contours in uncompromising style.

At Great Linford, Fred Roche, who had been appointed as Director of Design and Production in 1970, decided on a different approach, a more harmonious and sensitive model. Roche took the view that no individual architect should design more than seventy housing units – beyond that even the most brilliant designer ran out of ideas and started repeating (Lock, *op. cit.*). It was an inspired move. Today Great Linford has the feel of a place with depth and history, though most of it was constructed at the same time (there are some older buildings in a village core).

As so often in Milton Keynes a brilliant mind had seen the future – and it worked, paving the way for the later vernacular phase, built in brick and timber, with low-pitched roofs and a sense of context (Bishop, *op. cit.*). Post-1979, with Mrs Thatcher and the Conservatives in power, the new emphasis was on private building, right-to-buy and individualism. With private sector confidence growing, the house builder Bovis ushered in a third phase in 1980, when non-structural half timbering and a thatched roof was applied to a timber frame house, hiding the real structure. Jeffery characterizes it as 'radical eclectic' and argues that this was the true reflection of the values of freedom of choice on which the master plan was founded (Jeffery, *op. cit.*).

Much of this was anathema to architects. Writing in the *Architects Journal*, Julienne Hanson bemoaned the philistine products of the speculative builders. The new Milton Keynes housing market, she argued, was 'hard headed, materialistic and status seeking' (Hanson, 1992, p. 36). Housing designs and layouts reflected a distasteful individualist culture. Yet Derek Walker would not have been surprised (or perhaps offended) by consumerist culture: 'I saw the sixties as a time of aspiration, dissolving class structures. People were getting wealthier... The whole system of consumerism was being born, big time.' (Walker, quoted in Beckett, 2009, p. 425)

## Thatcherism Anticipated?

As it turned out, a great deal of the Milton Keynes project anticipated the social and political changes which came to Britain in the 1980s and later. Even the name, by strange coincidence, reflected two contrasting schools of economic thought which dominated the post-war years: Keynesianism and demand management, which prevailed pre-1970; and Milton Friedman's right wing monetarism, which rose to ascendancy post-1970. By 1978, with Callaghan's Labour government in office, yet merely clinging to power, the left wing optimism that launched the birth of Milton Keynes had evaporated. Callaghan had been forced to accept a loan from the International Monetary Fund, after the exchange markets lost faith in the British economy. Renouncing Keynesian economic orthodoxy, he told his party conference that by trying to spend its way out of trouble Britain had been living on borrowed time (Sandbrook, 2013). In parallel, Labour Environment Secretary Peter Shore fired the first warning shots on new towns, developing his new policy for the inner cities. A shift of government policy had started, away from state investment on green fields to regenerating older urban areas (HMSO, 1977). Callaghan's term of office ended in a series of strikes known as the Winter of Discontent; and on 4 May 1979 Margaret Thatcher entered Downing Street as Britain's first woman Prime Minister. A new era in political life, and a decided shift to the right in politics, had begun.

In late 1978, as Callaghan's administration limped on, the Development Corporation realized that it could soon be dealing with a Conservative Party in office. A weekend brainstorming session produced a provocative paper on future strategy by newly appointed Planning Director Lee Shostak, titled 'Here Comes Maggie'. Shostak argued that the Development Corporation might need to 'Think Tory', accepting Thatcher on her own terms as: 'queen of opportunity and individual intuition; patroness of the private sector; guardian angel of efficiency; and the enemy of public expenditure' (Shostak, undated, p. 2). Anticipating public expenditure cuts, reduced public investment in housing and increased reliance on market forces, it was time to operate like businessmen. The Development Corporation controlled the most attractive development site in Europe, with all services available at low cost, a new intercity railway station and an unlimited pool of housing. 'The pension funds and insurance companies', said Shostak, 'are bursting with used one pound notes. Why don't we offer them an investment opportunity which Maggie won't let them refuse' (*ibid*, p. 11). Even before Thatcher was elected, the Corporation was putting increased emphasis on building private rather than council homes (Beckett, *op. cit.*). Little was needed to shift strategy to the right, for the master plan had always been underpinned by flexibility and freedom of choice. Increasing individual freedom was at the heart of Mrs Thatcher's politics; it was the main issue in her foreword to the Conservative Election Manifesto in 1979 (Conservative Party, 1979).

Embracing the private builders proved to be crucial to survival. Ministers made it clear that the days of public renting were over, expenditure would be cut, and the public service oriented 1970s new town model would have to become a slim, self-financing, property investment machine. Michael Heseltine, as Thatcher's Environment Secretary, saw 'packaging' as a major task for the Corporation, by which he meant preparing opportunities for private sector investment (Bendixson and Platt, *op. cit.*).

An elegant new shopping centre (now a listed structure) was opened in 1979. It is the centrepiece of Milton Keynes and its best building, breaking out of the gently curving grid of roads to impose a formal layout based on avenues, boulevards and right angles. Derek Walker led a team of designers, happy to work on late into the night if need be: 'Architects were working till 11 or 12 at night ... you never had to ask anybody to do a little more. They'd all do it gratis – it was enormous esprit de corps' (Walker, quoted in Hill, 2007, p. 83). A team photo shows his bright, young, idealistic designs in front, and within the branches, of a huge spreading tree (Hill, *op. cit.*). In expression, clothing and body language, they could be posing for a 1970s album cover.

When first opened, at over one million square feet (92,900 square metres), it was the largest shopping centre in Britain. At that time no other new British shopping centre could emulate Central Milton Keynes. None had the design

Figure 8.3. *Central Milton Keynes.* Further homage is paid to architectural modernism (and to the rationality of grid squares).

clarity, and none tried to match European standards of public realm. Most were characterized by nondescript architecture and poor finishes, derived from the US out-of-town shopping mall model, even if located in town centres (Jeffery, *op. cit.*). Four months after taking office, Mrs Thatcher opened the new building. Her speech acknowledged the success of Milton Keynes, but underlined the changes to come – and especially encouraged people to own their own homes (Beckett, *op. cit.*).

The politics of middle-class individualism came to dominate British society during and after Mrs Thatcher's government. Milton Keynes was uncannily ahead of the trends, creating one of the new suburban 'edge city' developments, which would become home to newly aspirational middle-class voters. Philip Gould, Tony Blair's brilliant political strategist, saw the crucial importance of this group, arguing that 60 per cent of the population had come to regard itself as middle class. The middle class was no longer a privileged sub-sector of society: mass politics was becoming middle-class politics, and 'winning the century means winning middle class support' (Gould, 1998). It was here, in Melvin Webber's 'non-places', located between the poorest and wealthiest sectors of society, that general elections would be won or lost.

## A Measure of Success

Is Milton Keynes a success? For Bendixson and Platt (*op. cit.*) the question is meaningless. 'Is London a success?' they ask. For David Lock, planning consultant, former government planning advisor, and former Milton Keynes strategic planner, there are no doubts: 'Measured by any normal criteria, yes: indices of residents' satisfaction, economic prosperity, healthiness, business start-ups, levels of employment, net in commuting, ethnic diversity, demographic spread, and such like' (Lock, *op. cit.*). Lock's view is supported by the comparative city statistics produced by the Centre for Cities. Nationally, Milton Keynes is ranked first in terms of housing growth, second in terms of population growth, third in terms of employment in London headquartered firms, fourth in terms of business start-ups, fourth in terms of cities with the highest proportion of private sector employment, fifth in terms of businesses per resident, seventh in terms of average earnings. It is amongst the ten British cities with the lowest rise in house prices (Centre for Cities, 2014). As Britain struggled to rebuild its economic base after the 2008 financial crash, with soaring house prices and pitifully low levels of construction, Milton Keynes shone like a beacon of state led investment underpinning private success. Covering some 34 square miles (88 square kilometres), it is now home to almost a quarter of a million people. You wonder why, almost in a fit of absent-mindedness, the British simply walked away from the idea.

No city is without its critics. Michael Edwards was personally involved in the early planning processes. He argued that the planners could have delivered a much better physical environment and doubts whether the plan was in fact deduced from its set of abstract policy goals. Peter Hall was involved in those discussions and tends to confirm Edward's scepticism: 'Mel [Webber] came on a sabbatical to London and in momentous seminars convened by Richard Llewelyn Davies we sketched out the basic concept for Milton Keynes' (Hall, 2014, p. 272).

Those involved were determined to bury Pooley's plan – a plan that would have given priority to public transport at the expense of cars. According to Edwards, an early proposal from him and Nathaniel Lichfield for a systematic cost benefit study comparing the two approaches met with a frosty reception from the team, and was probably never put to the Board (Edwards, 2001). Thus the master plan and its more detailed implementation placed too much emphasis on cars at the expense of public transport; local shopping centres struggled to maintain viability, and pedestrians often had a long wet walk through woods to the bus stop. Encouraging development to turn its back on the main roads had been a mistake, creating a bland and featureless urban landscape, difficult to serve by public transport. The commitment to flexibility meant that the planners were less clear and forceful with private housing developers than they should have been. Yet even Edwards acknowledged the success of the segregated cycle path system and the huge commitment to green space planning and biodiversity. Milton Keynes is not perfect – what city is?

Our story might end here. At last, it seems, we have an example of British government in action, using public sector investment and mechanisms like development corporations and compulsory purchase to shape economic and social change. This is not mere regulation, but driven development, using the tools acquired in World War Two, especially the bureaucratic skills of state direction and land acquisition, and the technical skills of civil engineering, architecture and landscape architecture. The plan's leading objective might have been freedom of choice, but implementation was autocratic and state directed. Especially in the crucial early years, little or nothing was owed to private or voluntary initiative. Yet the response must be equivocal. For if we start to question how the new town idea emerged, why it got onto the political agenda, and who devised the mechanisms for development, a rather different and somewhat familiar set of answers starts to emerge.

## The Emergence of a Vision

British new towns were not a new idea. The conquering Romans and the Normans, conscious of the value of urban settlement in conquest and pacification, made their mark in planning new towns and cities. Edward I built his own examples, not least the towns that sit alongside his great castles in Wales, including Conway, Caernarvon and Harlech, designed to subjugate and intimidate the Welsh. Edward's enthusiasm for new towns had led him, in

1297, to summon a conference of experts in town planning from twenty-one English towns. At the port town of Winchelsea, which first applied for royal help in 1236, Edward's spacious plan was carried through to cater for a population three or four times the average thirteenth-century town. Edinburgh's new town, a Georgian masterpiece, was begun in the eighteenth century. 'Tied towns' were created by nineteenth century philanthropic industrialists, notably in Bourneville, Port Sunlight, Saltaire and New Lanark (Bell and Bell, 1972). But these were, by and large, conventional towns.

The story of post-war new towns, with Milton Keynes culminating in terms of scale and ambition, begins with a single man, Ebenezer Howard, and an extraordinary book (more pamphlet in terms of style and length) called *To-Morrow: A Peaceful Path to Real Reform* (Howard, 1898). Howard was an unusual author, with an unusual vision of the future, and a social reformer in the British tradition of civic duty and individual philanthropy. He was not an educated man, having left school at 14 to become a shorthand clerk. At 21 he left with friends for America, finding himself in the bleak state of Nebraska. This brief experiment as an American farmer was not successful and Howard headed for Chicago, just recovering from a great fire, and in the midst of massive planned rebuilding. Five years later he was back in Britain, finding work as a parliamentary shorthand reporter, and drawn, through his interest in social reform, into debates about housing and the future of London (Hunt, 2004). In the 1880s he attended lectures by Peter Kropotkin, the Russian anarchist and environmentalist. Howard began to formulate his own ideas on the future of city life, and on a planned alternative, his garden city.

Howard was as much 'doer' as thinker. He was engaged with practical problems; indeed the first lines in the first chapter of his (re-published) book deal immediately with the practical problems of estate management, not lofty concepts of social change (Howard, 1965 [1902]). His originality lay in his vision for a new form of urban society, which instead of harking back to an idealized past, harnessed modern technology to make his vision a reality (and in so doing, strangely anticipated Webber). Eight months after his book was published Howard took the lead in setting up a Garden Cities Association to take forward his ideas. A year later he formed the first Garden City Limited, with £50,000 capital; and two years later a Garden City Pioneer Company was registered to survey potential sites (Hall, 1988). Two practical attempts to build garden cities followed, at Letchworth in 1903 and Welwyn Garden City in 1919, with Howard personally involved (Meller, 1997). Howard continued to promote his ideas through the Garden Cities Association, which became the Garden Cities and the Town Planning Association, and subsequently the Town and Country Planning Association (TCPA). Howard and the Garden Cities Association campaigned ceaselessly for planning reform, powerfully so before, during, and after the Second World War.

In his proposal for a garden city Howard tried to bring together the best qualities of the countryside and of the city, so that future urban developments would not repeat the mistakes of the nineteenth-century industrial city. The garden city would unite the benefits of city life, especially culture and employment, with the best of country life, in gardens, open spaces, lack of pollution and the beauty of the natural environment. A private company, raising capital in conventional ways would develop it, but the land, once purchased, would remain the property of the local community.

Beyond the limited practical experiments, little progress was made in the inter war years. Yet the TCPA continued to campaign, and in 1936 secured one of its most powerful advocates, in Frederic J. Osborn. At the end of the 1930s Osborn mounted a sustained campaign to define the role of town planners, convinced that town planning should go hand in hand with economic planning, giving evidence to this effect to the government's Barlow Commission. It was, claims Helen Meller: 'A point where the old crossed the new. The old philanthropic private world of the garden city movement and voluntary pressure groups gave its views to the new social science based Royal Commission, looking at the location of industry. The only things both worlds shared was a belief in the need for more planning' (Meller, *op. cit.*, p. 66). The Second World War and its aftermath gave Osborn and the TCPA the opportunity to turn belief into reality.

Osborn has provided an insider's account of his tactical, political and personal manoeuvrings, which begins with a frank admission: the TCPA, that persistent and tireless advocate of new towns, was 'a propaganda society' (Osborn and Whittick, *op. cit.*). It fought a long slow battle of ideas, over nearly half a century, sometimes through long patches when little progress could be made. The Association languished in effectiveness between the wars. Osborn put this down to two periods of bad luck. The first came in the inter-war suburban boom, when electric subways, trams and the motor car made it possible for workers to commute longer distances and live in new suburbs on the edge of cities. The second was the great national housing drive in the 1920s and 1930s, when local authorities opted *en masse* for garden suburbs and edge of town housing, rather than discrete garden cities or new towns. The TCPA bent with the wind, supporting Hampstead Garden Suburb in 1907, but merely as a tactic. More tactical and politically astute decisions were to follow.

Two government Committees gave the Association a foothold in policy making. The first was the 1920 Committee on Unhealthy Areas, with Neville Chamberlain as its chairman. It recommended restrictions on factory building in the overcrowded London areas, along with movement to garden cities. This, it appears, was the origin of Chamberlain's interest in decentralization of economic activity and the garden city idea. The Association began to campaign from another angle – for necessary dispersal to complement restrictions. By then Osborn had become the TCPA's Secretary. When he became Prime Minister in 1938, Chamberlain appointed a Royal Commission under Sir Anderson Montague Barlow to examine the geographical distribution of industrial population. Two members of the Commission, Sir Patrick Abercrombie and Mrs Lionel Hitchens, were advocates of new towns.

Barlow's report was a turning point in government concern for urban development and planning. It itemized the disadvantages of excessively large cities and was unequivocal about the disadvantages of the biggest cities like London. The threat of air attack in the looming war with Germany added an extra dimension to the Committee's concerns. Yet it was divided on solutions. Some members wanted a national authority to redevelop congested areas and disperse industry and population, but the report was open on whether this should be an executive or merely advisory body. A minority report argued for the creation of a new planning ministry with powers to restrict as well as to develop. Though the Association was disappointed with the Barlow Report it decided that if the Report was welcomed as 'triumphant vindication of the Association's own policy it could be made so in fact' (Osborn and Whittick, *op. cit.*, p. 44).

## Lord Reith Takes Control

With the coming of war the Barlow Report was put on the shelf. It rapidly came off the shelf as the blitz began to create wide-open spaces in Britain's big cities, and thoughts turned to reconstruction. The government believed that encouraging this debate could help morale and Churchill appointed Lord Reith, architect of the British Broadcasting Corporation and then Minister of Public Works, to study and report on methods for post-war reconstruction (Ward, *op. cit.*). Reith moved the case for planning forward at astonishing speed. He looked again at the Barlow Report and in February 1941 secured Cabinet agreement to the principle of a national authority with a positive policy for transport, industrial development and agriculture. In February 1942 the government established a Ministry of Works and Planning and said that steps would be taken to implement Barlow's recommendations on dispersal. Yet the detail of post-war policy remained vague and it was far from clear what role, if any, would be played by new towns.

The ambitious and assertive Reith loathed Churchill: 'The sight of Churchill naturally bothered me. I absolutely hate him' (Reith, in Stuart, 1975, p. 59). Evidently the feeling was mutual, for only two days after the decision to establish a Planning Ministry, in 1943, Churchill dismissed Reith. Reith was mortified and, as his diaries show, spent the rest of the war in despair, frustration and depression.

Yet events were gathering pace. By establishing the Ministry for Town and Country Planning the first steps were taken to provide powers for acquisition of land in bombed and obsolescent urban areas. In the same year Abercrombie published his first plan for Greater London, recommending substantial dispersal of population and employment, followed by the Greater London Plan of 1944, which made proposals for a green belt encircling London and new towns beyond. Driven by the impetus of war, the stage was set for post-war planning.

The Labour Party had not made a feature of dispersal policy in its election campaign. A sub-committee chaired by Lewis Silkin had discussed reconstruction, but Silkin backpedalled on new towns and the messages remained mixed. Labour published Silkin's report as policy, yet issued a popular pamphlet spotlighting new towns. Following Labour's 1945 landslide election victory, Silkin was appointed as Minster of Town and Country Planning. Lord Reith was back, promptly appointed as the chairman of a committee charged with advising on the establishment, development and organization of new towns. Reith had spoken with Attlee in June 1940: 'He gave me very definite encouragement to do all the post war planning I was inclined to' (Reith, in Stuart, *op. cit.*, p. 256). Evidently, as Prime Minister, Attlee was as good as his word.

Reith knew nothing about the subject but threw himself into the role with the energy of a coiled spring. In only eight months three powerfully argued reports hit Whitehall desks and Reith secured unanimous support for his recommendation to create government appointed development corporations to build the new towns. The New Towns Act of 1946 closely reflected Reith's recommendations, with corporations given powers to acquire land and undertake development (Ward, *op. cit.*). Using government loans repayable over 60 years, the intention was to start twenty new towns. In the event twelve were started in England and two in Scotland. In 1955 another new town was started in Scotland under a Conservative government. In 1961 the second generation of new towns was begun, with, as we have seen, Milton Keynes designated in 1967.

## Planning by Propaganda Society

Here was final vindication of the power of a small group of determined individuals, shaping policy and ideas at the highest level of government by their persistence, intelligence and determination. It had taken almost half a century from 1898, the publication date of Howard's book, to The New Towns Act of 1946, just as it had taken slightly over half a century, from 1906 and the first private members Bill for motorway construction, to the opening of the Preston bypass, Britain's first motorway in 1958. Government had indeed created the plan for Milton Keynes. But government's policy had been driven from below the state machinery, by the members of a self-proclaimed 'propaganda society', not by the machinations of central bureaucracy. Individuals played a hugely important role in the creation of Milton Keynes – especially Crossman, Campbell, Llewellyn Davies and Roche – just as they did in the emergence of the new towns movement and its move to the centre of national policy. But this time the state provided and supported a powerful framework for implementation and action, albeit at arm's length from Whitehall. There are familiar strands in the Milton Keynes story, to be sure. But driven by the social, political and technocratic impetus that emerged from the Second World War, for 30 years at least, a rather different British plan had emerged, if only to disappear from view as events moved on.

## References

Beckett, A. (2009) *When the Lights Went Out: What Really Happened to Britain in the Seventies*. London: Faber.

Bell, C. and Bell, R. (1972) *City Fathers: The Early History of Town Planning in Britain*. Harmondsworth: Pelican.

Bendixson, T. and Platt, J. (1992) *Milton Keynes: Image and Reality*. Cambridge: Granta Editions.

Bishop, J. (1986) *Milton Keynes – the Best of Both Worlds: Public and Professional Views of a New City*. Bristol: School for Advanced Urban Studies University of Bristol.

Centre for Cities (2014) *Cities Outlook 2014*. London: Centre for Cities. Available at: http://www.centreforcities.org/assets/files/2014/Cities_Outlook_2014.pdf.

Clapson, M. (2004) *A Social History of Milton Keynes*. London: Frank Cass.

Conservative Party (1979) *The Conservative Manifesto 1979*. London: Conservative Central Office.

Edwards, M. (2001) City design: what went wrong at Milton Keynes? *Journal of Urban Design*, **6**(1), pp. 73–82.

Gould, P. (1998) *The Unfinished Revolution: How the Modernisers Saved the Labour Party*. London: Abacus.

*Guardian* (2005) Obituary of Peter Youngman. 17 June. Available at: http://www.theguardian.com/news/2005/jun/17/guardianobituaries.artsobituaries1.

Hall, P. (1980) *Great Planning Disasters*. London: Weidenfeld and Nicolson.

Hall, P. (1988) *Cities of Tomorrow: An Intellectual History of Urban Planning and Design in the Twentieth Century*. Oxford: Basil Blackwell.

Hall, P. (2014) Apologia pro vita sua, in Tewdwr-Jones, M., Phelps, N.A. and Freestone, R. (eds.) *The Planning Imagination: Peter Hall and the Study of Urban and Regional Planning*. London: Routledge.

Hanson, J. (1992) Selling the dream. *Architects Journal*, **195**(15), pp. 36–39.

Hill, M. (2007) *The Story of the Original CMK*. Milton Keynes: Living Archive.

HMSO (1977) *Policy for the Inner Cities*, Cmnd 6845. London: HMSO.

Howard, E. (1898) *Tomorrow: A Peaceful Path to Real Reform*. London: Swan Sonnenschein.

Howard, E. (1965 [1902]) *Garden Cities of Tomorrow*. Cambridge, MA: MIT Press.

Hunt, T. (2004) *Building Jerusalem: the Rise and Fall of the Victorian City*. London: Weidenfeld and Nicolson.

Jeffery, R. (2012) The centrality of Milton Keynes, in *The Seventies: Rediscovering a Lost Decade of British Architecture* (Twentieth Century 10, Journal of the Twentieth Century Society). London: The Twentieth Century Society.

Llewellyn Davies, Weeks and Partners (1966) *Washington New Town Master Plan and Report*. Washington UK: Washington Development Corporation.

Lock, D. (2014) Interviews and Discussion with the Author, April 2014. Lock was formerly Strategic Planner with Milton Keynes Development Corporation, and subsequently Chairman of David Lock Associates.

Mars, T. (1992) Little Los Angeles in Bucks. *Architects Journal*, **195**(15), pp. 22–26.

Meller, H. (1997) *Towns, Plans and Society in Modern Britain*. Cambridge: Cambridge University Press.

Milton Keynes Council (2010) *Milton Keynes: A Sustainable Future*. Milton Keynes: NHBC Foundation.

MKDC (Milton Keynes Development Corporation) (1970) *The Plan for Milton Keynes* (Presented by Milton Keynes Development Corporation to The Minister for Housing and Local Government, Llewellyn Davies, Weeks, Forestier-Walker and Bor in Wavendon). Milton Keynes: MKDC.

Osborn, F.J. and Whittick, A. (1977) *New Towns: Their Origins, Achievements and Progress*. London: Leonard Hill.

Pimlott, B. (1992) *Harold Wilson*. London: Harper Collins.

Rasmussen, S.E. (1982) *London: The Unique City*. Cambridge MA: MIT Press.

Sandbrook, D. (2013) *Seasons in the Sun: The Battle for Britain*, 1974–1979. Harmondsworth: Penguin.

Shostak, L. (undated) Here Comes Maggie... So What Are We Going To Do. Milton Keynes Development Corporation: Milton Keynes. Unpublished discussion paper.

Shostak, L. (2015) Discussion with the author, 11 April 2015. (Shostak was formerly Planning Director at Milton Keynes Development Corporation.)

Stuart, C. (ed.) (1975) *The Reith Diaries*. London: Collins.

Ward, S. (1994) *Planning and Urban Change*. London: Paul Chapman Publishing.

Webber, M. (1963) Order in diversity: community without propinquity, in Wingo, L. (ed.) *Cities and Space: The Future Use of Urban Land*. Baltimore, MD: John Hopkins University Press.

Webber, M. (1964) Urban place and the non-place urban realm, in Webber, M., Dychman, J.W., Foley, D.L., Gutenberg, A.Z., Wheaton, W.L.C. and Wurste, C.B. (eds.) *Explorations into Urban Structure*. Philadelphia, PA: University of Pennsylvania Press.

# 9

# The Dream of Caligula
## The Channel Tunnel and Its Rail Link

*This precious stone set in the silver sea,*
*Which serves it in the office of a wall,*
*Or as moat defensive to a house,*
*Against the envy of less happier lands,*
*This blessed plot, this earth, this realm, this England.*
              William Shakespeare, *Richard II*, Act 2, Scene 1

In a slightly perverse sense, the British could be said to have opened their first Channel Tunnel Rail Link on 9 March 1899. As a Bill to approve the Channel Tunnel received the Royal Assent in February 1987, and the tunnel officially opened on 6 May 1994, that link came almost 100 years too early. For in 1966 the Great Central Railway London Extension, to use its full title, had been closed as a trunk route, a casualty of the Beeching cuts in the 1960s. Thus the only properly engineered route in Britain for continental rail traffic was lifted, just as the British Prime Minister was finalizing negotiations with the French for a Channel Tunnel, and the French were planning their network of high-speed connecting lines. It was not exactly an auspicious start. But the irony had a certain resonance for what came after.

### Victorian Vision

That first link was the brainchild of the great Victorian railway baron and Manchester businessman Sir Alfred Watkin, a man condemned by historian Jack

Simmons as 'a megalomaniac and a gambler' (Simmons, 1978, p. 93). His dream was nothing less than to build the Channel Tunnel along with a magnificently engineered new railway, linking the north of England to the tunnel, and offering the prospect of railway travel directly from Manchester to Paris. Watkin's 'London Extension', subsequently known as the Great Central Railway, ran from Nottingham to Marylebone Station in London. It was engineered to the highest standards and was the last piece of main line railway built in Britain until the opening of the new Channel Tunnel Rail Link in 2007. Watkin's line was laid out for high-speed running, with a maximum gradient of only 1 in 176, and no curves of less than 1 mile (1.6 km) in radius. Ready to receive continental trains, all bridges and tunnels were built to the 'Berne Convention' loading gauge (Greaves, 2005), an engineering standard which still bedevils British railway operations in the twenty-first century. Berne Gauge is a common standard across continental railways, and allows for the passage of higher and wider rolling stock, including two-tier carriages and higher and wider container traffic. Only now are some main trunk routes in Britain being slowly and painfully upgraded to meet the standards Watkin set in 1899.

Figure 9.1. *Trackbed of the former Great Central Railway, Culworth.* The heroic scale of construction is evident even in dereliction, as is the unpopulated landscape through which this failed gamble ran.

In financial terms the London Extension was a total failure. It ran through thinly populated countryside with few major towns and never paid a dividend to its shareholders. Sir Sam Fay, the Great Central's manager, told a meeting of staff in the 1920s that 'the London extension was only kept solvent by the Grimsby fish traffic' (*ibid.*, p. 324) and by the 1950s that traffic had dwindled, lost to road haulage. Jack Simmons's verdict proved to be correct: Watkin was 'ambitious and wrong-headed' and his London Extension 'a wasteful extravagance which shows the Victorian devotion to the competitive principle at its worst' (Simmons, 1986, p. 32).

Yet even Simmons acknowledged that the line was an engineering and political triumph. In building the 94-mile (151 km) extension, Watkin won over his own shareholders, saw off objections from other companies and secured his parliamentary Bill against the objections of London's elite, not least the Marylebone Cricket Club and the artistic community of St. Johns Wood. The cricketers proved the biggest obstacles. As national cricketing hero W.G. Grace put it, the thought of steel rails running through this 'chief bulwark of our national pastime was repellent' (Greaves, *op. cit.*, p. 311). The artist Alma Tadema argued that vibration from trains would make it impossible for him to draw a straight line on canvas. Yet Watkin secured his Bill, compensating the cricket club with more land than it lost, taking the railway underground on its approach to Marylebone, and relocating the terminus to Marylebone and away from the artists and their sensitive brushwork.

Watkin was not the first to dream of a Channel Tunnel. A fixed crossing of the Channel was first proposed by the Roman emperor Caligula, who wanted a continuous bridge of ships, and commissioned a two mile trial pontoon jutting out from the Italian coast (Comfort, 2006). The first serious proposal dates back to 1802 when Albert Mathieu Favier, a French mining engineer, suggested it to Napoleon Bonaparte. But the Napoleonic Wars resumed soon afterwards and the vision – save Napoleon's wish for a distinctly one-way traffic – went into hibernation. By 1833 another Frenchman, Aimé Thomé de Gamond, proposed a new scheme, formally considered by the French and English governments. Napoleon was enthusiastic, as was Prince Albert, but Palmerston was scornful and it came to nothing. Yet the end of the 1860s saw the boat train routes between London and Dover and Paris and Calais completed, and the idea took off again. De Gamond produced a scheme for two parallel railway tunnels and went into partnership with the British engineer William Low. On 2 August 1875 the British and French governments passed Bills empowering a Channel Tunnel Company and French engineers began digging at Sangatte – until the British ran out of funds.

Here the energetic Watkin enters the plot, with his northern dream of running trains from Manchester to Paris via Baker Street, the East London line, and the South Eastern Railway's route from London to Dover. By 1880 he had already excavated an 800-metre tunnel bore, without authority. The following year he obtained powers for the engineer Low to start a tunnel from Shakespeare Cliff to meet the French (who were still digging). Almost a mile of tunnel had been dug before the Board of Trade ordered a halt. Undeterred, Watkin carried on and by then he had tunnelled further than the French.

## His Majesty's Opposition

Government and civil service alike were determined to stop Watkin. Whereas the French (not unlike Caligula) had given support, the British state objected, abstained, and eventually blocked the plan. Twice in 1881 Watkin wrote to the Board of Trade suggesting that an investment of such scale and importance should not be left to private initiative, but justified government funding. The reply was an emphatic no. Writing to his counterpart in the War Office in 1894, a Permanent Under Secretary in the Treasury said: '[I am] strongly opposed to this tunnel, and I believe its construction would be a national misfortune' (Greaves, *op. cit.*, p. 269).

A key political opponent was Joseph Chamberlain, President of the Board of Trade. In 1881 the Board suggested to the War Office that a departmental committee should be formed, and before long the Channel Tunnel plan had become a matter for national security. Evidence from the military, not least from the redoubtable General Sir Garnet Wolseley, was hostile: 'The tunnel would directly tempt invasion', claimed Wolseley, 'the successful invasion of England with the tunnel in enemy hands would be the permanent ruin of the country' (Wolseley, quoted in Greaves, *op. cit.*, p. 261). Whipped up by the press, politicians, and the military, public opinion became hostile and angry citizens smashed the windows of the Channel Tunnel Company's offices. Although he continued to introduce parliamentary Bills and Motions until 1895, all were defeated and Watkin's dream was finished.

Several further half-hearted attempts were made to resurrect the tunnel plan in the early twentieth century, but all foundered on lack of government support or continued military hostility. The truth was that Britain's rulers suffered from insularity and xenophobia. A rare public example was the evidence submitted by the Earl of Crawford to the Channel Tunnel Committee in 1929. Crawford argued that a tunnel would expose Britain to a torrent of criminality, homosexuality, pornography and drug trafficking – failings which he claimed were commonplace to foreigners (Gourvish, 2006). As late as 1949 the Foreign Office warned that a tunnel project would undermine 'that unquestioning sense of superiority which forms an essential element in British self-confidence' (quoted in *ibid.*, p. 16).

By 1953 Defence Minister Harold Macmillan had decided that there was no national security issue. In 1957 a Channel Tunnel Study Group had been re-launched; and a new head of steam was building. In 1966 the British and French Prime Ministers, Harold Wilson and Georges Pompidou, declared their support, and when Edward Heath's government later took office, committed to a European destiny for Britain, a scheme for twin rail runnels was swiftly drawn up. In 1973 both governments signed an agreement initiating tunnel boring, British Railways published its first plans for a high-speed link, and work started on a 300 metre pilot tunnel at Shakespeare Cliff. Still fretting about national security, the Chiefs of Defence Staff commissioned a study that proposed building into the tunnel a nuclear device, to be triggered if hostile forces appeared. Wisely the plan was dropped when it was realized that this device could turn the tunnel into a gigantic mortar, laying waste to the area of

Kent directly beyond it. Yet the Generals need not have worried; taking office in February 1974 and looking for spending cuts, Labour shelved the project (Comfort, *op. cit.*). The cutting machine's head was sealed in concrete (which proved difficult to remove when work resumed 12 years later).

The British Government's fleeting interest and support was thus ended, and the initiative passed once again to business interests, and of course to the French. French national railways (SNCF) and British Rail quietly began devising the most economical and low-cost scheme possible, announcing their plans in September 1978. The single-track tunnel – nicknamed the mouse hole – allowed for batches of trains running in opposite directions. There would be no high-speed link, and British Rail Southern Region, which argued that their saturated commuter lines could not accommodate any further services, were told that they would have to.

Like the ghost of Watkin, this austerity project attracted interest from banks and contractors. Margaret Thatcher, the incoming British Prime Minister, was no lover of railways (nor of Europe), but her Transport Minister Norman Fowler invited bids to build the tunnel, and was enthusiastically in favour of a privately funded scheme.

## The French Break Through

At last the French felt that the British might be serious, although government continued to prevaricate – economist Sir Alec Cairncross, for example, went out of his way to pour cold water on the scheme (Gourvish, *op. cit.*). Nonetheless the French and British Transport Ministers met in September 1981, followed a week later by the new French President, Francois Mitterand, and Margaret Thatcher, who committed themselves to a scheme starting by 1984.

The question is why. Doubtless Thatcher saw it as part of a wider deal; she was in difficult negotiations with Mitterand and other leaders to extract a major budget rebate from her European partners. Mitterand and French Prime Minister Pierre Mauroy (Mayor of Lille since 1973) were keen to use the project as a means of stimulating the depressed Pas de Calais region (Gourvish, *op. cit.*); French Transport Minister Jean Auroux wanted the French TGV trains to come to London (Henderson, 1987). The French were thinking on a strategic level; and it was on Mitterand's initiative, eager to stamp the project with his own authority, that the joint announcement was made. He saw it as a touchstone of Anglo-French relations.

The personal chemistry between Thatcher and Mitterand cannot be ignored. Thatcher admired Mitterand's intellectual quality; he in turn was fascinated by Thatcher, the woman, not least at the beginning of their relationship. He famously advised his Minister for Europe, Roland Dumas, to be aware of her dangerous qualities: '*Cette femme Thatcher, elle a les yeux de Caligule, mais elle a la bouche de Marilyn Monroe*'. Cheyson, the French Foreign Minister, observed their strange mutual fascination: 'Each looked at the other, wondering how something so strange could exist, trying to grasp who he or she was' (Young, 1998, pp. 320–321).

There was no doubting Thatcher's personal enthusiasm. She had told Sir Nicholas Henderson that she felt passionately in favour of some form of fixed link, and that the decision must be taken as soon as possible. Henderson, former UK Ambassador to France, became chairman of the Channel Tunnel Group (CTG) in March 1985, having first become involved in the tunnel project early in 1984, as a board member of Tarmac, one of the companies participating in the CTG (Henderson, *op. cit.*).

Rival groups now came forward with their bids for the project and in all nine schemes were submitted, including the Anglo French bid from CTG. Mitterrand told the British that he would only back the tunnel project if the plug was pulled on Channel Expressway, CTG's strongest rival, because it had no French business involvement. On 20 January 1986 Thatcher and Mitterrand announced that CTG and its French partner Trans Manche had won the concession. The agreement was enshrined in a Treaty signed in the Chapter House of Canterbury Cathedral on 12 February 1986. CTG had by now assembled private sector finance, and the project made its way through the British and French legislatures. The French Council of Ministers approved the choice, twin Bills were introduced ratifying the Treaty and the concession, and in April and June respectively the Chamber of Deputies and Senate agreed (Comfort, *op. cit.*).

In Britain legislation passed through a complex Hybrid Bill procedure, involving long sessions before a Select Committee, as well as consideration by the House of Lords. The Act received the Royal Assent on 23 July 1987 and work was ready to start after CTG (now Eurotunnel) assembled its final £5 billion loan and credit facility from 198 banks.

So the Channel Tunnel saga has the familiar hallmarks of great British infrastructure planning: high dependency on private individuals, and on individual political leadership. The British civil service performed with studied neutrality. Henderson recounts his early dealings with Andrew Lyall, the senior spokesman for Whitehall: 'He never showed any favour towards us, but his very frankness was invaluable … he answered our queries without equivocation and he certainly never gave us any encouragement' (Henderson, *op. cit.*, p. 38). In a real sense the Channel Tunnel was not a British plan at all. It was an Anglo-French plan, and relied heavily on French state initiative, support and involvement. Nonetheless it set the scene for Act 2: how the British wrestled with, and finally built, a high-speed rail link from the Channel to London, thus completing the first new trunk railway in Britain since Watkin's ill-fated and premature London Extension in 1899.

## The Missing Link

Nicholas Comfort gives an acid summary of the tunnel link saga:

> When the shambolic history of decision making in Britain on major infrastructure projects comes to be written, the Channel Tunnel Rail Link will come a close second to the tunnel itself in terms of time and money wasted, and false starts made by nervous officialdom' (Comfort, *op. cit.*, p. 167)

The story goes back to 1970 and the Southern Region of British Rail, who, as we have seen, insisted that the rail system between Dover and London had no capacity for international traffic. A new high-speed line was proposed, following the existing route to Tonbridge, thence to Redhill, Edenbridge and a new terminus at White City. The plan was quickly dropped after protests from the residents of Surrey.

The 1987 Channel Tunnel Act was passed on the expedient basis that no high-speed ink would be built, trains using the existing network. A 'usage contract' required SNCF to provide a high-speed link, but not its British counterpart (Gourvish, *op. cit.*). By avoiding discussion of the rail link the risk of organized opposition to the Bill had been much reduced. Eurotunnel, British Rail, French Railways and the Department of Transport all knew that this was absurd, and that a new line to the centre of London was essential. Yet Junior Transport Minister, Michael Portillo, insisted that the private sector must bear most of the cost. The 1987 Act included a ban on government subsidies to a public sector project, but did not preclude subsidizing a private sector project. If British Rail wanted new investment it had to demonstrate an 8 per cent return on investment. The Department for Transport could not assist. It was traditionally a weak Whitehall department (Hennessy, 1990) with rapidly rotating Ministers, whose term of office seldom lasted for more than 2 years; it was rarely able to see through any long-term strategy or initiative.

British Rail, left on its own, came up with a cleverly improvised solution. New trains were commissioned, built to cope with the constrained (non Berne standard) British loading gauge, relatively sharp curves on the route, three different power supplies, and two different platform heights. As an interim solution these would run on a lightly used line in Kent, formerly used by boat trains, until air traffic killed them off, going via Tonbridge to existing platforms at Waterloo, previously used for parcels. A wonderfully sinuous dedicated new station, designed by Nicholas Grimshaw, would be built there, at a cost of £190 million (only to become derelict when the new high-speed rail link eventually reached St Pancras in 2007).

By now we will be familiar with the theme of planning from below. So it will come as no surprise that the impetus for a new route came initially neither from government or British Rail, but from Kent County Council. Kent was a remarkably proactive local authority, in part because of the high calibre of its leading councillors. Kent's councillors wanted a culture which combined public service with making things happen. Their approach was in marked contrast to the 'stand to one side' ethos of central government. Working with a Junior Minister in the Transport Department, Kent published the Kent Impact Study in August 1987, setting out the need for new rail and road infrastructure. In parallel, forecasts of tunnel traffic were rising, and Alistair Morton, Eurotunnel's abrasive chief executive, was demanding action. A Treasury official responded drily: 'although BR think he is wrong, we do not intend to obstruct anybody else who wants to put *their* money where *his* mouth is' (quoted in Gourvish, *op. cit.*, p. 334).

Little interest was shown by Ministers. As Minister of State for Transport Michael Portillo had told the Commons that it had nothing to do with him (Gourvish, *op. cit.*). Portillo was simply following the party line. Attempts by the government to distance itself from the scheme continued; on several occasions Mrs Thatcher made it clear that the whole matter was the sole responsibility of British Rail.

As it turned out, the forecasts of rising traffic *were* optimistic, partly because they had not anticipated rising competition from airlines. In 1882 Watkin had forecast 4.5m passenger journeys per annum between Britain and France; in 1985 British Rail was forecasting 20.4m in 2003; Eurotunnel 17m; the Number Ten Downing Street Policy Unit 48m. The actual figure for 2003 turned out to be 6.3m – closer to Watkin's nineteenth-century estimate than any contemporary forecast (Faith, 2007). Evidently the science of forecasting techniques had not improved since the nineteenth century. Yet the British Treasury continued to regard cost benefit analysis, resting on the twin stilts of forecast cost and demand, as the touchstone for decision-making (Gourvish, *op. cit.*).

The pressure on British Rail was not merely political, nor related to long-term forecasts of Channel Tunnel demand (including its own). After 1984 it found that commuting passenger levels were rising at a rate of 4 per cent annually, as employment levels in London's booming economy rose. A new executive, John Welsby, was brought in to lead the project. Unfortunately he made a bad start by producing a report on options, showing four potential alignments through Kent, which leaked to the newspapers. Between them the alternatives blighted huge swathes of Kent and there was a storm of protest. As in the 1970s the railwaymen had slipped up again. Government continued to distance itself from the whole venture, Ministers taking the view that it was British Rail's report, and it was for British Rail to defend it (Gourvish, *op. cit.*).

The problem with British Rail's options was their scale and diversity, which increased the number of potential protestors, ranging from commuters in the Weald of Kent to young professionals gentrifying inner London. Kent County Council rejected all four British Rail options, continuing its argument for a route alongside the existing M20 motorway, and the opposition became still more intense when British Rail finally published its preferred route in March 1989. This ran close to the M20 corridor, diving into a long tunnel to reach central London. Yet the objectors were not appeased. An argument developed about the point in Peckham where British Rail's tunnel surfaced. Hundreds of homes were still at risk of blight or clearance and the mood of opposition was unwavering. It looked like stalemate, for both British Rail and the absentee Department of Transport (Faith, *op. cit.*).

## Enter Arup

Here the story takes a twist that is both strange and, in the context of what has gone before, utterly predictable. For leadership passed from Whitehall and nationalized industry to a small number of private individuals within a brilliant, yet somewhat idiosyncratic, British engineering consultancy – Arup.

Arup was (and is) an interesting organization. It was the creation of Ove Arup, a Danish engineer born in Newcastle upon Tyne, whose marble bust is still displayed prominently in Arup offices. Ove was an unusual engineer, starting his undergraduate studies in philosophy, and switching to engineering because he became convinced that he could never become an outstanding philosopher, and (he claimed) because he could think of no alternative other than to 'shoot yourself in the autumn' (Jones, 2006, p. 16). On a practical level he was rather disorganized, an archetypal absent minded professor type, kept on track largely by the efforts of his brilliant secretary, Ruth Winewar. Regarded

Figure 9.2. *Ove Arup*. Failed philosopher and brilliant structural engineer, Arup's lack of interest in management helped to found a business which was at once idiosyncratic, liberating and individualistic.

as a bohemian intellectual and champagne socialist, he remained a philosopher manqué to the end of his life (*ibid.*). It would not be difficult to imagine him as part of the eccentric intellectual culture of wartime Bletchley Park. Yet he had charm and self-confidence, mathematical skills, and proved to be an immensely talented structural engineer. Influenced by the architects Le Corbusier and Walter Gropius, Ove began to work with modernist architects on daring pre-war concrete projects. He specialized in experimental work in reinforced concrete.

It is only to be expected, therefore, that Arup would be very different from other engineering firms. Ove's obsession with ideas, his idiosyncratic style in recruitment (people were appointed whose core values motivated them towards open minded co-operation) and lack of interest in conventional management developed a culture which was at once liberating, individualistic, and slightly arrogant. The aim was to break the barriers to mutual understanding, and, following Ove's personal philosophy, create a 'composite brain' for each job (*ibid.*). Decision-making should be spread downward as far as possible and the whole pattern of activity flexible and open to revision. In 1970 Ove gave a lecture in which he defined the ideal organization: 'a relatively close knit team, working in the same place and having continuity of work on a few jobs at a time, so that the members could really learn to appreciate each other's qualities' (Arup quoted in Jones, *op. cit.*, p. 274).

By 1997 Arup's partners had given away their equity, and employee and charitable trusts owned the firm – rather like the British John Lewis Partnership. With no external shareholders, employees were less interested in financial rewards than in the creative excitement of a project; and they were given surprising freedom to do as they liked. Arup made their reputation in finding an engineering solution to the almost unbuildable concept for the Sydney Opera House, a project which many consulting engineers would have regarded as mission impossible (Hall, 2007). Again, parallels with the chaotic yet creative culture in Bletchley Park are uncanny.

Exploiting this freedom and lack of central direction, a small group inside the company began to develop a radical alternative route for the rail link (*ibid.*). Arup's involvement first began with a banker called Colin Stannard, who had been asked to evaluate the bids for the Channel Tunnel by the Department for Transport, an appointment that led to him becoming chief fundraiser for CTG. Michael Lewis of Arup heard Stannard speak in a meeting and got in touch. When government announced its decision to support a private sector led rail project they went into partnership. Stannard saw the potential synergy between the rail link and plans for redeveloping the Kings Cross area, then being advanced by developers Rosehaugh Stanhope. Stannard and Arup believed that government would not want a contractor led bid, which might lead to biased cost estimates. The outcome was a proposal for a joint venture with British Rail to select a route and deliver it, in a vehicle called Kent Rail. Arup would become involved in project initiation rather than consultancy: not without qualms, the

Arup board eventually approved the proposal and allocated £1 million for costs. Kent Rail was one of six bids for the project in the pre-qualification process. At Arup, Mark Bostock, Arup's first hired economist, was in charge. He had been described by one of his colleagues as a man 'who has only to see a box to start thinking about jumping out of it' (Faith, *op. cit.*, p. 106). As the Kent Rail bid developed, Bostock concealed the ever-mounting costs by dividing it into a selection of job numbers.

Stannard knew that Mrs Thatcher would not approve any scheme that did not have overwhelming backing from the private sector. But British Rail did not even call the Arup team for interview, and in July the Kent Rail bid was thrown out. British Rail, it seemed, wanted more direct control over the project. By September British Rail was down to a short list of two consortia and the winner was Eurorail, a consortium involving Trafalgar House and BICC.

Arup did not capitulate. Instead it decided to commit its own resources to find the best route for the rail link and soon decided not to approach London from the south. They realized that East London (unlike South London) was an area where local councils and local people actually wanted new development and jobs. The challenge was finding a route through the urban fabric, rather than fighting a war of attrition with well-informed objectors. Moreover Arup anticipated a different kind of railway. British Rail was thinking of a high-speed line which carried only long distance passenger traffic. Arup wanted to explore much wider options, including commuting and freight, and proposed a four-track railway to take this extra traffic (Gourvish, *op. cit.*). They announced their eastern route proposal in November 1989, just as British Rail was admitting that its own proposal for a tunnel through south London had failed because of cost increases. So trains would be back on the surface in British Rail's plan, to the consternation of objectors, and the parliamentary Private Bill for the British Rail/Trafalgar House project was shelved for a year.

Arup now had two tasks: to devise the optimum solution and to sell it to MPs, councillors and the general public. They took to lobbying and attending party conferences, soon realizing that the British Rail/Trafalgar House route was unpopular with MPs, whereas the eastern route was attractive to councils like Newham, who foresaw huge regeneration opportunities at Stratford.

By this time British Rail had a team of 340 people working on its proposal; Arup had five, two of whom were fitting in the Channel Tunnel work after hours. Despite (or perhaps because of) their loose management structure, with no clear lines of responsibility, Arup had spent £750,000 on the job. Their plan required no demolitions, acquisition of two houses, and affected only 115 properties within a 200-metre zone. British Rail's required the acquisition of 151 houses, and affected 5,900 in the 200-metre zone. By May 1990 British Rail and Eurorail had abandoned their partnership, though government continued to argue that the Arup scheme was too expensive.

In May Parliament saw its only full debate on the projects. Though some in government now wanted to abandon the British Rail plan, it was kept alive by looking at a new option – a fast link to the edge of London and use of existing rail lines within. The problem was that those rail lines did not have enough capacity. Government commissioned consultants to look at the comparative costs of the Arup and British Rail schemes and found that (with Arup's proposal pruned back to two tracks for comparison purposes) they were similar (Faith, *op. cit.*)).

## Enter Heseltine

Then politics intervened: Mrs Thatcher had resigned, and after a battle for party leadership with Michael Heseltine, was replaced by John Major. Major appointed Heseltine to his old post as Secretary of State for the Environment, where he would have to deal with the policy that had helped bring Thatcher down – the poll tax. It was astute politics. But it also gave Heseltine a platform for his ambitious interventionist brand of Conservative politics. The stage was set for the final act.

A senior civil servant who had known Heseltine in his previous incarnation in the Department for the Environment described the returned Heseltine as 'more autocratic and grand in manner', though still 'restlessly stirring things up' (Crick, 1997, p. 364). His role in Thatcher's downfall seemed to give him a new aura, that of a man whose place in history was assured. Never an orthodox politician, Heseltine was always decisive and often visionary; he became a presence in meetings and exploited his heavyweight reputation.

Heseltine's dream of regenerating East London and the wastelands beyond had taken root as a Junior Minister in the Heath government, when he had wanted a development corporation for the south bank of the Thames. In the early 1980s part of that dream was realized in the creation of the London Docklands Development Corporation, where public money was used, alongside planning powers, to attract large-scale private investment in property. Returning to his old Department Heseltine took a passionate interest in a massive redevelopment project for a linear city stretching from Docklands to Southend in Essex and the Medway towns in Kent – the so called Thames Gateway (known at first as the East Thames Corridor).

Thames Gateway had been inspired by Professor Peter Hall. He first suggested the idea at a conference in 1991, and subsequently became Heseltine's special advisor on planning. Heseltine believed that Thames Gateway could take forward his achievements in Docklands, whilst taking pressure for development off areas to the West of London. According to Hall: 'Heseltine sees himself as the master builder, a great planner like Napoleon III… The East Thames corridor was one of those rare political decisions that had everyone salivating. It took pressure off the Oxford and Berkshire area, and Labour boroughs were offered development they thought they'd been cheated of' (Crick, *op. cit.*, p. 376).

A central component of the vision was the Channel Tunnel Rail Link, which became a tussle between Heseltine and the Department of Transport, supporting British Rail's preferred route through south-east London. The railwaymen were unwavering in their belief in the southern route, even though thousands of homes might be affected; their Chairman Bob Reid shared the opposition to Arup's proposal.

Heseltine knew that consideration of the route was being confined to the Department of Transport and asked to be invited to the meeting at which the plans were being reviewed (Heseltine, 2000). Because of Heseltine's pressure an inter-ministerial steering group was established, with Heseltine heavily in support of the eastern route for environmental and social reasons, and Norman Lamont, the Chancellor, against the whole project. The Treasury view was that the forecast return was so low that there was no economic justification. They wanted the scheme killed off. Likewise, the Prime Minister's Policy unit said that the Arup scheme was more expensive, with lower benefits, and a 'net present value' in the range £660–800m (Gourvish, *op. cit.*).

The key meeting took place on 19 June 1991 when Arup made a presentation to Heseltine, Malcolm Rifkind, the Transport Secretary, and three junior minsters. A senior civil servant who attended the meeting said: 'It was unbelievable, Heseltine just ran the whole meeting and ran roughshod over Rifkind, and had this mania over the East Thames corridor and regeneration' (Crick, *op. cit.*, p. 376). When Arup ran through their case on costs, arguing that their route was better value if proper risk contingencies were included, Bob Reid

Figure 9.3. *Medway Viaduct under construction.* Arup's route diverted from the British Rail proposal in mid Kent, running sharply north-west through the North Downs and across the chalk pits of Kent Thamesside.

was furious. Yet Heseltine won the day. At the Conservative Party conference in October Rifkind announced that the route would be on the lines put forward by Arup. It was formally adopted in October 1990. In March 1993 another Transport Secretary, John Macgregor, announced that St Pancras instead of Kings Cross would become the terminal of the rail link, using a route closely reflecting Arup's proposal.

A consortium was now needed to take the project forward and in February 1996, London and Continental Railways (LCR – a consortium including Arup, Bechtel, Virgin, National Express, SG Warburg and others) was chosen. In return for agreeing to construct the link LCR was given a 999 year lease on the line, and gifted St Pancras, as well as at Stratford and other lands, the profits to be split with government. The Royal Assent was given to the link on 18 December 1996.

Unfortunately LCR soon ran into financial problems and in January 1998, asked John Prescott (the new Secretary of State for Transport, Local Government and Regions in Blair's government) for a further £1.2 billion to finish the project. Prescott refused, but later approved an arrangement where an extra £140 million would be contributed by government; with LCRs concession reduced (it would only retain a 99 year lease on the line). In effect Railtrack, the privatized railway infrastructure owner, was in the lead, managing the project on LCR's behalf with Bechtel. Three years later, when LCRs financial problems became acute, Bechtel took over the job of completing the line.

Financial structures changed again in June 2002 when Railtrack ran into severe problems and was wound up by government and replaced by Network Rail. Network Rail took Railtrack's place in the project; phase 1 of the link was acquired by LCR, who in turn sold the rights to operate, manage and maintain the entire route, including St Pancras, to Network Rail.

## Explanation and Evaluation

In October 1998 work was inaugurated on what was to become Britain's first new main line railway for over a century. Section 1 opened in September 2003, with trains still travelling to Waterloo on existing tracks. Section 2, through to St Pancras opened in November 2007. The quality of the engineering and design achievement, together with the restoration of Barlow's train shed and the gothic splendour of St Pancras station, are widely seen as triumphant success stories.

Yet at £5.2 billion, the Channel Tunnel Rail Link has cost around £50 million per kilometre. It is more expensive than any other high-speed rail line in the world, costing more than seven times as much per kilometre as the high-speed line between Madrid and Lerida, which opened at much the same time. Government had estimated the project cost in 1996 at £400m; British Rail at £700m in 1987; estimates for Phase 1 alone rose from £707 million in 1989 to £1.25 billion in 1990, the actual cost being £1.9 billion (Omega Centre, 2008).

Why were the comparative costs so high? Explanations include heavily built up terrain in the UK, the need to build a high-speed route to the heart of the capital, since existing tracks were congested with commuter traffic, and the fact that the Channel Tunnel link was built as a one off, rather than as part

Figure 9.4. *Eurostar high-speed train in mid Kent.* The Channel Tunnel Rail Link (now known as High Speed One) was the first, and only, new British railway route constructed in the twentieth century.

Figure 9.5. *St Pancras International Station.* The quality of engineering, conservation and design achievement is widely regarded as a triumphant success.

of a long-term programme of route building (*ibid*.). The financial packages and arrangements, born of the belief that the line should not be publicly funded are complex, and doubtless more expensive than a simpler public funding model. There can be little doubt that the Arup route, though lower in environmental impact, required much more costly and complicated engineering solutions.

The extent to which this was offset by regeneration gains has still to be proved. One early (and at the outset wholly unexpected) gain included the successful bid and staging of the London Olympic Games at Stratford in 2010, for which the Channel Tunnel Rail Link and new high-speed Javelin commuter trains acted as a key transport link to St Pancras and central London. Yet evaluating the project's regeneration benefits in 1991, consultants Pieda concluded sceptically that, while the easterly route did provide greater opportunities for regeneration, in itself it was neither a sufficient nor necessary condition for the regeneration of the East Thames corridor (*ibid*.). More recent reports tend to bear out these conclusions. Opinions have been divided on the success of Thames Gateway, with critics highlighting the complexity of governance arrangements, which included two urban development corporations, three sub-regional partnerships, seven local regeneration partnerships, an overarching strategic partnership group, and nineteen local authorities, not to mention twenty-five government departments. Heseltine had originally wanted a powerful single body – an English Development Agency – to lead, but his proposal was turned down by Cabinet colleagues (Crick, *op. cit*.). In March 2011 the new Coalition government announced the first stage in dismantling the Thames Gateway Development Corporation, as part of its move from strategic planning to localism, whilst the Thames Gateway bridge, seen as a crucial part of the project, was scrapped by Boris Johnson, London's Mayor, in November 2008 (House of Commons Library, 2011). The credit crunch and economic downturn brought virtually all new house building in the Gateway to a halt.

A final verdict on Thames Gateway and the regeneration effects of the rail link will take years to reach. Like all so called 'mega projects' it has been long in preparation; its objectives have tended to shift as time has passed; it has catalysed unexpected benefits like the Olympics; and it will take many more years to bear its full fruit. Evaluation of mega projects takes place on the shifting sands of context, including pure serendipity and happenstance, and other mega events, such as domestic political change and international decisions (Omega Centre, 2012). But that does not stop judgements on the project's characteristics and its planning gestation. Quite clearly, the rail link has all the hallmarks of earlier case studies, and resonance with the nineteenth-century attempt to build a Channel Tunnel and rail connections. Like Watkin's great project 100 years earlier, the Channel Tunnel Rail Link relied very heavily on private sector leadership and on individual initiative. Watkin's ghost was present in the management ethos and culture created by Ove Arup, in the Arup team which developed and continued to pursue its vision for an easterly route (sometimes at considerable financial risk to the company), and, it might be said, in the buccaneering leadership shown by Michael Heseltine and his advisor Professor Peter Hall. Neither should one forget the positive leadership roles played by local government in Kent County Council or the London Borough of Newham.

The same government machine which had so effectively blocked Watkin's nineteenth-century plans, stood quietly on the side-lines throughput the saga of the Channel Tunnel and its rail links, where once again private sector leadership took the initiative and civil servants acted as 'rubber stampers' and regulators, rather than as purposeful initiators. Only when Michael Heseltine, a particularly powerful and determined individual Minister, took the lead, was the government machine galvanized into action in what has been described as a 'triumph of political will and entrepreneurial optimism over economic scepticism' (Gourvish, *op. cit.*, p. 385).

For the most part the rail link project was kept discreetly at arm's length and left to British Rail, a body that simply did not have the political guile and capacity to deal with sensitive planning and public relations issues. The official history of British Rail concluded:

> Frequently disconcerted, and shunted around by the government as it wrestled with armies of consultants, British Rail made a substantial commitment to the Channel Tunnel in terms of investment, resources and management time. Some of its actions may be criticized and a substantial amount of public money was wasted. However most of the blame rests with the government... (Gourvish, 2002, p. 340)

## References

Comfort, N. (2006) *The Channel Tunnel and its High Speed Links*. Monmouth: The Oakwood Press.

Crick, M. (1997) *Michael Heseltine: A Biography*. Harmondsworth: Penguin.

Faith, N. (2007) *The Right Line*. Kingston, Kent: Seagrave Foulkes.

Gourvish, T. (2002) *British Rail 1974–1997: From Integration to Privatisation*. Oxford: Oxford University Press.

Gourvish, T. (2006) *The Official History of Britain and the Channel Tunnel*. London: Routledge.

Greaves, N. (2005) *Sir Edward Watkin, 1819–1901*. Suffolk: The Book Guild.

Hall, P. (2007) Foreword, in Faith, N., *The Right Line*. Kingston, Kent: Seagrave Foulkes.

Henderson, N. (1987) *Tunnels and Channels: Reflections on Britain and Abroad*. London: Weidenfeld and Nicolson.

Hennessy, P. (1990) *Whitehall*. London: Fontana.

Heseltine, M.(2000) *Life in the Jungle: My Autobiography*. London: Hodder and Stoughton.

House of Commons Library (2011) Thames Gateway Update. Available at: updatehttp://www.parliament.uk/briefing-papers/SN03894.pdf.

Jones, P. (2006) *Ove Arup: Masterbuilder of the Twentieth Century*. London: Yale University Press.

Omega Centre (2008) *Project Profile: Channel Tunnel Rail Link*. London: Omega Centre, Bartlett School of Planning, University College London.

Omega Centre (2012) *Mega Projects Executive Summary: Lessons for Decision Makers*. London: Omega Centre, Bartlett School of Planning, University College London.

Simmons, J. (1978) *The Railway in England and Wales 1830–1914*. Leicester: Leicester University Press.

Simmons, J. (1986) *The Railways of Britain*. London: Macmillan.

Young, H. (1998) *This Blessed Plot: Britain and Europe from Churchill to Blair*. London: Macmillan.

# 10

# The Pedaller's Tale
## Pioneering the National Cycle Network

*On the way cycling here tonight I stopped next to a woman at the traffic lights and I said 'Hello'. I was wearing a helmet and dark glasses. 'It's a lovely sunny day today'. She sort of peered at me and said 'I can't recognise you, you're in disguise' and I said 'Oh no, we've never met before'. In the twenty years I've been cycling I always speak to other cyclists; and it's something that car drivers can't do, the only way they tend to communicate is through road rage.*

George Platts, Sustrans founder, 1997

By the time that the former Somerset and Dorset Railway started to build its Bath extension in the early 1870s, the failing enterprise was increasingly short of money. So the single line route from Midford to Bath, including two long tunnels, was built to very minimum standards of clearance, without any ventilation shafts. Conditions on the engine footplate in the mile long Combe Down tunnel must have been like a scene from Dante's Inferno, with choking dust, smoke, fire and steam. In 1966 the line was closed and its days as a transport link seemed gone forever (Atthill, 1985). Yet in 2013 it was reopened, this time as one of the 'Two Tunnels', the longest cycling and walking tunnel in Britain. It is an exhilarating experience to pedal through the atmospherically lit void; not least as the deepest section features an eerie audio visual artwork that sounds like a demented string quartet, trapped forever underground and endlessly playing Stockhausen.

## A National Network

The Two Tunnels is not a one off scheme, but the latest element in an enormous infrastructure project known as the National Cycle Network, which attracted three-quarters of a billion user visits in 2012–2013 (Sustrans, 2013). Stretching from Lands End at the South West tip of England, to John O'Groats in the far north of Scotland, and from Dover through Wales to Ballyshannnon in the west of Northern Ireland, in all there are 14,700 miles (23,700 km) of cycling, wheelchair and walking routes, many on safe 'off road' sections. It is an astonishing new national asset, connecting all the major cities of the UK and the most extensive transport network construction in Britain since the building of the motorways. Linking together ancient paths, Roman roads, canal towpaths, disused railway lines, drovers roads, country lanes and 'traffic calmed' roads, about a third of the network is on traffic free routes, with the remaining two-thirds on minor roads. Maintenance is shared between hundreds of partners. Local authorities look after sections within highways. Traffic free sections are maintained by councils, owners or by charitable trusts, where contractors and several thousand volunteers do the work. Creating the network has involved countrywide partnerships between local authorities, businesses, land owners, environmental groups and many others (Wickers, 2000).

Much of the funding for the project came from the National Lottery, through its Millennium Lottery fund, although it did not attract the fame (or perhaps infamy) attached to more grandiose Millennium projects, such as the Millennium Dome – the latter a costly and embarrassing fiasco that was driven by the misplaced ambitions of national politicians like Tony Blair (King and Crewe, 2013). The cycleway network was a low-key affair, spread through Britain rather than focused on a single big project that could make the front pages of newspapers. Apart from several significant new bridge structures (some of which are of great beauty), the network is a modest linear necklace in the landscape.

Figure 10.1. *National cycle network route on the Kennet and Avon Canal towpath.* The Network links together ancient paths, drovers' roads, disused railways, towpaths and minor roads.

Figure 10.2. *The Two Tunnels, Bath.* The longest cycling and walking tunnel in Britain.

In itself all this would be a significant achievement, arguably as significant as the creation of the UK's National Parks. But the wider objectives have been more ambitious and wide ranging than just providing for an occasional outing. They include changing national transport policy, promoting cycling as an alternative form of transport, providing tourism resources, creating places where people who do not cycle could be encouraged to do so, providing new green space, encouraging biodiversity, commissioning public art, and not least getting an increasingly obese and illness prone generation out of their cars, off their sofas and onto a bicycle, or their feet. About half the journeys on the network are by bike and the remainder by walkers. According to a formula devised by the World Health Organization, a calculation in 2008 showed that the total value in health benefits to cyclists using the (then much smaller) network was £270 million (Davies, 2010). So in creating the network, health, aesthetic, ecological, social and artistic objectives became almost as important as transport objectives.

All this was achieved – and indeed is still being achieved – without government initiative or central direction, and in the earlier stages without support. Pam Ashton, who was closely involved (as Sustrans Chair between 1987 and 1991), recalled an early meeting with a civil servant: 'I went to see someone in a government department who sat there with his arms folded and said, you're never going to do this … government was uninterested and supercilious. They had better things to do' (Ashton, 2014). There was little direct support at any stage (former Transport Secretary Steven Norris being the honourable exception) and only a little from professional institutions, through the Institution of Civil Engineers (Grimshaw, 2014). Everything rested on the initiative of a small number of committed and determined individuals (and one individual in particular) working in a charitable body, dependent on loose partnership arrangements with local authorities, and supported by grants from the UK Lottery. The charity is known as Sustrans (short for sustainable transport) and the story of its birth, growth and evolution takes us back to the 1970s, a sometimes despairing, yet surprisingly pivotal era in recent British history.

## Sustrans and Cyclebag

The 1970s are not often seen as Britain's finest hour. Yet they were certainly eventful. On 4 March 1974 the OPEC oil shock created a political and economic crisis that led to a three-day working week and the collapse of Edward Heath's Conservative government. After 20 years of growth, real earnings fell in 1976 and 1977. Though living standards improved through much of the decade, Britain's economy, politics and cultural life seemed to falter. The electorate turned its back on socialism as a solution. Collective working-class culture, like manufacturing employment, was waning, with individualism emerging as a dominant ethos. Two Prime Ministers – the Conservative Heath and Labour leader Callaghan – were unable to control the power of the trade unions.

These were the years of the IMF crisis (with Britain supplicant to its lenders), the IRA Birmingham bombings, and the Grunwick strike, culminating in the period of industrial strife known as the 'Winter of Discontent'. They were also the years of youth unemployment and the emergence of rebellious punk rock music led by the Sex Pistols – a group whose anarchic discontent seemed to reflect the spirit of the age as closely as had the wit and optimism of the Beatles in the 1960s (Sandbrook, 2013). Environmental activism and protest rose through the 1970s, in Britain as well as other Western countries. It heralded the end of London's motorway plans, and new motorways in general. The decade ended with the election of Margaret Thatcher and an enduring shift to the right in politics.

While protestors like John Tyme led the frontal attack on motorway building (see Chapter 7), a subtler mind was questioning the whole basis of post-war transport policy. That man was Mayer Hillman, a researcher at a London think tank called Political and Economic Planning (PEP). I met Hillman in the 1970s, when my university tutor suggested (hesitantly) that Hillman might be a useful contact for a planning thesis. Hillman proved to be a man of passionate, unconventional, even outlandish, views on transport policy and at least 20 years ahead of his time. His report 'Personal Mobility and Transport Policy' turned conventional wisdom on its head. It argued that personal mobility in a car-borne society could become very limited for those without cars, including the young and the old. People's needs, and their ability to get around, must become the starting point for policy, with the focus on walking, the mode most frequently used and the most universally available (Hillman *et al.*, 1973). It was a startling, if prosaic, observation. For transport policy had turned its back on muscle power in favour of cars, trains and planes. Even now a standard textbook on transport planning devotes only a few cursory paragraphs to cycling (Headicar, 2009). In the 1970s anyone who championed the cause of feet and pedals would have been regarded as utterly eccentric.

One man who shared Hillman's views was a Cambridge educated civil engineer called John Grimshaw. The son of a British Army officer, Grimshaw was brought up in a family with a strong belief in public service. He lived in East Africa until the age of 12, thereafter being educated at a minor English public school (Grimshaw, *op. cit.*).

Grimshaw is something of an entrepreneur, an outsider, a man who does not easily take no for an answer. After an early career working for transport consultants in the UK and overseas, he decided to break with transport orthodoxy. Like Hillman, he came to believe that traditional transport planning had completely overlooked the needs of cyclists and pedestrians: 'I think I really decided that a lot of what we were doing was dishonest. Professionalism was being abused. You would stand up in front of a client and say that such a scheme was wonderful when in fact you thought it was ridiculous. I felt that traffic engineers were on a road to nowhere' (Wray, 1987). A man of commanding physical and charismatic social presence, Grimshaw quite literally decided to take another path.

Sustrans came into existence in Bristol towards the end of the 1970s. Bristol is a relaxed, cultured and relatively prosperous English city, sitting roughly midway between London and Cornwall, that seems to have some attraction for bohemian, environmentalist, artistic, if not vaguely anarchist types. The key date is 7 July 1977, when a group of about thirty people met in the upstairs room of the Nova Scotia pub. Nearly half of the group were artists or film makers, including art therapist George Platts and film maker Dave Sproxton, later a co-founder of Aardman Animations, the 'Wallace and Gromit' film animators (this artistic connection was not without significance for the way events developed). Alongside were John Grimshaw, and civic entrepreneurs like architect George Ferguson, who in 2013 was to become Bristol's independently elected city mayor, and Alistair Sawday, who went on to develop a respected environmental guide business (Grimshaw, *op. cit.*; Platts, 1997).

Sustrans' precursor was known as Cycle (Conserve Your Calf And Leg Muscles) and subsequently Cyclebag (add Bristol Action Group). Cyclebag was essentially an environmental campaign group, initiated by a group of cycling enthusiasts. As well as campaigning, the group wanted to build a short stretch of cycleway between Bristol and Bath on a disused railway line, but it was getting nowhere with the local authorities. Keen to make progress on the ground, Grimshaw had been offered a £10,000 grant from the Clarks shoe business in Glastonbury, to fund the costs of building the Bristol to Bath path. It was an act of philanthropy from the old established Quaker firm. The problem was that Cyclebag, although it had 2,000 members, was only a pressure group. Simply to receive the grant an 'enabling company' had to be created, which it was hoped could receive grants for similar projects elsewhere in the UK. That company, Sustainable Transport Limited, was born in 1979. As a trading company it was required to meet once a year for its Annual General Meeting. Both Grimshaw and Platts became Directors, along with representatives of other English cycling campaign groups (Platts, *op. cit.*).

Grimshaw became the company's chief engineer. Apart from his technical skills, working on an extension to the preserved narrow gauge Festiniog Railway in Wales, he had acquired an understanding of how volunteers could undertake major civil engineering tasks. This would be useful for, despite the grant, practical progress was slow, bogged down in negotiations. According to Platts the point came when Grimshaw thought: 'Well, they're not going to build it for us. We've got these 2,000 loyal members. Maybe we'll see if they can do it' (Platts, *op. cit.*, p. 5).

## The First Miles

Thus in summer 1979 5 miles (8 km) of cycle path were built in only ten weeks, using the Clarks grant for materials, and volunteer labour. Apart from the tipping of materials for the path surface, everything was done with hand tools. Avon County Council, who had purchased the old line for an abandoned road scheme, gave Cyclebag an annual licence to use the site for £1. Although it was not the first off-road cycle route in the UK (that distinction belongs to the Manifold railway path in Derbyshire, created in the 1930s) it was the first city centre to city centre route, with potential for attracting large numbers of commuters, as well as recreational users.

In 1980 the Private Secretary to the Minister of Transport visited the project. Not long afterwards John Grimshaw and Bill Clarke (Cyclebag Secretary) were commissioned to produce a report on the potential of all disused railways in England and Wales as cycle routes. Published officially by Her Majesty's Stationery Office, the report estimated that of the 10,000 miles (16,000 km) of disused railway line, around 8,000 miles (13,000 km) would be impossible to recover, being fragmented or lost to various private ownerships. However, the remaining 2,000 miles (3,200 km) had potential for re-use. Concerned that their report might end up on the shelf, the authors prepared thirty-three appendices, each setting out detailed proposals (Department for Transport, 1982). So the report became an outline feasibility study and the basis for implementation, rather than conversation (Wickers, *op. cit.*).

Bath to Bristol was only a beginning. Cyclebag believed that every town needed a safe place to start. Flushed with their success, the campaigners began looking at opportunities to repeat the formula in the West of England. From the outset these projects were viewed as linear open spaces, with the potential for nature conservation and visual art installations, rather than mere cycle paths. Partnerships with sculptors and arts organizations naturally followed (Platts, *op. cit.*). But this is jumping ahead a little.

Wherever there was a positive response from a local authority Sustrans would open negotiations for another scheme. It so happened that many of the positive responses came from the north of England rather than the south-west. In 1984, Sustrans was approached by the Countryside Commission, asking if they would like to buy the disused railway line between York and Selby. Taking on ownership, and the responsibilities of a landowner, would be a new departure, and Sustrans was therefore swiftly morphed from Company to Registered Charity. Subsequently there were hundreds of similar land agreements. Amongst other things, ownership enabled the sale of surplus land in order to cover long-term liabilities, like bridge maintenance.

An early route in Barnsley started with a phone call from the local authority. The council wanted to build a short stretch; Grimshaw suggested a national coast to coast route – the Trans Pennine Trail – which was completed as a later Millennium project, involving twenty-six local authorities working in partnership (Ashton, *op. cit.*). Sustrans was developing a national profile, and as luck would have it, a new source of funding and labour was emerging. Youth unemployment was increasing, the government had started to fund a whole range of job creation schemes through its Manpower Services Commission.

With funding available, several new construction projects emerged: including Bristol and Pill, supported by Bristol City Council; the Plym Valley path, involving agreements negotiated with many landowners; and at Swindon, built with help from Nacro, the national body which aims to rehabilitate criminals. The Bristol to Bath path was visited in 1982 by Kenneth Clarke, then Minister for Transport. Grimshaw recalls how he and Clarke set off on bicycles for an hour's cycling and conversation, soon leaving behind the Ministerial retinue, including all Clarke's security men (Grimshaw, *op. cit.*). Sustrans was building a national reputation, the success of its early schemes helping to persuade politicians and officials that these ideas could be tried elsewhere.

Major expansion followed in the mid-1980s. Projects at Selby, Derby, Consett, Sunderland and Liverpool were under way. Although Grimshaw remained Sustran's sole employee, as many as 800 people were working on site through the government's Community Enterprise Programmes. For every ten people employed Sustrans could take on one supervisor, and many of these individuals later joined the organization on a permanent basis. Shortly afterwards Sustrans carried out a major study for the Scottish Office on the potential of disused railways as cycle ways in Scotland, and work began on routes between Glasgow and Dumbarton.

Yet planning and organization remained complex and before schemes started there were invariably many objections. Objectors worried about crime, vandalism and stone throwing. Most of these vanished after construction was completed. Grimshaw recounted his favourite objection: 'The best comment I've actually had was in Bristol last summer when we had a person ring in to complain that he was woken early in the morning by people going down the path singing' (Wray, *op. cit.*)

Serious problems developed in the late 1980s and early 1990s as the government ended its Community Enterprise projects. Sustrans soldiered on to fulfil its commitments. As cash ran out for paying the employees, Grimshaw took out an overdraft against the value of his home. Fortunately the cash flow problem resolved itself in 1993 when a large site, which had been transferred to Sustrans, was sold to offset maintenance liabilities. The company was solvent again; a new membership organization was created, boosting numbers to 40,000 by 1999; and high-profile patrons including media personalities were recruited. The problems did not dent morale. Sue Bergin, who joined Sustrans in April 1993, recounted her huge personal commitment and enthusiasm for her job: 'I always thought we were on the edge of something very big… It was very very exciting' (Bergin, 1997). She was right, for an extraordinary new opportunity lay ahead.

## The Millennium Opportunity

In February 1994, John Major's Conservative government had established a body called the Millennium Commission to authorize grants from National Lottery funds for projects to mark the new millennium. Comprising representatives of all

Figure 10.3. *Manchester Road Bridge, Bradford*. Opening of new bridge for walking and cycling across a busy road in 2012.

Figure 10.4. *Diglis Bridge*. Cyclists on National Route 46 beside the Worcestershire riverside.

political parties and men and women selected to represent Britain's geographical and cultural diversity, the Commission was a short-life organization, meeting for the first time in February 1994 and for the last in November 2006. Using £2.7 billion of National Lottery money, projects worth £4 billion were funded, eventually creating 225 different capital projects across 3,000 sites. Some of those projects secured international recognition almost as soon as they opened – such as Tate Modern and the Eden Project in Cornwall. Projects were asked to prove they could raise significant support from others before the fund would invest. On average, it paid for less than half the cost of a project and did not provide long-term revenue support (Big Lottery Fund, 2011).

Already skilled at working with local government and assembling projects with mixed funding, Sustrans quickly realized that Millennium funding could be the catalyst for an enormous new programme of work. They had already started to develop long distance projects, like the Trans Pennine Trail, the Sea to Sea route in northern England and even an Inverness to Dover route, the latter first discussed at a meeting in 1992 (Sustrans, 1994a). Now a truly national project could be realized. Backed by its experience, and the support of its growing membership base, Sustrans could make a realistic bid for funds for a National Cycle Network, creating a 6,500 mile (10,500 km) UK wide network by 2005, with the target of 2,500 miles (4,000 km) delivered by 2000 (Cotton and Grimshaw, 2000).

From the outset the Network was seen as a campaigning device with very broad objectives. Sustrans argued that any transport policy designed to meet environmental targets, reduce congestion and improve health must provide a real choice, allowing for higher levels of cycling. Three-quarters of all journeys made in Britain were less than 5 miles (8 km). If one-third of these were made by cycle, it would mean a tenfold increase in cycle use, bringing Britain into line with many other European countries. A national network would raise the status of cycling; demonstrate its popularity amongst all ages; reduce congestion; act as a catalyst for making entire urban areas cycle friendly; provide quiet routes through beautiful countryside; extend provision for walkers and wheelchair users; achieve improvements in health and fitness; and help to reduce $CO_2$ emissions (Sustrans, 1994*b*). On the global stage, Sustrans argued, Western countries had a moral responsibility to champion the bicycle: 'If the West can demonstrate that cycling is modern, then the Chinese, Indians, and others may be happy to keep their bikes rather than exchanging them for cars… If they don't, if aspiring to western standards of living goes hand in hand with car ownership, then we are all doomed' (Wickers, *op. cit.*, p. 44).

Creating the plan for the National Network was entirely pragmatic. It would simply take all the projects already completed or in progress, and join them together with new routes, off road or on minor roads, to create a network that would cover the country. Each new section was carefully itemized with route maps, mileages and key contacts, with calculations of projected use, based on official data (Sustrans, 1995). At the last minute concern was raised that the bid did not include projects in Northern Ireland, so three Sustrans supporters in the Province drew up proposals over a weekend. They went into the plan (Grimshaw, *op. cit.*).

HRH Prince Charles launched the bid in March 1995. By now Sustrans had enlisted fourteen high-profile patrons, including celebrities, opinion leaders, and politicians. The bid totalled £42.5 million, a figure which seemed realistic, given that the maximum grant available for a project was officially said to be £50 million. Nonetheless the bid was less than a quarter of the estimated total cost of the network. Sustrans realized that it could not compete with high-profile projects like the Dome, the government led project which eventually cost the Lottery £628 million, three times its original grant (King and Crewe, *op. cit.*). In any event, every Sustrans project so far had been funded from half a dozen different sources. In this context it seemed reasonable to ask for only 23 per cent of the total cost. Since many other projects received 50 per cent funding, the Cycle Network bid, in percentage terms, turned out to be the smallest of all.

In September 1995 the National Cycle Network was the first large project to be awarded Millennium Commission grant and Sustrans was presented with a cheque for £42.5 million. The Trans Pennine Trail, a joint local authority led project inspired by Sustrans, also obtained Millennium funding of £6m, eventually receiving £19m in funding from various sources (Ashton, *op. cit.*). It was time to start building.

Of all the partnerships forged, the relationship with local government was the most critical. Local councils were responsible for planning permission, for highways, and were capable of integrating schemes in an overall plan. Within each partner authority one individual officer would invariably emerge, beavering away as unofficial project champion. Their technical status varied. Sometimes it might be a town planner, sometimes an engineer, sometimes a relatively junior technician. 'It can't be done without a friend in the council', said Grimshaw, 'People worked it so that we got the cash' (Grimshaw, *op. cit.*).

By June 2000 all mileage targets had been exceeded. A little over 1,000 miles (1,600 km) of route on minor roads was projected; 3,008 miles (4,841 km) were completed. Less than 100 miles (160 km) of new railway path was projected; 219 (352 km) were completed. In all the bid target was to deliver 2,500 miles (4,000 km) by 2000; in fact 5,500 miles (8,850 km) were completed. Different elements in four different countries and the efforts of almost 400 local authorities and other bodies had been coordinated and the network has never stopped growing. In 2013 500 new miles (800 km) were added, bringing the total to 14,700 miles (23,700 km).

Artists played a key role in creating Sustrans – Cyclebag as it then was – in the 1970s. Perhaps it was this connection that led to the policy of commissioning sculpture, so that these new public spaces would be seen as friendly and benign. Certainly it was not long before it could be claimed that the Cycle Network had become Britain's largest outdoor sculpture park. Mileposts were featured on the York and Selby project in 1985. A series of mounds and lookout points were built from scrap. Much of the sculpture commissioned since has reused industrial materials. Spoil heaps became Andy Goldsworthy's Lambton Worm;

Figure 10.5. *Andy Goldsworthy's 'Lambton Worm', County Durham.* Sculptures were commissioned along the Network to add interest: Andy Goldswothy's Lambton Worm was formed from reshaped spoil heaps.

Figure 10.6. *David Kemp's 'Lost Legion', Glasgow to Greenock Cycleway.* Kemp's mysterious sculpture used old gas bottles and transformers.

gas bottles and transformers became David Kemp's mysterious Lost Legion; the same artist used an old ventilation shaft as the basis for his King Coal (Sustrans, 1993). The latter forms part of the Consett and Sunderland Sculpture Trail, a 22-mile (35 km) stretch, which, within weeks of completion, became the second most visited tourist attraction in County Durham (after Durham Cathedral). In 1992, the Sculpture Trail received a Gulbenkian/Independent award, and in the same year Sustrans itself received an Arts Council award for art in public spaces.

## An Idea Ahead of Its Time

The National Cycle Network is the most recent of nine case studies and perhaps it is too soon yet to claim that it is a successful achievement. It has yet to pass the test of time and may yet encounter real problems. Sustrans is shifting the emphasis of its activity towards campaigning and education and away from infrastructure, although it retains an enormous maintenance responsibility. But there seems little doubt about the enduring need to promote healthier and more active lifestyles. The UK All Party Parliamentary Commission on Physical Activity has pointed to an 'epidemic of physical inactivity', because people have simply stopped moving, in schools and workplaces, towns and cities. Only 61 per cent of adults meet the Chief Medical Officers guidelines for daily physical activity; a problem, it is believed, which causes 37,000 premature deaths a year.

Even fewer children, as a percentage, reach the recommended activity target. In comparison with the 1960s the UK population is now 24 per cent less physically active. Physical activity, research indicates, reduces the risk of all mortality by 30 per cent, of heart disease by 20–25 per cent, of diabetes by 35–50 per cent, and dementia by 40–45 per cent (All Party Commission on Physical Activity, 2014).

What is more, this is a fast growing international problem: in only 44 years physical activity in the United States has declined by 32 per cent and is projected to fall by 46 per cent by 2030. China's 1.3 billion citizens are becoming less physically active at a higher rate than any other nation. In 18 years, physical activity has fallen by 45 per cent (Nike Inc. *et al.*, 2013). Research and official policy has caught up with Cyclebag and Mayer Hillman.

The parallels between the creation of the Cycle Network and great plans from the past are inescapable. All the hallmarks are here: the lack of initiative and drive from central government; creativity and innovation outside the formal structures of government; the determination, vision and passionate drive of a small number of individuals. Improvisation, informality and local initiative sometimes move at astonishing speed: a plan for cycle routes in Northern Ireland was completed in a weekend, the Millennium targets were achieved twice over. Support – often highly informal support – from the structures of local government is vital. A national plan seems somehow simply to evolve from below, with almost accidental grant aid support from the centre. We have seen the same characteristics at work in plans as diverse as the London Squares and Birkenhead Park, in the building of the national motorways, the Channel Tunnel Rail Link, and even in the wartime invention and use of the world's first electronic computers. In Part Three we start to identify the common threads, review the case studies, and move towards an explanation of why and how things have worked as they have.

## References

All Party Commission on Physical Activity (2014) *Tackling Physical Inactivity – A Coordinated Approach*. London: All Party Commission. Available at: http://parliamentarycommissiononphysicalactivity. files.wordpress.com/2014/04/apcopa-final.pdf.

Ashton, P. (2014) Interview with the author, Liverpool, August.

Atthill, R. (1985) *The Somerset and Dorset Railway: New Edition.* Newton Abbot: David and Charles.

Bergin, S. (1997) Interview of Sustrans employee by Jennifer Bourdillon, unpublished transcript, Bristol, April.

Big Lottery Fund (2011) *Millennium Now: Celebrating the Legacy of the Millennium.* Available at: http://www.biglotteryfund.org.uk/millenniumnow.

Cotton, N. and Grimshaw, J. (2000) *The Official Guide to the National Cycle Network*. Bristol: Sustrans.

Davies, H. (2010) Transport in a Low Carbon Managed Future, Paper presented as Sustrans National Cycle Network Director at Institution of Civil Engineers Seminar. Birmingham: Sustrans (unpublished).

Department for Transport/John Grimshaw and Associates (1982) *Study of Disused Railways in England and Wales: Potential Cycle Routes.* London: HMSO.

Grimshaw, J. (2014) Interview with the author, Bristol, August.

Headicar, P. (2009) *Transport Policy and Planning in Great Britain*. London: Routledge.

Hillman, M., Henderson, I. and Whalley, A. (1973) *Personal Mobility and Transport Policy* (Broadsheet 542). London: Political and Economic Planning.

King, A. and Crewe, I. (2013) *The Blunders of Our Governments*. London: One World Publications.

Nike Inc. with American College for Sports Medicine and International Council of Sport Science and Physical Education (2013) *Designed to Move: A Physical Activity Action Agenda*. Available at: https://s3.nikecdn.com/dtm/live/en_US/DesignedToMove_FullReport.pdf.

Platts, G. (1997) Interview of Sustrans founder member by Jennifer Bourdillon, unpublished transcript, Southampton, March.

Sandbrook, D. (2013) *Seasons in the Sun: The Battle for Britain, 1974–1979*. Harmondsworth: Penguin.

Sustrans (1993) *15 Year Review incorporating Annual Report, 1992–1993*. Bristol: Sustrans.

Sustrans (1994a) Inverness to Dover Cycle Routes: A Review Programme, November 1994. Bristol: Sustrans.

Sustrans (1994b) The 5000 Mile National Cycle Network, Incorporating the 1,000 mile Inverness to Dover Route (leaflet). Bristol: Sustrans.

Sustrans (1995) *The National Cycleway Network: Appendix*. Bristol: Sustrans.

Sustrans (2013) Millions of People on the Move: Usage and Benefits of the National Cycle Network. Bristol: Sustrans. Available at: http://www.sustrans.org.uk/sites/default/files/file_content_type/sustrans-ncn-report-2013.pdf.

Wickers, D. (2000) *Millennium Miles: The Story of the National Cycle Network*. Whitley: GB Publications Limited/Sustrans.

Wray, I. (1987) Why the cyclists burst into song. *Architects Journal*, **185**, 15 April, p. 15.

Part Three

# EXPLANATIONS AND IMPLICATIONS

# 11

# **The Common Threads**
## Drawing Together the Case Studies

*As a nation we do seem to be empiricists, extremely cautious about principles, strong on pragmatism – we just are a 'back of envelope' type race.*

Philip Ziegler, 1996

It is time to bring together what we have learned in the case studies, and, if we can, identify the common threads. Despite their diversity in time period and subject matter it proves easy to do so, as the same features crop up with surprising regularity. So our recapitulation is grouped around the following themes:

- The role of the state;
- The role of individuals and individualism;
- Innovation;
- Flexibility and improvisation;
- Institutions and platforms.

## The Role of the State

The first and most obvious theme is the limited, almost passive, indeed sometimes wholly negative, role of central government, or 'the state', even in constructing national networks. The first Private Members Bill for a motorway standard road was considered in 1906. Construction of the first stretch of motorway began only in 1958. During the 1930s, though progress was made with new road schemes in the provinces, especially in Liverpool, central government remained indifferent or hostile. These new roads were not required, according to a Royal Commission on Transport in 1931; and in any event they could not be built because the country was already so 'densely roaded'. Incremental improvement to the existing system – patch and mend – was the better solution. In 2006 the Eddington Report, commissioned by Tony Blair's government, expressed uncannily similar views, hostile to *grands projéts*, and in favour of small-scale improvements to an existing system. In particular, high-speed rail, it argued, was not needed in Britain. Britain's towns and cities were so much closer together than their equivalents on the continent. A map showing the distances between major cities served to underline the point; or more accurately to distort it, since it left off the connections to more distant Scottish cities (HM Treasury, 2006). The initiative for motorway building came from outside the government machine, from a small group of committed professionals, operating within professional institutions and within local government.

The Channel Tunnel was indeed driven by government initiative. But it was the initiative of the French government, not the British, who had opposed or failed to support a succession of construction projects from Sir Alfred Watkin's great Victorian dream in 1897 through to the mid-1980s. At the Board of Trade, Joseph Chamberlain went out of his way to kill off the Watkin plan. With the tunnel built, after the final agreement between Thatcher and Mitterrand, the need for a high-speed link to London was obvious. Yet the responsible department – Transport – failed to take the lead, swiftly passing the problem to an ill prepared nationalized industry in British Rail. It was only when Michael Heseltine personally championed the project that government eventually committed itself to the link. The Channel Tunnel rail link needed the support of government, which was long in coming. Yet it depended in large part on personal initiative, entirely outside the confines of government and the civil service. In the Channel Tunnel saga the British government proved more obstacle than activist.

It was much the same story for the National Cycle Network. The project emerged, not from government, but from the efforts of a small committed group of individuals. There was little or no positive support from the centre for cycling. A positive policy for cycling emerged as government responded to the pressure of campaigners; and before that happened it was openly sceptical.

Thus the twentieth century's big plans follow a course charted in the seventeenth, eighteenth and nineteenth centuries, and in London we can see the failure to enact plans to startling effect. For the state made two bold attempts to re-plan and restructure the city's road and infrastructure networks. In 1666, after the Great Fire, Wren's master plan for reconstruction swiftly won the King's support; equally swiftly it lost it. Pragmatism and the pluralistic interests of property owners prevailed, as the city was rebuilt on original alignments and to original land ownership boundaries. Before leaving the burning city the civil servant Samuel Pepys buried his wine and parmesan cheese in his garden, confident that when the fire was burned out he would return to his land and recover his property. Central London *was* re-planned throughout the eighteenth and nineteenth century (and indeed into the twenty-first century), and what emerged was a city fabric almost unique to the city. But the lead certainly did not, and does not, come from state direction or control.

In the twentieth century, government made a second attempt to instil order into London's diversity. Once again the impetus was large-scale fire damage and destruction, this time caused by the Blitz. Government encouraged the preparation of ambitious plans for post-war reconstruction by Sir Patrick Abercrombie, later setting up a Greater London Council as the driving force for building a new network of urban motorways, thus implementing Abercrombie's great plan. The planners imported new techniques of forecasting and rational planning, developed in the United States during and after the Second World War. Yet to no avail; history simply repeated itself. The road plans were not implemented on any scale and only scattered fragments of the road network were built. They were opposed by intelligent and well-organized individual objectors; eventually political change took place and they were abandoned. Only an outer ring road, built through the undeveloped area beyond the city, was constructed, as part of the national motorway system. It is now the M25.

The literature on Bletchley Park and its code breakers has a tendency to focus on the technicalities of code breaking and its military impact. Rather less attention has been paid to the basic question – how was this organized and by whom? It might reasonably be assumed that a national code breaking institution, passing secret intelligence to the highest levels and utilizing the revolutionary infrastructure of information technology would have been brought into being by government. Yet here again government's role was passive. The War Office did not support the Bletchley Park initiative. Later in the war, the Bletchley Park authorities did not support a proposal to commission an electronic computer. To repeat West's conclusions on the Radio Security Service in a much wider context, all this was a classic example of time honoured British improvisation with voluntary workers making considerable sacrifices to rescue an ill prepared Whitehall establishment (West, 1986).

Remarkably, it seems that in many respects twentieth-century governments played as limited a role in British plans as their eighteenth- and nineteenth-century counterparts. The great landscapes of Capability Brown, admired around the world had absolutely nothing to do with state planning or sponsorship. Government had no role in creating the world's first public park in Birkenhead, or indeed in any of the numerous nineteenth-century projects it inspired. A House of Commons Select Committee certainly identified the problem and made cogent arguments for new urban green space (SCPW, 1833). But it left open the issue of whether government should take a lead.

There is one important exception to all this, although with hindsight it appears to have been more a blip than a structural change. The Second World War had an enormous impact on British society, on public administration, on civil engineering, on planning and design, and subsequently on politics. Britain's economy was crippled by the costs of fighting the war; parts of its cities were destroyed by the Blitz; its infrastructure was worn out; new techniques in large-scale engineering had been invented in building airfields and clearing bomb damage; and war socialism had reshaped the civil service as a machine for doing, rather than regulating. The country wanted change and a better future.

A new Labour government committed to socialist policies and reconstruction set the stage. It supplied the impetus for major post-war projects, including the creation of the Welfare State, large-scale public house building and the National Health Service, as it did for physical plans. In Britain, as elsewhere in the western world, the three decades after the war were a high point of state led planning and change, only to falter in the late 1960s and early 1970s as the public mood changed and economic progress stalled. These were the years of government commitment to motorways and new towns, including the new city of Milton Keynes. Even so, initiative was often left to local government, which led the way in lobbying for the motorways and substantially built them (at least until Barbara Castle introduced government Road Construction Units in the mid-1960s). The new towns and their development corporations *were* absolutely clear examples of government taking the initiative. Yet in inspiration and leadership they owed everything to individuals outside the government machine.

The post-war plan for Cambridge was a small, yet critical, example of the plans created under the provisions of the Labour government's 1947 Town and Country Planning Act. Led by local government and external consultants, its call for restraint could be construed as a failed plan. Planned restraint helped create the conditions in Cambridge for a particular type of growth, a type anticipated and supported by the planners. Yet there is no doubt that in Cambridge government was never in charge of events. The extraordinary growth of the Cambridge economy was not driven by government action or direction.

## Individuals and Individualism

If government in Britain rarely drives change or implements big plans, who does? The answer will already be obvious. They are driven from below by individuals, acting in autonomous institutions, or, if you prefer, on autonomous institutional platforms. Indeed the planning processes (if they can be so described) prove to be surprisingly non-hierarchical.

London was not shaped by Wren's great plan, but by the forces of individual objection and individual land ownership, subtly modulated by regulation and the rule of law. Objectors blocked the post war motorway proposals as surely as they had blocked the development of Lincoln's Inn Fields for housing in the seventeenth century. The great estates shaped the developed form of inner

London throughout the eighteenth and nineteenth centuries. They are still a force to be reckoned with, owning perhaps more than 50 per cent of the current central area (the figure has been estimated from a slightly fuzzy map in the frontispiece to NLA, 2013).

What is more the great estates are growing, not shrinking, as new landlords enter the field to take forward the redevelopment and regeneration of areas which have slipped into decline. The most important examples of new great estates are the redevelopment proposals for the area around King's Cross and St Pancras. The most fascinating is the Soho Estate, created by incremental post-war acquisition by one man, Paul Raymond, and now being managed and regenerated by his two grand-daughters.

Birkenhead Park, the world's first public park, like so many others, was the creation of local government, in the form of the Birkenhead Improvement Commissioners, and specifically the two men who were prime movers: Isaac Holmes, a Liverpool councillor, and Sir William Jackson. Birkenhead's designer Sir Joseph Paxton owed much to the naturalistic school of English landscape architects, best known through the works of Capability Brown.

Thus were the landscape innovations of the English school rooted in the earlier works of William Kent and others, and in the minds of Pope, Milton and Evelyn, transmitted into Victorian landscape design. Private landowners commissioned every one of Brown's landscapes. These were landscapes born of, and created for, wealthy independent private individuals and their families. Indeed at Stowe, the site of Brown's earliest work, the wider landscape was intended as an iconographic celebration of individualism and of Whig political sentiments.

We might have expected such stories from the eighteenth and nineteenth centuries. What is astonishing is the re-appearance of individual initiative and charitable activity for creating green space and transport facilities in the late twentieth century. The National Cycle Network, all 14,700 miles (23,700 km) created since 1977, together with the sculpture and art work along the routes, owes nothing to government, and everything to the persistence of a small number of determined individuals and a private charity. The initiative depended crucially on partnership arrangements with many other bodies, and especially with local government, where one individual in each and every authority (sometimes senior, sometimes junior) played the key role in making things happen.

We find further resonance in the creation of the world's first computer and in the plan for Cambridge and the later explosive growth of science-based industry in that city. Bletchley Park was turned down for funding by the War Office and created at the personal initiative of Admiral Sir Hugh Sinclair. He bought the site and buildings with his own funds, recruiting a chef and waitresses to look after the code breakers. Colossus, the code breaker's computer, was built at the personal initiative of Thomas Flowers with the support of his immediate line managers in the Post Office Research Establishment, Dollis Hill, after the authorities had turned it down (Copeland, 2006b).

For good or ill, the post-war plan for Cambridge owed everything to Lord William Holford, as well as to the initiative of the Planning Minister Lewis Silkin, who made sure that planning powers rested with the county, rather than city, council and was instrumental in Holford's appointment. With the benefit of hindsight it is evident that Holford's plan was carefully nuanced and supplied the right physical framework to support the city's growth. That growth was predetermined not by government but by the university, through its history, its long tradition of scientific excellence, and the brilliant minds it had attracted.

One private initiative played a crucial role in re-establishing the scientific pre-eminence of Cambridge after its eighteenth-century torpor: the establishment of the Cavendish Laboratory, a personal gift from the Duke of Devonshire. It became the platform for individual scientific brilliance in the early twentieth century, and later for crucial wartime atomic research. The Cavendish also attracted key technologists like William Pye, founder of Pye Electronics, to the city in the nineteenth century.

There was more than individual excellence to the Cambridge story, to be sure. Government did play a crucial 'walk on' role from time to time. Spurred by the growth of dissenting academies and redbrick universities in the nineteenth century, government insisted that Cambridge should modernize. During Harold Wilson's 1960s Labour government, a final flowering of post-war intervention and state planning helped to bring the Computer Assisted Design (CAD) centre to Cambridge. Government funding of facilities like Addenbrooke's Hospital remained critical in securing the bedrock of first-class research institutions. But government had little or no hand in masterminding a strategy. Strategic direction came from the policies, actions (and doubtless high-level lobbying) of an autonomous institution – the university itself.

Unquestionably, government was more active and purposeful in the decades after the Second World War. Yet in a massive national project like the building of the motorways, personal initiative remained vital – as we saw in the case of Sir James Drake – as was the role of local government as a prime mover in physical delivery. Milton Keynes, designated by Harold Wilson's Labour government, was state action on a heroic scale. But individual initiative remained vital, in the form of the Development Corporation's chairman, Lord Campbell, in the pre-war visions and campaigning of Frederic Osborn and the Town and Country Planning Association (who had set the scene for post-war implementation) and not least in the extraordinary drive and resourcefulness of one rather maverick and unconventional figure – Lord Reith.

Consider finally the Channel Tunnel and its rail link. The Tunnel itself was of course a government initiative. But essentially it was a French government initiative, a deal struck between Mitterand and Thatcher after years of indecision and vacillation. The Link itself – now known as High Speed One – remains the only section of high-speed railway in the country. It owed nothing to the efforts of government departments. Progress came from two sources –

from the unpaid and un-commissioned work of a company of brilliant British consulting engineers, and later from the personal leadership of one politician, Michael Heseltine – bent on making the government machine deliver a *grand projét*. Heseltine's style was perhaps as much a rarity in central government as it was an everyday reality in local government and the other institutions in this story.

## Improvisers, Innovators and Objectors

As one might expect, the informality of a planning style outside the confines of central leadership lends itself to, and perhaps requires, a degree of improvisation. We saw in Chapter 1 that critics of the rationalist comprehensive approach to planning (such as Lindblom, Popper, Taleb, Kay and to an extent the Omega Centre) advocated a more flexible 'trial and error' approach to building policy. We can see that approach in practice in many of the case studies.

The plan for the National Cycle Network was largely pragmatic, designed to link up projects already underway. A meeting of activists and creative types in a pub kicked off the events that led to the creation of Sustrans. The evolution from campaigning group to a land-owning trust was not thought out at the outset. It simply evolved. A plan for Northern Ireland was drawn up over a weekend. The programme was opportunistic, responding to opportunities for projects and for funding. Led by a charity this might be expected. But we can see traces of a similar approach in the evolution of ideas and plans for national motorway building.

The Ten Year Trunk Road Plan, including 800 miles (1,290 km) of motorways, announced by the Labour Transport Minister in 1946 (Edbrooke, 1971) was essentially the proposal drawn up by activists in the Institution of Civil Engineers in their spare time. The route eventually accepted for the Channel Tunnel rail link was proposed and thought through by a small group of individuals in Arup in complete informality; the work was charged to other projects to keep the activity undisclosed to senior management. Bletchley Park was an extraordinarily informal, at times almost chaotic, institution. Ideas were shared at informal events, to which there was an open invitation (the so-called tea parties, at which tea was never served). Eccentricity and non-mainstream behaviour was accepted and tolerated. The decision to build the Colossus computer was taken informally without recourse to higher authority. Significant resources were drawn into the process of building the machine without, it seems, any government approval. The phenomenal process of post-war economic growth in Cambridge was entirely reliant on informal meetings of key individuals in a network so loose that it was difficult to define.

Of course, Milton Keynes *was* led by a powerful government funded bureaucracy. Yet the emergence of the proposal for Milton Keynes had as much to do with ideas emerging through local government, in both Bletchley and Buckinghamshire Councils as with central government diktat. And the conceptual basis for the Milton Keynes master plan arose from an American academic, Melvin Webber.

So far as can be seen the same process of improvisation and informal decision-making was at work in the earlier case studies for Birkenhead Park, Brown's landscapes and the London Squares. London's planning via the Great Estates showed a similar 'trial and error' ethos. Paul Raymond created the Soho Estate – one of the newest – after deciding to buy up properties within walking distance of his strip club. Decisions came, not from a government master plan but from private individuals.

Innovation in policy and strategy went hand in hand with improvisation. The Cambridge story, post-1970, is almost entirely a tale of brilliant innovation, by individuals working in a supportive context. Arup's answer to the Channel Tunnel Rail Link dilemma was an innovative and daring (though far from cheap) engineering solution. Birkenhead Park was an innovation in urban policy without parallel. No one had conceived of a National Cycle Network until Sustrans came into being. Though the true innovations came from others, Capability Brown's works nonetheless spread the gospel of a new landscape aesthetic around the world. As the first step towards the practical realization of Turing's conceptual machine for thinking, Colossus was the ultimate innovation. Improvisation and informality played central roles in its public sector conception and birth.

Objectors sometimes played as large a role as activists. Objectors forced a compete rethink on the route of the Channel Tunnel Rail Link in the twentieth century, just as objectors stopped the development of Lincoln's Inn Fields in the seventeenth century. Objectors derailed Wren's plan for rebuilding the city of London, just as they derailed the London motorways plan.

## Non Hierarchical Institutions

No matter how brilliant, individuals cannot achieve things alone. They need some form of institutional platform to supply resources and serve as a focus for activism. Every case study in this book has a clear institutional focus. It might be a large landowner or a great estate, some form of local government body, a private design company, a campaign group, a charitable trust, a state-backed development corporation, or a wealthy and well connected university. Sometimes a relatively weak institution will need support from others: Sustrans, for example, needed support from local government officers for every project.

Few plans made use of the techniques of rational planning, even those implemented after the introduction of technocratic models in the 1960s. A simple form of cost benefit analysis was used to justify motorway proposals, and cost benefit analysis still remains a critical hurdle for transport investment today. But it was not used in evaluating the options for the Milton Keynes master plan, and seems to have had little or no impact on the Channel Tunnel Rail Link decisions. A form of 'objective led' rational planning appeared to inform the Milton Keynes master plan, though the truth seems to be that its development form had already been settled in those academic seminars with Melvin Webber. Numerical forecasting had little impact on the other plans. Bizarrely, forecasts of demand for a Channel Tunnel appear to have been more accurate in the nineteenth than the twentieth century. Lindblom's notion of 'disjointed incrementalism' was often to the fore, as was Self's conception of planning as a process rooted in empirical studies, imaginative synthesis, medium- to long-term time scales and generalized physical and social effects. We can trace elements of all this, in case studies as diverse as the behaviour of London's great estates, the emergence of public parks and even in the evolution of English landscape design.

Perhaps none of this should come as a surprise. For the techniques of rational planning implicitly assume that decisions are taken on the basis of objective evidence by a single higher planning authority, whereas the evidence from the case studies suggests that this is not a characteristic of the British planning style. Instead decisions are often taken in what might best be described as *non-hierarchical* institutions. Often plans are prime examples of the 'trial and error' informality espoused by Taleb and others (Taleb, 2007; Self, 1975; Kay, 2011), rather than an exercise in top down centralism. For good or ill, there was very little of the latter on display.

But this is as far as we can go in inductive reasoning, extracting common threads from the case studies. While there is substantial common ground, these conclusions need to be reinforced by analysing British institutions and their evolution, and by a rather more theoretical approach. We turn to that task in the following chapters. If theory and history begin to mesh with empirical observation then a much stronger explanation can be forged.

## References

Copeland, B.J. (2006*b*) Machine against machine, in Copeland, B J. (ed.) (2006*a*) *Colossus: The Secrets of Bletchley Park's Codebreaking Computers*. Oxford: Oxford University Press.

Edbrooke, B. (1971) Motorway planning, in *Motorways in Britain: Today and Tomorrow*. London: Institution of Civil Engineers.

HM Treasury/Department for Transport (2006) *The Eddington Transport Study: The Case for Action: Sir Rod Eddington's Advice to Government*. London: The Stationery Office.

Kay, J. (2011) *Obliquity: Why Our Goals Are Best Achieved Indirectly*. London: Profile.

NLA (New London Architecture) (2013) *Great Estates: How London's Landowners Shape the City*. London: NLA.

Select Committee on Public Walks (SCPW) (1833) *Report of the Select Committee on Public Walks*, Cmnd 448. London: HMSO.

Self, P. (1975) *Econocrats and the Policy Process: The Politics and Philosophy of Cost Benefit Analysis*. London: Macmillan.

Taleb, N. (2007) *The Black Swan: The Impact of the Highly Improbable*. Harmondsworth: Penguin.

West, N. (1986) *GCHQ: The Secret Wireless War 1900–1986*. London: Weidenfeld and Nicolson.

# 12

## Who's in Charge?
## The British Government Machine

*The answer we received to the question 'who does UK grand strategy?' is no one... There is little idea of what the UK's national interest is, and therefore what our strategic purpose should be.*

Conclusion of the House of Commons Public Administration Select Committee, First Report of Session 2010–2011

Richard Crossman was an irreverent and intellectual Cabinet Minister. An Oxford don and former editor of the *New Statesman* magazine, throughout his career, beginning as Secretary of State for Housing and Local Government, Crossman kept detailed diaries to cast light on how the institutions of government worked, as experienced from the inside. In them he conveyed the full extent of the power of the civil service, and the power of senior civil servants, including Dame Evelyn Sharp, his own permanent secretary.

While Crossman admired the intellect and commitment of individual civil servants – not least Dame Evelyn – his views on how strategy was shaped and implemented were less than complimentary. In January 1965, barely three months into the job, Crossman was reflecting on the quality of his department: 'The personnel is second rate and unimpressive. They are extremely good at working the procedures of the civil service. What they lack is a constructive apprehension of the problems with which they deal and any kind of imagination' (Crossman, 1979, p. 57).

## Crossman's Critique

By June 1965 Crossman was questioning how strategy was shaped at the heart of government: 'Policy is formulated by the various departments and merely coordinated by [Prime Minister] Harold Wilson at the last moment. There is no inner cabinet with a coherent policy for this government' (Crossman, *op. cit.*, p. 103). He returns to the theme in July 1966: 'In the case of defence and foreign policy the Defence Committee, on which the Chiefs of Staff are at least present, is a central instrument which has worked for thirty years and gets some coherent decisions taken. When defence problems come up there may be wrong decisions, but at least decisions and contingency plans are made. Nothing of this sort exists to deal with the economy' (*ibid.*, p. 210).

Much the same view was shared by his Cabinet colleague Roy Jenkins in an aside recorded in December 1966: '"Heavens' I said to him 'I wish we could have been given a clearer vision of his [Wilson's] long term policy in Rhodesia'. He replied 'I'd give anything for evidence that we have a long term plan for any part of this government's policy thank you very much Dick'" (*ibid.*, p. 253).

Crossman's critique of civil service culture was repeated in his later lectures at Harvard University: 'Architects have always been recognized as people you can have in Ministries alongside gentlemen. But quantity surveyors are not and statisticians have only recently graduated to the genteel class. When I got to Housing I asked about my statistical staff, and I was told that we had an establishment of three but an actual staff of one, because they hadn't bothered to fill the other two places (Crossman, 1972, p. 70) … The idea that in order to be a good Permanent Secretary of Education you must know about education is long since defunct… Non expertise is the hallmark of a man who is going to get right to the top of the British civil service' (*ibid.*, p. 66).

In his American lectures, Crossman advanced uncharacteristically sanguine views about the virtues of British government. One of his American questioners was not convinced: 'A great many ideas in this country come from inside the bureaucracy… The most dramatic example that I can think of is the Marshall Plan, which came from inside the bureaucracy. I think it is hard to imagine something as innovative as that coming from inside the machinery you're describing…' (*ibid.*, p. 81)

Perhaps Harold Wilson's cabinet was singularly inept. Perhaps Crossman, by temperament both an academic and a critic, was simply hypercritical of the government machine. Perhaps both are true. Yet the problem is that he is far from a lone dissident, and views like his are certainly not unique. Nor, as the Chapter's introductory quote makes clear, has criticism of the central strategic capacity of British government weakened with time. There is a distinct resonance here with the evidence that has emerged from the case studies.

So it is time to put the operations of British government under the microscope and ask how Britain has been governed; how that style of government relates to the characteristics of wider British society; and how these characteristics originated. Then we should be able to move towards a clearer explanation of why things are as they are; whether this is a terrible weakness or a peculiar strength (or perhaps even a little of both); and not least how successful British plans reflect and resonate with the particular culture of British government.

## The Rise and Fall of Central Strategy

When Margaret Thatcher's Conservative government abolished the British government's Central Policy Review Staff (CPRS) in June 1983 there were no objectors. It was apparently accepted that the CPRS Think Tank, established in 1970 by Edward Heath's Conservative government, was superfluous and unnecessary. Yet the case for some form of Think Tank had been around for a very long time. The view that government should actually do some coherent long-term planning seems to have first originated in 1916, during the First World War at a time when, as the historian A.J.P. Taylor reminds us, the British state was still a small fragment of its later reality: 'Until August 1914 a sensible law abiding Englishman could pass through life and hardly notice the existence of the state, beyond the post office and the policeman. He could live where he liked and as he liked. He had no official number or identity card. He could travel abroad or leave his country forever without a passport or any sort of official permission' (Taylor, 1970, p. 25).

The pressure for strategic thinking began when Lloyd George replaced Asquith as Prime Minister in 1916. Both the office of Prime Minister and the Cabinet, in their modern form, date from that moment. Lloyd George established the War Cabinet Secretariat led by Colonel Maurice Hankey, so that the process of strategic decision-making at the centre could be structured and recorded. Yet the Secretariat, as its name implied, was merely an administrative device for processing decisions, rather than assessing their content or securing implementation. Alongside them Lloyd George established a personal policy team, in the form of the so-called 'garden suburb', located in temporary huts in the garden of Number 10 Downing Street and comprising just five men. Led by an Oxford don, Professor W.G.S. Adams, it was the first attempt to strengthen the Prime Minister's power and control. During the closing months of war Lord Haldane's Committee tried to distil the lessons, noting the previous lack of capability for the organized acquisition of facts and information and for the systematic application of thought (Ministry of Reconstruction, 1918).

No notice was taken of Haldane and the garden suburb was quietly demolished. Only the Secretariat survived, evolving into an Office staffed entirely by civil servants. In a sharp criticism of the inter-war Cabinet policy-making which echoes down the years, Leo Amery said: 'One thing that is hardly ever discussed is general policy … there is little Cabinet policy as such on any subject. No one has time to think it out, to discuss it, to coordinate its various

Figure 12.1. *Lloyd George.* On becoming Prime Minister in 1916, Lloyd George created pressure for strategic thinking, establishing a personal policy team known as the 'garden suburb'.

elements … there are only Departmental policies' (Amery, quoted in Blackstone and Plowden, 1988, p. 3).

When Winston Churchill became Prime Minister in 1940 he rapidly took personal control. 'Churchill is the government in every sense of the word' Harry Hopkins reported to President Roosevelt in early 1941, 'He controls the grand strategy and often the details' (Hopkins, quoted in Daalder, 1964, p. 85). Churchill brought with him a small personal staff, led by Professor Lindemann, to give advice on scientific and statistical matters, and half a dozen young academic economists were recruited. The team briefed Lindemann (who became Lord Cherwell in 1941), as well as Churchill, building contacts with nearly every Ministry.

Work was informal and intimate and Lord Cherwell spent much time in discussion with his staff, and with the Prime Minister; advice from Cherwell and his staff often resulted in a Prime Ministerial directive. Unsurprisingly Cherwell was disliked by civil servants (*ibid.*). Yet even these arrangements did not go far enough for Stafford Cripps, who was brought into the war Cabinet in 1942. Cripps wanted a War Cabinet of non-departmental ministers who could act as a central thinking and planning machine and complained that 'Problems of strategy are conceived by the war cabinet hurriedly, without sufficient information and often in isolation' (*ibid.*, p. 90).

Churchill was an authoritarian and absolutist ruler, whose methods were acceptable in time of war, but not of peace. When the Conservatives were defeated in July 1945 Cherwell and his team were swiftly done away with. In

1946–1947 a new centralized economic policy team was created with Sir Edwin Plowden as its Chief Planning Officer. But when Cripps became Chancellor of the Exchequer he took Plowden with him to the Treasury, and non-departmental strategic advice was once again lost.

The idea did not emerge again until the mid-1960s, when Edward Heath, as new leader of the Conservative Party, commissioned advice on the structure of government. Young Conservatives like David Howell and Mark Schreiber were arguing for a centralized capability, including a Crown Consultancy Unit. In parallel Heath asked a group of retired civil servants chaired by Baroness Evelyn Sharp to give personal advice. Sharp said that 'In the particular sphere I had worked in, the machinery did not work well … sometimes disputes were taken to Cabinet … but there seemed no way of settling the departmental pattern in the interests of good government'. She recalled a lunch with Prime Minister Harold Macmillan: 'One thing he said was: "It's a strange thing that I have now got the biggest job I have ever had and less help in doing it than I have ever known". And that clicked with my growing notion that there was a gap in the machinery of government at the centre' (Sharp, quoted in Blackstone and Plowden, *op. cit.*, p. 7).

In November 1968 Sharp's group recommended the creation of an Office of the Prime Minister and Cabinet. Its central role would be 'the crucial task of enabling the government to identify its main objectives, to relate individual decisions to their wider context, and in doing so to coordinate its own activities' (*ibid.*, p. 8). This was just too much to swallow. What eventually emerged was a proposal for the creation of a small staff reporting to the Prime Minster, which became known as the Central Policy Review Staff. Its abolition only 13 years later marked the end of a short-lived (and not altogether successful) experiment in peacetime strategic planning. Whitehall reverted to normal.

## Contemporary Critique

But the problem has not gone way. In April 2011 a report from the independent Institute for Government complained that no one in departments or in the centre of government had responsibility for ensuring that policy-making was of high quality, or met Minister's needs. The Cabinet Office (ostensibly a central coordinating function) did not cover policy making: 'Number 10 tries to anticipate the political problems policies may generate, but mainly exists to further the Prime Minister's agenda and put out fires' (Hallsworth and Rutter, 2011, p. 11). As a result, the authors argued, there was little counterweight to day to day pressures; pressure to maintain a steady flow of initiatives; pressure to keep decisions closed until they can be announced; and pressure to place short-term departmental advantage over long-term collective benefit. Those who succeeded best in this system were able to make a splash or manage a crisis, rather than oversee long-term results. Many of the civil servants interviewed reported that they felt unclear about the overall objectives of their Ministers and the government in general (*ibid.*). The Institute's researchers concluded that there was a case for 'a whole of government strategy' and recommended a greater role for the centre through the creation of a Head of Policy Effectiveness. All this echoed Peter Hennessy's earlier conclusions that there had been a strong tendency amongst Ministers and civil servants to 'eschew the rational, the written, the planned, or the strategic', in favour of 'understated, pragmatic, occasionally inspired ad hocery and last minute improvisation' (Hennessy, 1997, p. 13). Hennessey's conclusions are sharper than his analysis, but he was right to attack the pretence that this trait was not only deliberate, but desirable. With Whitehall facing up to an unstable future alongside deep cuts in departmental expenditure a more realistic, professional and informed notion of choice through politics seemed crucial.

The Institute's 2011 report followed a similarly unsettling analysis issued just a year earlier (Parker *et al.*, 2010). It confirmed the power of individual departmental baronies, and the weakness, if not irrelevance, of centralized direction and planning. Whitehall, the authors concluded, was highly capable of containing public spending. The UK's strong control over tax and spending made it almost uniquely placed to hit any spending target. But the same characteristics were also at the root of Whitehall's weakness. Departments and 'silo based' providers were likely to protect their own existence and squeeze out collaboration and innovation elsewhere.

Quotes from anonymous senior civil servants amplified the message: 'If I sat out in a department' said a Director General, 'I'd say that the Cabinet Office is sometimes irrelevant – I'm vaguely aware that they do some things but it doesn't matter to me' (*ibid.*, p. 22). A Permanent Secretary was equally doubtful: 'They've never really come out with a view of what the Cabinet Office is for' (*ibid.*). Others concurred: 'Departments are very powerful' and 'I actually think that pushing some of the other government departments to be joined up is important' (*ibid.*, p. 25). There was a gap at the centre of Whitehall, the authors concluded: a conspicuous lack of a single coherent strategy for government as a whole.

Whitehall's non-strategic ethos sits alongside another repeated critique – the generalist and non-expert ethos of senior civil servants. In January 2013, *The Times* quoted Lord Adonis, the former Labour Cabinet Minister: 'We have a non-expert civil service, characterized by very poor training. The civil service itself has much lower prestige in England than in continental countries, because the State itself is held in much lower esteem' (Sylvester and Thomson, 2013, p. 8). The same article quoted critics ranging from former Prime Minister Tony Blair, to Steve Hilton, David Cameron's former director of strategy, who characterized the government machine as slow moving, closed off, and self-serving.

## Civil Service Reform

These are precisely the criticisms voiced in the *Civil Service Reform Plan*, published in June 2012 – a document that, as if to underline its urgency and authority, enjoyed three forewords: one from the Prime Minister; another from the Minister for the Cabinet Office; and a third from the Head of the Civil Service (HM Government, 2012). While acknowledging the traditional and valuable virtues of impartiality, objectivity and honesty, and the agility of civil servants in responding to the crises – an improvisational skill we have noted before – the plan was filled with (suitably discreet) criticism.

Civil service culture, said the report, was slow and resistant to change; it was cautious, too focused on process not outcomes, bureaucratic and hierarchical. It needed to be pacier and more flexible, adapting swiftly to the needs of the day. There were few incentives for change in the *status quo* and too few capable project managers. Whitehall had a monopoly on policy development, where the civil service acted as a blocker or filter on policy advice from others. The quality of policy advice was inconsistent, reflecting too narrow a range of views. Policy design was considered separately from implementation and there was a lack of management information across government. Only one-third of recent major projects have been delivered to time and budget. There were too few people with commissioning and contracting skills and such capabilities as did exist were too 'siloed'. Turnover in critical posts was high and this led to a lack of collective corporate memory. Barriers between the civil service and the private sector should be broken down to encourage interchange of staff and learning. Within the civil service the authority and influence of the professions should be strengthened. The report said that: 'Operational management and delivery has been undervalued compared with policy development, an issue first identified in the Fulton Report in 1968' (*ibid.*, p. 22).

Early in 2013, dissatisfaction with the civil service spilled over into newspaper reports. *The Times* ran several pages alleging a bitter power struggle in Whitehall between ministers and mandarins. Ministers were said to be exasperated with their staff. Former Prime Minister Tony Blair described the government machine as hopelessly bureaucratic. Amongst the specific allegations, it was said that civil servants had tried to subvert a transparency drive; that only 15 per cent of documents sent between departments related to the coalition agreement (a sort of manifesto in government for the Coalition); and that ministers did not trust figures supplied to them by civil servants. More seriously the coverage expressed concern about project management skills, with few projects being delivered on time and to budget. An anonymous minister claimed that the mandarins were a roadblock to reform, as levers were pulled but nothing happened. Blair complained that: 'The traditional skill set of the civil service is not what is required if you want to drive change … there is an inherent dysfunctionality in the gap between what we really want those systems to do

Figure 12.2. *Tony Blair.* Like others before him, Blair came to believe that 'the traditional skill set of the civil service is not what is required if you want to drive change'.

today – implementation, delivery, performance – and what they are traditionally geared up to do, which is analysis and policy advice' (Sylvester and Thomson, *op. cit.*, p. 8). Shortly afterwards came a civil service response. Speaking at the Institute for Government, Sir David Normington said that Ministers had opened up 'a much wider questioning of whether the present model of a civil service, politically impartial, recruited on merit, through fair and open competition, is still valid' (Neville, 2013, p. 2). It was not clear, however, that they had done any such thing.

In 2014 the critics re-engaged. The Confederation of British Industry returned to the theme that civil servants were ill fitted to manage public sector contracts (Plimmer, 2014, p. 2). The Treasury was reported to be considering applications for a new post of chief financial officer charged with securing better value for money from public expenditure. The new post was part of Whitehall's response to a report by the management consultants McKinsey who argued that Britain had lessons to learn about breaking down departmental silos and securing better value for money. Speaking at the Institute for Government, the official who had conducted a recent spending review said that the data and evidence to back up decisions could be 'patchy' (Neville, 2014, p. 2).

The problems itemized in the *Civil Service Reform Plan* (and in part rehearsed by this press coverage) made for a startling list. Yet little or none was new. In

1964 a review of the civil service by the Fabians led its authors to ask: 'Is the civil service the best service we could have to meet the needs of today? Our answer is emphatically no' (Fabian Group, 1964, p. 15). The Fabians claimed that civil servant policy-makers lived in isolation from industry, local government and the rest of society, were omniscient all-rounder's rather than experts, living in an administrative hierarchy as closed as a monastic order, and, without provision for appointments from outside, out of touch with the times. As a consequence they cited the failure of the Labour post-war government to draw up any long-term plan (apart from the 4-year programme required by the American Marshall Plan as a means of obtaining aid) whilst in France Monnet had established his Commissariat du Plan and built the foundations for French indicative planning. Civil servants, the Fabians concluded, were amateurish, negative, closed, and secretive in their approach to policy.

In a similar vein Thomas Balogh, one of Labour Prime Minister Harold Wilson's advisors, had described the Whitehall mandarins as 'the Apotheosis of the Dilettante'. Balogh launched a blistering attack on the way recruitment favoured the smooth extrovert conformist with good connections and no knowledge of modern problems, flitting ineffectually from one subject to another (Balogh, 1968). 'No one would be mad enough to advocate the periodic interchange of dentists and surgeons, solicitors and barristers, engineers and musicians. Yet surely the problems that most of these professions encounter are simple in comparison with the complexities of the social and economic system in the modern state' (*ibid.*, p. 16).

According to Balogh the problems were rooted in Victorian Northcote-Trevelyan reforms. The Victorians, he argued, wanted an absence of corruption, and reticence from bureaucratic pretension. Positive knowledge and imagination, and an assertion of public against private interest were not wanted. These qualities were best secured through a purposefully useless and somewhat dilettante learning, which would keep dangerous thoughts away. The cultivation of tolerant scepticism was obtained by insisting on a formal education which only developed the powers of debate and argument, rather than knowledge of the world and its problems. Vocational and technical knowledge was strongly discouraged; classics and the abstractions of pure mathematics were the ideal.

After 1914, Balogh argued, the system of civil service organization planned by the Victorian reformers was realized. A vast unitary machine was created, where the influence of the Treasury became paramount. Officials were no longer dependent on the success of their departments, and constructive thinking became a secondary quality. Instead a generalist tradition prevailed, where civil service recruits with professional or technical qualifications were not favoured. In the absence of purposeful government, led by committed experts in their field, Balogh concluded, successive British governments had proved unable to devise policies to strengthen the country's diplomatic, political and economic base. Others were to reach very similar, though perhaps less biting, conclusions.

## Two Failures:
## The Fulton Report and the Department of Economic Affairs

As early as 1942 future Prime Minister Harold Wilson and his friend John Fulton, both then employed in the Mines Department of the Board of Trade, had begun to form their views on the future of the civil service, whilst fire watching when their rotas overlapped. Both had a similar dislike of the entrenched administrative class. Wilson thought it failed to give weight to professionals like him, Fulton believed it lacked drive, originality, inventiveness and the will to innovate (Kellner and Crowther Hunt, 1980).

In 1966 Wilson's government made a determined attempt to secure change, setting up a Committee of Inquiry chaired by Lord John Fulton to examine the structure, recruitment, management and training of the home civil service and to make recommendations. Fulton's report concluded that the civil service was in need of fundamental change and identified six key inadequacies. The most important of these was that the Service was based on a belief in the supreme virtue of the generalist all-rounder (or amateur) at the highest levels in the administrative class; a concept which the Committee thought was obsolete at all levels and in all parts of the Service. Echoing Balogh, the report emphasized the virtues of professionalism. But public debate focused unhelpfully on the supposed contrast between amateurs and professionals, when it should have homed in on the more subtle and important distinction between professional generalists and professional specialists. The familiar argument from senior civil servants was that putting a specialist like an engineer into a senior role would be damaging; he or she would simply be unable to take a broader view (*ibid.*).

Fulton's research bore out Balogh's conclusions. In France, West Germany, Sweden and the United States, higher civil servants were recruited on the basis of their qualifications and the tasks that they would undertake in running the state. Fulton found that that over 70 per cent of graduates in the administrative class had degrees in the arts and humanities. Yet in the United States only small proportions were arts graduates, the rest coming from the social sciences, natural and applied sciences. In France the counterparts of the administrative class were graduates of the Ecole Nationale, where they had two and a half years of general education in social sciences including economics, law, public administration and statistics. The British recruitment process seemed to discriminate against those with a vocational educational background. And in conformity with the ethos of generalists, administrators were not kept in any job for a long period; they were rapidly rotated from one job to another, usually staying for little over two years. Thus the generalist learned a great deal about government as a whole, yet had little deep understanding about any particular job. Fulton's proposals were defeated. Aiming at the cult of the generalist, his committee had attacked the ethos and power base of the high command itself. The proposals were watered down and lost (*ibid.*).

Wilson made one other attempt at radical change in the machinery of government. The Department of Economic Affairs (DEA) was to be a keystone in his plans for economic revival – a purposeful and modernizing Ministry which would challenge the dead hand of the Treasury. It survived for less than 5 years. On day one there were no chairs, desks or telephones. Except for the First Secretary of State, the mercurial George Brown, everyone 'sat on the floor like Buddhas ... the chaos was terrible with George erupting the whole time' (Hennessy, 1990, p. 183). It was not an auspicious start.

Despite Brown's extraordinary personal style, rushing from meetings, upsetting Ministerial colleagues and outraging officials, the DEA was a serious attempt to meet the criticism that the Treasury had sustained a 'stop go' economy and held production in contempt. Pride of place was given to Brown's National Plan of 1965, an exercise in indicative planning designed to do for the British economy what Monnet's Commissariat du Plan had done for the French. The National Plan survived for four months, destroyed by the balance of payments crisis of July 1966. The DEA itself was killed off by Roy Jenkins when he became Chancellor in 1969. It proved no match for the powers, information, or expertise of the Treasury. The former Treasury Permanent Secretary Sir Douglas Wass clearly regarded the DEA as weak and emasculated from day one: 'All the important operational tools of economic management were in the hands of the Treasury ... [the DEA] did not have departmental responsibility for anything apart from prices and incomes that really affected day to day business. It really was left beached studying the longer term problems of the British economy' (Wass, quoted in *ibid.*, p. 187).

It might be argued that all this is a rather one sided analysis, which overlooks the unquestionable virtues of the civil service machine – the underlying values of integrity, transparency, objectivity and responsibility, identified in the Civil Service Reform Plan in precisely the same terms used by a group of retired and former senior civil servants (Better Government Initiative, 2010). None of these need be disputed. Yet they do nothing to contradict the essential characteristics of the machine described by its critics and set firmly within its history – a 'night-watchman' rather than a chief executive, a skilled improviser and crisis manager, a machine that pursues smooth continuity, rather than purposeful strategic change, and (save in time of war) an organization without strong leadership and control from the centre. How can these deep-seated characteristics best be explained?

## Regulatory States and Developmental States

In his seminal study of the post-war Japanese economic miracle, the American writer Chalmers Johnson offers an illuminating distinction between two basic forms of government. Reflecting Weber's distinction between a market economy and a planned economy, Dahrendorf's distinction between 'market rationality' and 'plan rationality' (Dahrendorf, 1968), and Kelly's distinction between a 'rule governed state' and a 'purpose governed state' (Kelly, 1979), Johnson introduces the concepts of *developmental state* and *regulatory state* (Johnson, 1982).

Regulatory states are those which were first to industrialize. Government had little to do with their new forms of economic activity, but towards the end of the nineteenth century took on regulatory functions in the interest of maintaining competition, consumer protection and so forth. In states which were late to industrialize, the state itself led the drive to industrialization, taking on developmental functions. The United States is a good example of a state where the regulatory function is prominent. It has, for example, many regulations concerning the anti-trust implications of the size of firms, but does not concern itself with which industries should exist and which should not. Johnson argues that, 'the developmental state by contrast has as a dominant feature the setting of such substantive social and economic goals' (*ibid.*, p. 19). In other words the developmental state has a strategic or goal driven approach to its economy, and by implication much else.

In regulatory or market rational states, such as the United States, public service does not normally attract the most capable individuals and national decision-making is dominated by elected representatives and lawyers rather than bureaucrats. Decisions in regulatory states are judged first and foremost by their economic efficiency. By contrast, in developmental states goal orientated activities are judged by their effectiveness in achieving goals. A developmental state should not, however, be confused with a Communist style command economy, where state ownership and planning are not simply a means to an end but are fundamental values in themselves. In these states, plans are more ideology than instrument.

Johnson argued that Japan was just such a developmental or 'plan rational' state. The post-war Japanese economic miracle was the result of developmental planning, carried forward especially by MITI (the Ministry of International Trade and Industry). Industrial and economic policy in Japan was unashamedly interventionist. In the words of Sahashi Shigeru, a former Minister at MITI: 'It is an utterly self-centred [businessman's] point of view to think that the government should be concerned with providing only a favourable environment for industries without telling them what to do' (*ibid.*, p. 11).

Home demand led Japan's growth for the two decades after 1955. The economy was driven by private investment, nurtured by confident expectations for the long term, created by government. Finance was highly dependent on city bank loans, which were in turn guaranteed by the Bank of Japan and the Ministry of Finance. So government had direct involvement in strategic industries and economic bureaucrats were accorded high position and status. Official agencies attracted the most talented graduates from the best universities and the positions of the high-level officials were the most prestigious in society, led by the dominance of MITI in creating and executing industrial policy. On retirement, between the ages of 50 and 55, these bureaucrats moved from government into banking, politics and the industrial sector. Thus, the powerful and prestigious bureaucracy was a central component of Japan's developmental state.

A developmental state has to rest on consensus. Without consensus there could not be agreement on overarching social and economic goals, or the plans which follow from them. Where consensus exists, said Johnson, the developmental state will outperform the regulatory state. But when consensus does not exist the developmental state will be adrift and unable to address its problems. Japan experienced just such drift after the oil price shock in 1973. Crucially, Johnson concluded that: 'The great strength of the plan rational system lies in its effectiveness in dealing with routine problems, whereas the great strength of the market rational system lies in its effectiveness in dealing with critical problems' (*ibid.*, p. 22).

First into the industrial revolution, Britain is perhaps the prime example of a country with the culture and institutions of a regulatory state. Like the United States, it is in large part an individualistic society, where government is seen more as umpire than actor. We can see its characteristics clearly through the lens of Johnson's illuminating theory. Bureaucrats in Britain do not have particularly high prestige or status. There is little coherent strategic planning, and when attempts are made to introduce such institutions, they have little grip on events and a relatively short life. Big decisions often rest with lawyers and the legal system, rather than planners and the planning system. There are few long-term plans and, save in times of war, there is relatively little central direction (or indeed control) within the government system. Industrial and economic planning is weak and ineffectual. Talented individuals with high-level professional skills have tended not to move into the civil service. Indeed there seems to be reluctance to accommodate such individuals in government. A generalist ethos prevails. Most attempts to create and wield a more strategic and purposeful set of central state institutions have failed or been disbanded, be they Lord Fulton's civil service reforms, Edward Heath's Central Policy Review Staff, Harold Wilson's unsuccessful Department of Economic Affairs, his successful Ministry of Technology (Coopey, 1993), or more recently John Prescott's Regional Development Agencies.

All this is the corollary to the inspired individuals and autonomous institutions that lie behind so many successful British plans. It all seems rooted very deeply in British culture. The question is why; and in searching for answers, it is time to turn to history, and from British weakness to British strength.

## References

Balogh, T. (1968) The apotheosis of the dilettante, in Thomas, H. (ed.) *Crisis in the Civil Service*. London: Anthony Blond (Balogh's paper was first published in 1959).

Better Government Initiative (2010) *Good Government: Reforming Parliament and the Executive*. Available at: http://www.bettergovernmentinitiative.co.uk/sitedata/Misc/Good-government-17-October.pdf.

Blackstone, T. and Plowden, W. (1988) *Inside the Think Tank: Advising the Cabinet 1971–1983*. London: William Heinemann.

Coopey, R. (1993) Industrial policy in the white heat of the scientific revolution, in Coopey, R., Fielding, S. and Tiratsoo, N. (eds.) *The Wilson Governments 1964–1970*. London: Pinter.

Crossman, R. (1972) *Inside View: The Godkin Lectures at Harvard University, 1970*. London: Jonathan Cape.

Crossman, R. (1979) *The Crossman Diaries: Selections from the Diaries of a Cabinet Minister 1964–1970*. London: Hamish Hamilton and Jonathan Cape.

Daalder, H. (1964) *Cabinet Reform in Britain 1914–1963*. Stanford, CA: Stanford University Press.

Dahrendorf, R. (1968) Market and plan: two types of rationality, in *Essays in the Theory of Society*. Stanford, CA: Stanford University Press.

Fabian Group (1964) *The Administrators: The Reform of the Civil Service*. London: Fabian Society.

Hallsworth, M. and Rutter, J. (2011) *Making Policy Better: Improving Whitehall's Core Business*. London: Institute for Government.

Hennessy, P (1990) *Whitehall*. London: Fontana.

Hennessy, P. (1997) *Muddling Through: Power, Politics and the Quality of Government in Post War Britain*. London: Indigo.

HM Government (2012) *The Civil Service Reform Plan*. Available at http://www.civilservice.gov.uk/wp-content/uploads/2012/06/Civil-Service-Reform-Plan-acc-final.pdf.

Johnson, C. (1982) *MITI and the Japanese Miracle: The Growth of Industrial Policy, 1925–1975*. Stanford, CA: Stanford University Press.

Kellner, P. and Crowther Hunt, N. (1980) *The Civil Servants: An Inquiry into Britain's Ruling Class*. London: Macdonald.

Kelly, G. (1979) Who needs a theory of citizenship? *Daedalus*, **108**(4), pp. 21–36.

Ministry of Reconstruction (1918) *Report of the Machinery of Government Committee*. Cmnd. 9230. London: HMSO.

Neville, S. (2013) Tensions escalate in civil service dispute. *Financial Times*, 29 January.

Neville, S. (2014) Hunt for finance chief to rule mandarins nears end. *Financial Times*, 4 March.

Parker, S., Paun, A., McClory, J. and Blatchford, K. (2010) *Shaping Up: A Whitehall for the Future*. London: Institute for Government.

Plimmer, G. (2014) Civil servants' contract skills are 'lacking'. *Financial Times*, 18 February.

Sylvester, R. and Thomson, S. (2013) Whitehall at war. *The Times*, 14 January.

Taylor, A.J.P. (1970) *English History 1914–1945*. London: Pelican.

# 13

# How Britain Works
## Pluralism, Autonomy and Individualism

*If Aristotle were to come again to this world he could not find words to explain the manner of this government… It has a monarchical appearance, and there is a king, but it is very far from being a monarchy.*

The French Ambassador in Charles II's London

For Ralf Dahrendorf, German sociologist and director of the London School of Economics, alongside continuity and excellence, liberty was the central strength which had underpinned Britain's market society. 'By market is meant', he said, 'the free interplay of autonomous and decentralized units for the welfare of the whole' (Dahrendorf, 1982, p. 26).

In most European countries, mediaeval battles between kings and barons were invariably won by the king. Absolute power – the power of kings or dictators – thus prevailed. But this was not so in Britain, where the rights of the King remained circumscribed, even before Parliament could rise to check them. Barons and king had established the limits of their respective rights. Sometimes the barons remained autonomous, sometimes they granted the king rights. The history is more complicated, as Dahrendorf admits (we shall come to it), but it illustrates what he saw as a critical feature of British society: the autonomy of its institutions.

## The Autonomy of Institutions

Dahrendorf brings the insight of a sympathetic outsider. The BBC for example, he said (writing in 1982), is publicly financed, like radio and television in

Figure 13.1. *Ralf Dahrendorf* (to left). Sociologist, anglophile and former LSE Director, Dahrendorf saw the autonomy of its institutions as a defining characteristic of British society.

continental countries, and could be expected to be run by the state as in France, or by councils on which the state is represented, as in Germany. Yet it is an autonomous institution run by the Director General accountable to Governors of the Corporation, appointed by the Queen in Council for a fixed term. They do not represent interest groups and their independence is expected and assumed. The British professions have public functions, the law originating in Parliament. It could be argued that the legal profession (for example) should be controlled by government with a public system of professional ethics, as is the case on the Continent. But in Britain the professions have retained an independent status. They organize education, admission to the profession and the maintenance of professional standards. They are, he says, 'the institutional barons of a society that has never become a state society' (*ibid.*, p. 27).

Dahrendorf gives other examples. The City is largely self-governing, with the Bank of England playing the role of referee. The Bank itself was privately controlled until 1946. Universities are almost entirely publicly financed yet the allocation of government funds is organized by a University Grants Committee on which there are more academics than administrators. The Civil Service is independent and non-political in a way that has become unknown in other European countries. The same Secretary to the Cabinet may serve two or three different Prime Ministers and will do so fairly and competently, without bringing his own views to bear on decisions. Traditionally people in Britain do not wait for the state to come to their help. There is a remarkable tradition of self-help. Voluntary organizations have always blossomed and it is more usual to rely on voluntary action than to ask government to step in. The state is far from omnipresent in British society. Where in Britain a man's or woman's word is sufficient, someone from the Continent always needs an official stamp. Dahrendorf concludes that 'the autonomy of institutions is the most effective institutional guarantee of liberty' (*ibid*., p. 28).

Some things have changed since Dahrendorf wrote his account. The BBC is governed by a Trust. The Universities are now financed by the Higher Education Funding Council. Local government is more tightly controlled and subject to centralized direction – a centralizing process which, Simon Jenkins argues, started in Margaret Thatcher's governments and continued through those of John Major and Tony Blair (Jenkins, 2006). The number of quasi autonomous governmental agencies (quangoes) has grown; the very use of the term is revealing.

But much remains as it was. The institutional framework Dahrendorf described certainly existed in one form or another when many of the plans described in this book took shape. Indeed for a short while David Cameron's Coalition government flirted with the virtues of a 'big society' in which voluntary organizations and personal initiative would play a wider role. Thus Dahrendorf's arguments begin to provide an explanatory momentum for the regulatory concept outlined by Johnson (1982). To understand how such widespread institutional autonomy and pluralism came into being, and persisted, we need to turn to history.

## The Rise of Pluralism

MIT economist Daron Acemoglu, and Harvard political scientist James Robinson, set out to explain the origins and global distribution of power, prosperity and poverty (Acemoglu and Robinson, 2013). Their argument is beguilingly simple. Countries differ in their economic success as a result of their institutional structures, the rules governing economic behaviour, and the incentives that motivate individuals. In successful economies institutions are fundamentally inclusive; that is to say they allow widespread participation in the economy, they make good use of individual skills and talents, and they let individuals make free choices. Inclusive institutions therefore secure private property, unbiased law and public services, which provide a level playing field to enable exchange and contract. The theory is essentially liberal and does not consider the potential for state-led development. But it is a useful framework for thinking about economic and political institutions, and, in our discussion, how these might influence the development of plans and the practice of planning.

Acemoglu and Robinson argue that the reason the Industrial Revolution started and made its rapid progress in Britain – especially, though not at all exclusively, in England – was the result of uniquely inclusive economic institutions, built on the inclusive political institutions introduced during the Glorious Revolution in 1688. These included stronger and rationalized rights in property, better financial markets, and the weakening of state monopolies in foreign trade. The political system was made more open and responsive to economic imperatives. In turn inclusive economic institutions gave early entrepreneurs the opportunity and incentive to develop their ideas and pursue technical innovation.

According to this reading of history, the political developments leading to the Glorious Revolution were shaped by several processes. The most important of these was political conflict between absolutism and its opponents. The latter did not want to rebuild a different form of absolutist government, but a new regime based on constitutional rule and pluralism – in other words the dispersal of power. The story began, as Dahrendorf had suggested, with Magna Carta, which set out some basic principles for constitutional rule, whilst curtailing the powers of the King.

After the Black Death, Western Europe began to drift away from Eastern Europe; constitutional documents like Magna Carta seemed to have greater traction in the West. Equally, political power began to drift away from elites to citizens, as exemplified in England by the Peasants Revolt in 1381. Magna Carta can be seen as a first hesitant step towards pluralism. Forced to sign the charter at Runnymede in 1251, the king accepted that he should consult the barons before raising taxes. The barons formed a council to ensure that the king implemented the charter, and in its absence the barons had the right to make amends by seizing land and property. King John had the charter annulled by the Pope at the earliest opportunity. Yet the influence remained.

England's first elected Parliament was created in 1265, consisting largely of nobles and aristocrats, but later a broader class was represented, including minor gentry and a new class of commercial farmers. After 1485 the Tudors increased political centralization by effectively removing military powers from the aristocracy and introducing the beginnings of a bureaucratic state, a revolution in government engineered by Thomas Cromwell, Henry VIII's first minister. Henry broke with Rome and dissolved the monasteries, expropriating all the lands of the mediaeval church and removing the power of the Catholic Church. The 400 or so smaller monasteries were dissolved by statute; the rest were seized by various methods, their confiscation ratified by statute in 1539. This gigantic transfer of land had no parallel in English history. It was the gentry who kept what they received and augmented it with acquisitions from other groups (Bindoff, 1950). They were represented in the House of Commons, their power and social significance based on sheep farming and agricultural production for the market. The King could not rule without the support of this newly expanded landed class (Hill, 1969) and, arguably, these acts of political centralization increased the demand for broader based political representation. In the fifteenth and sixteenth centuries, the barons and local elites made efforts to use Parliament as a counterweight to the powers of the King. Acemoglu and Robinson argue that: 'The Tudor project not only initiated political centralization, one pillar of inclusive institutions, but also indirectly contributed to pluralism' (Acemoglu and Robinson, *op. cit.*, p. 187).

Both James I and his son Charles I were determined to strengthen their position and to re-establish absolutist institutions. Conflict culminated in the late 1620s, with the Crown seeking to grant more monopolies as a source of revenue. Coming to the throne in 1625, Charles ignored the tradition established in Magna Carta that Parliament should give its approval to new taxes. He introduced 'forced' loans and refused to pay his debts, causing resentment, especially amongst the merchant classes. In 1642 the Civil War broke out. The outcome was trial and execution for Charles and his replacement by the dictatorship of Oliver Cromwell.

Following Cromwell's death the monarchy was restored in 1660, but James II's attempts to reassert the power of kings led to a further crisis. Parliament invited the Dutch Stadtholder William of Orange, and Mary, James's protestant daughter, to replace James, William ruling not as an absolute but a constitutional monarch. The Declaration of Rights, approved by Parliament in 1689, removed the monarchy's power to dispense with laws and to raise taxes without Parliamentary approval. Thus the Glorious Revolution, as it is known, handed power to Parliament and created a set of pluralistic institutions.

Power was indeed dispersed, but Parliament remained an elite institution; as late as 1917 only 28 per cent of the adult population could vote in elections (Marquand, 2008). Yet Parliament could be petitioned. Property rights were strengthened. Royal monopolies like the Royal African Company were removed. The Bank of England was created in 1694. The state began to expand, not least in the appointment of more excise tax collectors. The late seventeenth and early eighteenth centuries saw a transformational change in the scale and nature of British government and the rise of what can be described as a 'fiscal-military' state (Brewer, 1988). Taxes rose, the public debt rose, and a sizeable public administration was devoted to the state's military and fiscal needs. Between 1688 and 1714, 75 per cent of England's public expenditure went on waging war. The rise of the fiscal military state helped to create a financial community – what is now the City – whose influence on politics was profound, and remains so. The military state grew in scale and strength, yet the domestic state remained liberal in policy and outlook, and weak in its dealings with its own subjects. Brewer concludes: 'The overweening power of the Treasury, a highly centralized financial system, a standing Parliament, heavy taxation, an administrative class of gifted amateurs lacking training in the science of government but with a strong sense of duty, government deficits … all these features of modern British politics began under the later Stuarts and Hanoverians' (Brewer, *op. cit.*, p. 250).

## An Exceptionally Free Society

The inexorable drift toward pluralism took place alongside a massive expansion of trans-Atlantic trade. The power of Parliament meant that the Tudor and Stuart monarchs could not easily monopolize the new Atlantic trade and a new class of businessmen and merchants arose, with a vested interest in pluralism and hostility to absolutist rule. By 1686 there were 702 merchants in London exporting to the Caribbean, and a further 1,283 importing. Other ports like Bristol and Liverpool developed an expanding and wealthy merchant class. Similar processes were at work in France and Spain, but here the hold of kings on trade was much stronger. The merchant classes were pivotal to British politics. When the English Civil War broke out in 1642, the merchants largely sided with the Parliamentary cause. In the 1670s they were heavily involved in the formation of the Whig Party, opposing Stuart absolutism. In 1688 they were central to the deposing of James II.

Perhaps the most important feature of the political opposition to absolutism was its breadth. Apart from the merchant class, other economic groups were present: these included the gentry, commercial farmers (emerging in the Tudor Period) and the early manufacturing classes. So the coalition of opposition to the Stuarts was relatively diverse in its origins and interests. The replacement of one king by another was less attractive and less likely. By the same token, an English Parliament consisting of a broad coalition made it more willing to listen to petitions and less likely to support narrow or monopolistic interest groups. Thus the breadth of the coalition strengthened the hand of Parliament after 1688, whilst weakening the power of individual interests. It underlay the development of inclusive rather than exclusive institutions.

The English historian Christopher Hill shares many of these conclusions. From 1688 onwards England was, for the propertied class, an exceptionally free society. It would have been impossible for a king to rule without a Parliament and in contravention of the law. After 1701 judges were no longer dependent on government and juries were not accountable for their own verdicts. The supremacy of the common law had emerged. The press was the freest in Europe. With the Navigation Act of 1651 securing a national trading interest over the separate interests and privileges of the old monopoly companies, merchants could work out their own destiny, free of formal organization, yet within a protective framework of national legislation: 'The seventeenth century economic crisis which affected the whole of western Europe led to a strengthening of absolutism in most continental countries ... in England alone it created a system in which commercial and industrial capital had freedom to develop (Hill, *op. cit.*, p. 14). Even the left wing political scientist Andrew Gamble accepts that the seventeenth century English revolution had cut short royal absolutism, subordinating state power to the interests of a parliament, and creating a society that, for all its inequalities, ranks and titles: 'was more flexible and open to change and its property owning classes more unified than in any other urban society in Europe' (Gamble, 1981, p. 68).

The theory is persuasive as an explanation for the rise of industry and empire. It is reticent on less savoury explanations for the rise of British power and the wealth of its merchant classes, not least imperialism, conquest and war. The slave trade, for example, was central to the rise of several British ports, and the associated growth of merchant wealth. Between 1699 and 1807, Liverpool traders transported 1,364,930 African slaves in 5,249 voyages, London 744,721, and Bristol 481,487 (Liverpool City Council, 2003). Perhaps reference to this cruel trade dents the benign narrative.

Yet the view of British history as an unfurling of pluralism and the growth of a wide coalition of interest groups looks sound. With nearly 1,000 years of continuous political development, relatively secure in an island location and without the disruption of invasion or revolution, a gradual transfer and dispersion of power and wealth had occurred: from king to barons, in Magna Carta; from Catholic Church and monasteries to king and landowners, after the break with Rome; from king to Parliament after the Glorious Revolution; from landowners to merchants and financiers; and later to manufacturers. The conditions were met for the rise of industrial innovation, for the development of a distinctively British set of autonomous institutions, and for a dispersed distribution of power and influence.

## The Logic of Collective Action

Acemoglu and Robinson (2013) were not the first to recognize how continuous and stable government under the rule of law might lead to the steady diffusion of power. Mancur Olson's interest was not so much in explaining growth but in charting the causes of national economic decline: in his words: '... the mysterious decline or collapse of great empires and civilizations and the remarkable rise to wealth, power or other cultural achievement of previously peripheral or obscure peoples' (Olson, 1982, p. 1). Olson's theory drew on earlier work into the logic of collective action and, like Acemoglu and Robinson, he focused on the importance of institutions and behaviour. His argument is that some groups (those subject to particular incentives) are much more likely to act collectively to obtain collective goods, and crucially that smaller groups have a greater likelihood of engaging in collective action than larger ones. Thus societies will never achieve equity or efficiency through comprehensive bargaining between groups. Stable societies with unchanged boundaries will tend to accumulate more collusions and organizations for collective action over time, with members of smaller groups having disproportionate organizational power for collective action. The disproportion diminishes but does not disappear over time.

Seen through the lens of Olson's theory, it is apparent that there is a downside to the stability and endurance of institutions, political entities and states, since a process of institutional sclerosis can occur within their boundaries. To explore his hypothesis Olson looked at the historic economic performance of states and cities in the United States. His statistical tests indicated that older states did indeed perform less strongly: 'We found that there is the hypothesized negative relationship between the number of years since statehood for all non-confederate states and their current rates of economic growth, and that this relationship is statistically significant' (Olson, *op. cit.*, p. 99). The same was true of US cities and metropolitan areas: places which had the longest time to accumulate special interest groups had a similar tendency to decline.

Writing in the early 1980s, and doubtless with the economic troubles of 1970s Britain uppermost in his mind, Olson saw British industrial and economic decline echoing his theory. He noted the sharp contrast between Britain's political and institutional continuity (it had not been invaded) with the huge, almost revolutionary, impact of defeat and destruction in the Second World War on other European powers, and on Japan, alongside cathartic events like the French Revolution and the coming to power of Napoleon. In part medieval institutions had crumbled in Britain too. But they had not been pulverized in the same way as French institutions. The importance of the House of Lords, Oxbridge and the established church could perhaps be exaggerated, but they were symbols of Britain's legacy from the pre-industrial past. Extraordinary turmoil had occurred in the decades before the industrial revolution, and this doubtless played a part in opening British society to new talent and enterprise. But since then Britain had not suffered the institutional destruction, the forcible replacement of elites or the decimation of social classes observed in other European countries. Olson concluded that his theory: 'suggests that the unique stability of British life since the early eighteenth century must have affected social structure, social mobility, and cultural attitudes, but not through class conspiracies … the process is far subtler'. Equally, we might ask: what were the implications for British plans?

## War Socialism and Its Consequences

Britain escaped invasion in the Second World War. Nonetheless, total war brought profound changes, not least the arrival of huge numbers of women in the labour force. According to A.J.P. Taylor, there was a revolution in economic life. In the end, direction and control of industry turned wartime Britain into a country as socialist as Soviet Russia. Industrialists got into a habit of turning to government for help before the war and welcomed government controls for increased production. The administration of war socialism was more efficient than anything achieved in the First World War. More civil servants were used to working with industry and had encountered modern ideas. Trade union officials were closely involved as administrators rather than agitators, as were university intellectuals, who had often studied practical affairs and taken part in them. There was a readiness to use the same methods and to move towards the same results: 'People no longer asked about a man's background, only what he was doing for the war. This was especially true in the civil service' (Taylor, 1965, p. 617).

Peter Hennessy shares Taylor's optimistic reading of wartime production. Wartime Whitehall, he says, was an outstanding success, a crucial factor in producing high levels of mobilization: 'The mix of career regulars and outside irregulars blended between 1939 and 1945 represents *the* high point of achievement in the history of the British civil service' (Hennessy, 1990, p. 88). Edgerton is equally certain that wartime plans were successfully achieved. Britain, he argues, was a first class power with the capacity to wage a devastating war of machines. It was a great power which thought of war in material rather than martial terms, an industrial giant which remained at the centre of world trade (Edgerton, 2011).

The Regional Commissioners appointed in 1939 never had to use their powers in the event of invasion. Nonetheless they became critical elements in the conduct of wartime administration, coordinating all the separate ministries responsible for production at the regional level. A crisis was met immediately by the regional authorities without waiting for central government to act. This was a real improvement on the traditional apparatus, where nothing existed between Whitehall Departments and local government. But regional government did not last. Central government departments and local government bodies were jealous of the powers of the regions. Although regional offices were kept, the Commissioners were abolished after the war (Taylor, *op. cit.*). Yet it seems fair to say that the basic elements of a developmental state had been created. Doubtless the outlook, skills and attitudes were preserved by the generation that moved into post-war governance.

## Driven from Below – with One Exception

We can move toward conclusions. Britain is indeed a regulatory rather than developmental state, as Johnson (*op. cit.*) suggests. The Civil Service reflects this reality both in terms of its outlook, attitudes, values, and in the overriding lack of strategic thinking and project management skills at the centre. In part, as Johnson argues, this reflects the fact that Britain was first into the industrial revolution; thus the state played no positive or developmental role in the process. It merely arbitrated and regulated to remove the worst excesses of a process led by entrepreneurs and private capital. But that is not the whole story. The conditions that led to the emergence of an industrial revolution in Britain are reflected in the nature of its institutions and its history. Pluralistic institutions had developed steadily in Britain since Magna Carta, as the absolutist powers of the monarchy were reduced and eventually dispensed with. Parliament became the centre of power and its operations, especially the importance of petition, reflected the importance of diverse lobbies in a pluralistic society. More than this, many British institutions, as Dahrendorf (*op. cit.*) argued, are highly if not wholly autonomous – the judiciary, the universities, the internally regulated professions, even the supposed state broadcaster, the BBC.

Beyond the military sphere (and not always there) there is no tradition of centrally exercised power, of centrally driven strategy. Rasmussen (1982) perceptively identified this tendency in his study of London's development. On the other hand (and as one might expect), there is a powerful tradition of objections and objectors, which in terms of environmental planning can be traced back at least as far as the creation of Lincoln's Inn Fields, starting with a protest in 1613 (see p. 33). Britain's long and stable history means that a vast array of small pressure groups (often very well informed pressure groups) has developed. Their ability to block, stall and challenge big plans is considerable.

It is almost a natural consequence that British plans should be driven from below, as we saw in many of the case studies. Outstanding individuals invariably lead, based in autonomous intuitions, in charities, private companies, great estates, universities, or local government. In so far as the state has any role, it comes into play in picking up or supporting initiatives already being driven by others. The tradition of individualism is paramount: the tradition of hierarchical, state-led, initiative is almost non-existent. Implementing big infrastructure plans in Britain is frustrating and often frustrated.

There is an important exception. The Second World War had a profound impact on Britain's economy, its society, its government and its Civil Service. Perforce, the state became an initiating and implementing force in many fields, from armaments to clearance, from construction to reconstruction. What is more, the public mood seemed to change. Under the pressure of a war for national survival people accepted the overriding imperative of state directed action. Much of this survived the war, especially in plans for construction and reconstruction. Even so, the state's role (in building motorways, for example) was surprisingly limited, and much depended on local initiative. It was in the new towns that we can see the clearest evidence of purposeful state-directed action. Yet the importance of individuals and philanthropic effort should not be understated. The new town concept had been fought over for nearly 50 years by committed individuals and a private charity. It was driven forward by one brilliant and rather maverick individual, Lord Reith, in the heart of immediate post-war government.

The wartime state was unquestionably a centralizing institution. Although the most important consequences for development and construction now belong to history, in one respect the centralizing process initiated in the 1940s still reverberates. It is the impact on local government.

## Regulatory Centralism: Worst of All Worlds?

The golden age of British local government occurred in the 50 years leading up to the Second World War, culminating in the Local Government Act, 1933, a consolidating measure which confirmed structures, powers and functions. For the next 40 years, and especially after the Second World War, local government was on a downhill path. It lost a whole range of functions. Post-war nationalization saw many authorities lose control of municipal gas and electricity supplies, these utilities moving to electricity and gas boards in 1947 and 1948. Many local authorities lost their responsibility for water supply after the 1945 Water Act, as smaller authorities were absorbed into bigger joint boards. Under the Water Act 1973 these functions passed to regional water authorities which were subsequently privatized. It was the same story in health services. Under the 1946 National Health Service Act, local authority hospitals (there were around 1,700) were transferred to Regional Hospital Boards. Under the National Health Service Act 1973 local government lost its remaining personal health services, such as health centres and district nursing services. In 1934 government set up its Unemployment Assistance Board, later becoming the Supplementary Benefits Commission. As a result local government lost the function of public assistance. Maintenance of trunk roads passed from local to central government under the Trunk Roads Acts of 1936 and 1946 (Byrne, 1985).

Local government failed to attract new functions, such as the new towns programme, and, in later years, the motorway programme passed to the regional Road Construction Units. Crucially, financial independence was lost. Local government has received increasingly large amounts of grant aid from central government, in many respects becoming an agency of its paymaster. In 1913 local government received only 15 per cent of its total income from central government; by 1949 this had grown to 34 per cent; by 1973 it received £4,422m, 45 per cent of its total income, from the centre (Layfield, 1976). Layfield argued that local authorities should be responsible to their electorates for their expenditure, and this could not be achieved if central government continued to finance growth.

Closely connected with its loss of financial independence, local government was subject to ever increasing levels of central government control. Post-war legislation setting up the health, education and welfare services required local authorities to seek central government approval for their projects. Central government developed powers to intervene in local government decisions and to inspect their services. A huge volume of government regulatory advice, guidance, policy and ministerial circulars and letters was churned out by the post-war Whitehall machine (Byrne, *op. cit.*).

Before the Second World War, as the LSE's Professor Tony Travers argues, government had an Empire to run. As the Empire declined and welfare services grew, Westminster turned its attention from Canada and India to Ipswich and Carlisle: 'Since then, Britain has been overcome by the centripetal force of national government' (Travers, 2014). The financial statistics certainly bear out his argument. Britain's cities now receive only 17 per cent of their revenues from local taxes; on average, cities in OECD countries receive 55 per cent of their income from local taxes (Centre for Cities, 2014).

In the 1980s, the extreme centralizing tendencies of Margaret Thatcher's years were further accentuated, rather then reversed, by John Major's government and the Labour governments led by Tony Blair and Gordon Brown.

Figure 13.2. *Margaret Thatcher.* A committed centralizer, Thatcher's target was local government, whose traditional role as a bulwark of democracy was not accepted.

Far from reducing the role of central government, Thatcher had seemed to regard its superior wisdom as a benefit. Her target was local government, whose traditional role as a bulwark of democracy was no longer accepted. Repeated attacks on the financial independence of local government weakened its power and significance. In the poll tax, the reform that led to Thatcher's downfall, the aim was to ensure that 75 per cent of local spending would be determined by Whitehall (Young, 1989).

The Thatcher, Major and Blair governments can all be seen as centralizers. Thatcher's NHS reforms introduced a class of managers who logged waiting lists, appointments, referrals, lengths of stay, operations, and mortality rates. Her reform of university funding saw grants moving from a five year to a one year cycle, so that detailed reviews could be carried out of a university's work. Some public sector inputs were privatized, but for the most part, schools, universities, hospitals, law and housing fell under central measurement and control. The academic output of universities was measured numerically by means of a 'citation index' (how often published research was cited by other authors), with government research funding distributed accordingly. Major's government followed suit, as the Audit Commission drew up league tables of councils and hospital boards. By 1995 there were fifty-one so called 'Next Steps' agencies, and over 500 government-funded 'quangoes', responsible for over half of central government activity. Accordingly the Comptroller and Auditor General, the National Audit Office and the Audit Commission all expanded their roles, measuring effectiveness, efficiency and value for money in the arm's length agencies (Jenkins, 2006).

Blair followed where Thatcher and Major had led, his dislike for local government first developed in his experiences in the London Borough of Hackney. He was openly centralist: 'People need to know that we will run from the centre and forever from the centre' (Blair quoted in *ibid.*, p. 232). There was more than a whiff of absolutism to Blair's presidential style. But it was his Chancellor Gordon Brown who created the decisive mechanisms for centralized control, in the form of Whitehall and Treasury set targets. A policy and performance unit set up in the Cabinet Office was supplemented in 2001 by a delivery unit headed by Sir Michael Barber, a former academic. The Unit later moved to the Treasury. The targets were central to delivery, fixed jointly by the Treasury and spending departments, and monitored by the Audit Commission and the delivery unit. At his 1999 Party Conference, Blair claimed that he had 500 specific targets for the public sector. In 2000, his Deputy Prime Minister, John Prescott, said that he alone had imposed 2,500 targets on local government and transport (*ibid.*). Targets were meant to focus the efforts of public servants and make them work more closely with others. But the risk was that they would reduce professionalism, encourage game playing to meet targets at the expense of other priorities, and reduce common sense and trust.

From our perspective there is a much deeper risk. Whatever their beneficial effects, the deeper consequence was that autonomy, flexibility, discretion and initiative was steadily eroded at lower levels of government, and in civil

Figure 13.3. *John Prescott, former Deputy Prime Minister.* Prescott promoted regionalism whilst practising centralism, imposing 2,500 central targets for transport and local government.

institutions like the universities, as much in the withering away of independence as in the 'rule following' procedures of target delivery. A profoundly centralized mode of operation was thus imposed on a government machine which, by values, outlook and tradition, was essentially regulatory. In their different ways, the achievements demonstrated by each of the case studies serve to emphasize the importance of individualism, initiative and innovation, outside the formal machinery of government. In Britain, the imposition of central rule, through a government machine designed to regulate rather than take the initiative, does not sound like a winning formula. It sounds like the worst of all worlds.

## References

Acemoglu, D. and Robinson, J. (2013) *Why Nations Fail: The Origins of Power, Prosperity and Poverty*. London: Profile Books.

Bindoff, T. (1950) *Tudor England: The Pelican History of England*. Harmondsworth: Pelican.

Brewer, J. (1988) *The Sinews of Power: War, Money and the English State, 1688–1783*. Cambridge, MA: Harvard University Press.

Byrne, T. (1985) *Local Government in Britain*. Harmondsworth: Pelican.

Centre for Cities (2014) *Cities Outlook 2014*. London: Centre for Cities.

Dahrendorf, R. (1982) *On Britain*. London: BBC.

Edgerton, D. (2011) *Britain's War Machine: Weapons, Resources and Experts in the Second World War*. Harmondsworth: Allen Lane.

Gamble, A. (1981) *Britain in Decline: Economic Policy, Political Strategy and the British State*. London: Macmillan.

Hennessy, P. (1990) *Whitehall*. London: Fontana.

Hill, C. (1969) *Reformation to Industrial Revolution: The Pelican Economic History of Britain*, Volume 2, 1530–1780. Harmondsworth: Pelican.

Jenkins, S. (2006) *Thatcher and Sons: A Revolution in Three Acts*. London: Penguin.

Johnson, C. (1982) *MITI and the Japanese Miracle: The Growth of Industrial Policy, 1925–1975*. Stanford, CA: Stanford University Press.

Layfield, F. (1976) *Local Government Finance: Report of the Committee of Inquiry*. London: HMSO.

Liverpool City Council (2003) *Nomination of Liverpool – Maritime Mercantile City for Inscription on the World Heritage List*. Liverpool: Liverpool City Council.

Marquand, D. (2008) *Britain Since 1918: The Strange Career of British Democracy*. London: Weidenfeld and Nicolson.

Olson, M. (1982) *The Rise and Decline of Nations: Economic Growth, Stagflation and Economic Rigidities*. New Haven, CT: Yale University Press.

Rasmussen, S.E. (1982) *London: The Unique City*. Cambridge MA: MIT Press.

Taylor, A.J.P. (1965) *English History 1914–1945*. Harmondsworth: Pelican.

Travers, T. (2014) Long live borough hall – it is working better than Whitehall. *Financial Times*, 24/25 May.

Young, H. (1989) *One of Us: A Biography of Margaret Thatcher*. London: Macmillan.

# 14

## British Futures, British Plans
### Conclusions and Implications

*A key element in [Ming] China's retreat was the sheer conservatism of the Confucian bureaucracy … the all-important officialdom was concerned to preserve and recapture the past, not to create a brighter future…*

Professor Paul Kennedy, 1988

Britain is essentially a regulatory state. Central government does not drive development and change, but acts as a mediator, regulator or 'night watchman'. The civil service and the operations of the central government machine reflect this truth. We may not have the civil service some might wish for, but we have the one we should expect. All this is deeply rooted in the evolution of the country's unwritten constitution and its political and other institutions. It is a history that can be traced back as far as Magna Carta, and is reflected powerfully in the pluralistic distribution of power, the relative autonomy of institutions, and indeed in the ability of objectors, as individuals, associations, and indeed private companies, to use the legal system, the planning system and the political system to obstruct change.

Various attempts at reform over the last century have failed, or come to very little, with the important exception of the huge shock to the system which came from total mobilization and war socialism in the Second World War, and its aftermath until the early 1970s. Mrs Thatcher's government and its successors dismantled much of this settlement.

There is little positive planning for social and economic outcomes of the sort which underpinned the post-war Japanese economic miracle (Johnson,

1982) and the emergence of dynamic industrial competitors in Asia (Studwell, 2013). Further, there is little long-term central strategy and correspondingly little continuity within the central government machine, and various attempts to address the issue have foundered.

## The British Model

A different planning style seems to have prevailed in Britain. There has been relatively little impetus from above, little sense of hierarchical institutions, and indeed little or no dictatorial and technocratic direction. Instead initiative has characteristically come from below. Passionate and well-informed individuals, often with a high degree of determination, invariably drive change. They sometimes go to extraordinary lengths to have their visions adopted and their plans implemented, using a wide range of autonomous institutions as platforms for their campaigns and objectives: private companies, landed estates, charitable trusts, professional institutes, campaigning societies; universities; and most of all local government. Local government has often proved an essential support (and sometimes a driver) for initiatives launched elsewhere, just as central government has often proved to be indifferent or even hostile to change.

The same hallmarks or *modus operandi* emerge repeatedly: improvisation, flexibility, informality, and individualism. The dispersed and often organic nature of planning activity has made it a fertile breeding ground for innovation, in terms of concept, vision and implementation. Dispersed initiative and power has also provided an environment which is often conducive to 'trial and error' rather than top down directives. It is the very system advocated by writers like Taleb, Popper and Kay (see Chapter 1). Broadly speaking that is how the system has operated, and how significant plans have been implemented, and indeed are still being implemented, on a very large scale. It may not be ideal. But evidently it is a system that has worked in the past (including the very recent past).

In his discussion of the Japanese developmental state Chalmers Johnson reflected on its potential application to the United States, another prime example of the 'light touch' regulatory state. He wondered whether Japan was an appropriate model for Americans. The Japanese built on their own strengths: their bureaucracy, their banking system, their homogeneous society and the markets available to them. The institutions of the Japanese state were products above all of Japanese innovation and experience. But those seeking to emulate Japan's success needed to secure their own solutions from their own materials. So it might be argued that what the United States needed was not more state direction, but less regulation and more incentives from government for people to save, work and invest. The Japanese had learned their cooperative model as a matter of national survival; their defeat in the Second World War led them to maintain what were largely wartime forms of social and economic organization. Lacking this consensus on goals, the United States might be better to build on its strengths and unleash the competitive instincts of its companies and citizens. On the other hand, Johnson concluded, given the need to reinvigorate its economy, coordinate environmental, welfare, education and other policies, and stop living off its capital, whilst maintaining the military balance, perhaps the United States should be thinking about a pilot for developmental planning (Johnson, *op. cit.*). That dilemma has an acute resonance for Britain, as well as for the United States.

We must not become misty eyed about the British planning style. It has advantages and disadvantages. Decisions can take a very long time to enact. Sometimes plans that should have been implemented long ago hang around through the years. The long and unfinished saga of London's third airport is a case in point. Delay adds to costs in terms of blight, accelerating construction costs, and to the costs of congestion and delay imposed on users of sub-standard facilities, sometimes over long periods.

## Reforming the Centre

The question is what can, or should, be done about this. One obvious and perfectly reasonable response would be to urge the creation of a better coordinated government machine: perhaps a central policy unit, or a properly resourced Prime Minister's department, or a national infrastructure commission, or even a strengthening of that most powerful of central government departments, HM Treasury. Some recent proposals are in this tradition of reform. The Institute of Government has argued that the Cabinet Office and Treasury should refocus on a core role of coordinating strategy in government; departments should become capable of holding themselves to account; and collaboration between departments should move from aspiration to reality. The Cabinet Office should set strategic goals for government and these should become the basis for departmental spending allocations (Parker *et al.*, 2010). A year later the Institute followed up with a further report (Hallsworth and Rutter, 2011). No one in the current system, said the report, had responsibility for ensuring that policy was of high quality. Every department should have a policy director and the centre should oversee policy-making. A year later, the Civil Service Reform Plan criticized inconsistent policy-making and policy advice that drew on too narrow a range of evidence and views (HM Government, 2012).

A more recent report from the Institute for Government follows through the theme of central weakness and lack of strategic discipline, focusing on the lack of support for successive Prime Ministers. Unlike other countries, Britain's Prime Minister enjoys very little dedicated support. Power and resources are established in the individual departmental baronies, including the Treasury. In Australia or Canada, premiers enjoy a dedicated department with, respectively, fifty-six and ninety politically appointed advisors, alongside separate central civil service departments. British Prime Ministers have a private office designed to manage the Whitehall 'paper flow' and a tiny policy unit which works as a loose network of individuals, looks ahead in terms of days and is endlessly buffeted by short-term pressures. There is no space for long-term thinking. Thus government remains weak at handling long-term and cross-cutting issues (Harris and Rutter, 2014). Gently airing some modest proposals for a longer-term policy unit, the authors find themselves tellingly attracted to the more coherent and corporate approach to government in Scotland.

On infrastructure planning, Sir John Armitt's review for the Labour Party recommended the creation of a national infrastructure commission, producing a 25–30 year national infrastructure assessment. This would be submitted to the Chancellor and laid before Parliament. Individual government departments would be required to produce sector plans within 12 months. These too would be laid before Parliament for approval, with individual departments responsible for implementation. Therein rests the problem. As Armitt's own analysis found, when responsibility for the previous 'national policy statements' was left with individual departments: 'this has often resulted in policy and bureaucratic drift' (Armitt, 2013, p. 5).

The British could no doubt build a better and more purposive central machine. They certainly did so between 1939 and 1945 (though even then old ways often prevailed – as the story of the first computers so amply demonstrated). Yet peacetime experience is not at all encouraging, for the old problems seem to emerge again and again. Pluralism, dispersed power, and well-organized objectors are so often anathema to decisive central plans.

## Shrinking the Centre

Steve Hilton, Prime Minister David Cameron's former director of strategy, took a different, indeed revolutionary, view. Hilton wanted a 90 per cent head count reduction in the civil service, with the entire operation housed in a single building like Somerset House. Later he argued for a 70 per cent reduction written into civil service legislation, with power shifted to local communities and neighbourhoods (D'Ancona, 2013).

Hilton left Downing Street in March 2012 for a post at Stanford University, his reforms foiled. They were never likely to succeed, for like Lord Fulton before him he had tried to launch a direct attack on the high command. But perhaps they contained an element of rationality. Rather than seek to centralize initiative, within a machine that is not designed for initiative, perhaps another option beckons: to decentralize, reversing many of the centralizing trends of the last few decades.

Powerful centralizing tendencies still prevail. In December 2014, Mark Easton, the BBC's Home Editor, reported that: 'In the spring of 2011 … for the first time probably in living memory, central government was bigger than local government. The number of people in the UK employed by Whitehall overtook the number employed by the town hall' (Easton, 2014). Yet a seismic

Figure 14.1. *Alex Salmond, former Leader of the Scottish National Party.* Salmond came close to winning the Scottish referendum on independence; in the 2015 general election his Party swept aside all opposition in Scotland.

political dynamic is moving in another direction. Devolution for the Celtic fringes in Scotland, Wales and Northern Ireland is well advanced, the result of policies introduced by the Blair government (Morrison, 2001). London has a degree of independence through its effective and powerful metropolitan mayor. It is seeking more control over its own finances. The Scots are seeking much higher levels of devolution, having seen high, although not majority, support for complete independence in the 2014 referendum. As Harris and Rutter (*op. cit.*) noted, a new approach to government as a single organization has emerged in Scotland under the Scottish National Party. It has transformed the role of the centre, with a shared common purpose, aligned around cross-departmental 'performance outcomes'. Individual government departments have been abolished (Elvidge, 2011)).

The Coalition government in 2010 swiftly demolished Labour's regional apparatus, partly it seems on the basis of cost savings (Cable, 2009). But as a form of devolution, the regional tier counted for little. The Government Offices for the Regions were essentially monitoring outposts for the central civil service, with little discretion or independence; the Regional Development Agencies were, as their title implies, merely agents of government; the Regional Assemblies had no directly elected political leadership. At the same time, proposals first developed under Labour to give the largest cities and their hinterland statutory status as 'Combined Authorities' are now well advanced (Sandford, 2015). The Combined Authorities are not directly elected, but once established could provide the administrative structures on to which a metropolitan mayor on the London model might be grafted. However, there is no hierarchical element to the current Combined Authority model and the principles of governance might aptly be described as distributed or polycentric.

Lord Heseltine's report *No Stone Unturned* made a powerful case for decentralization of power from Whitehall to the English cities. Heseltine argued that central government had reserved for itself the majority of economic decisions and relegated local authorities to roles as service providers and agents of the centre. The involvement of local communities and of local business leaders had been lost and with it their energy and innovation. With responsibilities divided between the different Whitehall baronies, no one was in a position to take a holistic view. His solution was to bring together the Whitehall funding streams into a huge single pot, worth almost £50 billion and to make this available, on the scale of the (essentially county based) local enterprise partnerships (Department for Business, Innovation and Skills, 2012). While government accepted many of his recommendations, it balked at the scale of his financial restructuring, proposing a single pot no bigger than £2 billion – precisely the same as the budget deployed by the former regional development agencies (Cable, *op. cit.*).

Heseltine's unacceptable recommendation went far beyond the Coalition government's commitment to 'localism', championed by Eric Pickles, the Secretary of State for Communities and Local Government. Pickles dispensed with local government targets. He scythed through central government guidance to planning authorities, reducing 1,000 pages of national policy to a mere 50-page statement (House of Commons, 2014). But localism was rarely synonymous with a commitment to local government. In many ways it was simply the reverse; the advocates of localism wished to see responsibilities pushed below or outside democratic local government to a plethora of new or enhanced single-purpose institutions, some at the neighbourhood level – such as statutory neighbourhood plans and academy schools, as well as directly elected local police commissioners and directly elected city mayors. It has to be said that there has been little public support for either directly elected mayors or police commissioners. Only two cities agreed to move forward with directly elected mayors, one of them (Liverpool) without a referendum; electoral turnout for the police commissioners was extremely low. Localism can have the effect of undermining the power of directly elected local government. In so doing it perversely paves the way for a form of 'mass society' where there are no democratic institutions of any substance between the individual and central government. Localist institutions would not have the independence or significance to act as institutional platforms for key plans. They would be little more than micro-scale delivery agencies. When things go wrong with a localist institution, it is the centre that must intervene. Recent concerns about the policies of independent academy schools in Birmingham led to calls for reform and the introduction of an enhanced national inspectorate for all academy schools (Adams, 2014).

## The Case for Orderly Disorder

Should Britain strengthen its central institutions or decentralize? Readers by now will be in a position to draw their own conclusions. Ideally it should do both; although in practice reforming the central institutions may prove to be intractable, while decentralization may be feasible. Protecting and enhancing the autonomous status of local government, and many other elements in civil society (such as universities, professional institutions, charities and landed estates) would run with the grain of the British planning style.

What seems indisputable is that top down central planning works best in a relatively stable era, when trend based forecasts and extrapolations are inherently more reliable. In conditions of greater uncertainty and turbulence a different model might work more effectively: something that is more reliant on trial and error, encourages dispersed and decentralized initiative, and is inherently flexible. It sounds extraordinarily like the traditional British planning style.

Edmund Phelps, economist and Nobel Prize winner, believes that the public sector is incapable of innovation and enterprise. Only new and dynamic private sector organizations can deliver the goods (Phelps, 2014). The evidence in our case studies suggests that this is largely true of central government in the UK. But decentralized civil society below that level, including local government, can be extraordinarily creative, and in many respects the handmaiden to innovation.

Mariana Mazzucato, Professor of Economics at the Science Policy Research Unit in Kent, takes a diametrically opposite (and better evidenced) view (Mazzucato, 2014). She sees the state as a critical player in innovation and economic development, with the potential for significant entrepreneurial behaviour. Yet it must be said that many of her case studies present governments as, at best, accidental entrepreneurs. They may commission hugely expensive research programmes, often with military or pure science objectives, which spawn technologies with extraordinary civil and commercial potential. Individuals working within or close to these technologies, not governments, see and realize their wider potential.

The adoption of touch screen and GPS technologies, first incubated by US military research programmes, were profitably borrowed and exploited by Steve Jobs and Apple, rather than the US government. Tim Berners Lee invented the Hyper Text Transfer Protocol (http), the basis of the World Wide Web, implementing the system on computers installed at CERN (the organization for European nuclear research) a public institution with rather different goals. Thus change and innovation can occur at the interstices rather than the centre, through an informal and almost chaotic process. There are few British examples in Mazzucato's pages, with the intriguing exception of our old friend the British Post Office (see Chapter 5). Unable to secure support from the established US computer companies, who (correctly) perceived the internet as a disruptive threat to their businesses, the US government's Defense Advanced Research Projects Agency (DARPA) created a networked system in the United States, with the help of the public sector British Post Office.

Three American academics who studied the process of serial innovation in large corporates found that effective managers of what they describe as 'serial innovators' allow these bright, yet sometimes unworldly, individuals to 'fly under the radar' for significant periods. The managers 'let the birds fly', attending meetings with senior managers themselves, thus freeing the innovators from bureaucratic responsibilities and giving them creative freedom to pursue their ideas. Sometimes an innovator's projects were deliberately kept off the company's official books (Griffin et al., 2012). We saw examples of this practice in the case studies. Needless to say, acute resource shortages and demanding formal targets from above are anathema to these practices; just as the traditional British style is complementary.

Elinor Ostrom, political scientist and Nobel Prize winner, has developed a concept of 'polycentric governance' (Ostrom, 2010) which has extraordinary resonance with the British planning style. Ostrom rejects the notion that the world can be explained by invoking patterns of interaction in markets, alongside a state imposing rules which force otherwise self-serving individuals to contribute to wider social needs. She advances polycentric governance as a more productive arrangement and one better able to explain the activities of a diverse array of public and private agencies. By this she means a system of governance which has several centres of decision-making, formally independent of each other, that can enter into competitive relationships, or into contractual or cooperative undertakings. Her early studies of police departments showed

Figure 14.2. *Elinor Ostrom*. Nobel prize winner and political scientist, Ostrom argued the case for polycentric and non-hierarchical forms of governance.

not a single case in which a large centralized department outperformed smaller departments, serving smaller areas. Duplication rarely occurred, and metropolitan areas with large numbers of autonomous suppliers achieved higher technical levels of efficiency. Complexity was not the same as chaos. In subsequent research into resource and infrastructure systems across the world the same lesson was learned. Even in a study of policy in developing countries Ostrom and her colleagues reached a similar conclusion: 'There are numerous examples of polities ... lacking a single political leader. The principles underlying these non-hierarchical institutions offer a genuine alternative to systems which rely on hierarchical decision making' (Ostrom *et al.*, 1993, p. 191).

Ostrom concluded that a core goal of policy should be creating diverse polycentric institutions which can influence innovation, learning, trust, and adaptation, whilst producing effective and sustainable outcomes. The lesson from the case studies in this book is that, in contexts as diverse as engineering, city planning, landscape architecture, information technology and green space provision, polycentric governance has long been a staple of the British style. All this is congruent with the remarkable findings that Britain has some of the densest networks of civic association (or 'social capital') in the world, and that overall levels of sociability and civic trust have remained robust since the 1950s (Hall, 2002). Suitably revivified, all this could yet serve Britain well in the turbulent and unpredictable future which appears to lie ahead.

Perhaps there are lessons for other countries too, with different planning styles and a greater tradition of centrally driven and developmental plans. If they wish to support a more innovative, freewheeling, and perhaps more trusting culture, whilst coping with a rising tide of middle-class objectors, they may have much to learn from the orderly disorder that lies at the heart of great British plans.

## References

Adams, R. (2014) Trojan horse schools have done little to fix problems – Ofsted. *Guardian*, 14 October.

Armitt, J. (2013) *The Armitt Review: An Independent Review of Long Term Infrastructure Planning Commissioned for Labour's Policy Review*. London: Labour Party.

Cable, V. (2009) Tackling the Fiscal Crisis: A Recovery Plan for the UK, Reform Paper. Available at: http://www.reform.co.uk/client_files/www.reform.co.uk/files/Tackling%20the%20fiscal%20crisis%20FINAL.pdf.

D'Ancona, M. (2013) *In It Together: The Inside Story of the Coalition Government*. London: Penguin.

Department for Business Innovation and Skills (2012) *No Stone Unturned in Pursuit of Growth – Lord Heseltine Review*. London: The Stationery Office.

Easton, M. (2014) Whitehall versus town hall. 18 December 2014. Available at http://www.bbc.co.uk/news/uk-30520065.

Elvidge, J. (2011) *Northern Exposure: Lessons from the First Twelve Years of Devolved Government in Scotland*. London: Institute for Government.

Griffin, A., Raymond, L. and Vojak, B. (2012) *Serial Innovators: How Individuals Create and Deliver Breakthrough Innovations in Mature Firms*. Stanford, CA: Stanford University Press.

Hall, P.A. (2002) Great Britain: the role of government and the distribution of social capital, in

Putnam, R. (ed.) *Democracies in Flux: The Evolution of Social Capital in Contemporary Society.* Oxford: Oxford University Press.

Hallsworth, M. and Rutter, J. (2011) *Making Policy Better: Improving Whitehall's Core Business.* London; Institute for Government.

Harris, J. and Rutter, J. (2014) *Centre Forward: Effective Support for the Prime Minister at the Centre of Government.* London: Institute for Government.

HM Government (2012) *The Civil Service Reform Plan.* Available at: http://www.civilservice.gov.uk/wp-content/uploads/2012/06/Civil-Service-Reform-Plan-acc-final.pdf.

House of Commons (2014) *Communities and Local Government Committee: Operation of the National Planning Policy Framework, Fourth Report of Session, 2014–2015.* London: The Stationery Office.

Johnson, C. (1982) *MITI and the Japanese Miracle: The Growth of Industrial Policy, 1925–1975.* Stanford, CA: Stanford University Press.

Kennedy, P. (1988) *The Rise and Fall of the Great Powers.* New York: Random House.

Mazzucato, M. (2014) *The Entrepreneurial State: Debunking Public Versus Private Sector Myths.* London: Anthem Press.

Morrison, J. (2001) *Reforming Britain: New Labour, New Constitution?* London: Reuters/Pearson Education.

Ostrom, E. (2010) Beyond markets and states: polycentric governance of complex economic systems. *American Economic Review,* **100**(3), pp. 641–672.

Ostrom, E., Schroeder, L. and Wynne, S. (1993) *Institutional Incentives and Sustainable Development: Infrastructure Policies in Perspective.* Boulder, CO: Westview Press.

Parker, S., Paun, A., McClory, J., and Blatchford, K. (2010) *Shaping Up: A Whitehall for the Future.* London: Institute for Government.

Phelps, E. (2014) *Mass Flourishing: How Grassroots Innovation Created Jobs, Challenge and Change.* Princeton, NJ: Princeton University Press.

Sandford, M. (2015) Combined Authorities – Commons Library Standard Note. London: House of Commons. Available at: http://www.parliament.uk/business/publications/research/briefing-papers/SN06649/combined-authorities.

Studwell, J. (2013) *How Asia Works: Success and Failure in the World's Most Dynamic Region.* London: Profile Books.

# Index

*Note*: figures are shown by italic page
numbers, tables by bold numbers


Abercrombie, [Sir] Patrick  28, *29*, 134,
  173
    Greater London Plan [1944]  28, *91*,
      134, 173
    road plans for London  28–29, 31,
      43, 44, 173
absolute power  194
    and pluralism  197
academy schools  213
Acemoglu, Daron [economist]  196,
  197, 200
achievement criteria  17
Acorn Computers  94, 99
Act for the Rebuilding of the City of
    London [1667]  27, 33
Addison, Joseph [essayist]  53
Adonis, Andrew [Lord Adonis]  185
agglomeration economics  99
All-Party Parliamentary Commission
    on Physical Activity [2014]  166–167
Allen, Woody  60

Alma Tadema, Lawrence [artist]  140
Altshuler, A.  115
'American Pastoral' landscape style  61
Amery, Leo [politician]  182–183
Anglo-French projects  6, 143
Arcadian picturesque  *47*, 54
Argent [development company]  40
ARM microprocessors  94–95
Armitt, [Sir] John [civil engineer]  5,
  211
Arup [engineering consultancy], and
    Channel Tunnel rail link  146–149,
    150–151, 153, 177, 178
Arup, Ove [structural engineer]  146–
  147, 153
Ashton, Pam [Sustrans Chair]  157
Astra Zeneca, Cambridge R&D site  93,
  97
Atlantic trade  198–199
Audit Commission  205, 206
Auroux, Jean [French Transport
    Minister]  142
*autobahnen*  107, 110
autonomy of institutions  83, 194–196
*autostrada* programme  106

Bacon, Francis [philosopher]  51, 52
Baldwin, [Sir] Peter [civil servant]  112,
    116–117
    quoted  104
Balfour, Arthur [British PM]  105
Balogh, Thomas [economist], on civil
    service  188
Bank of England  195, 198
Barbon, Nicholas [17th c. financier]  43
Barlow Commission (and Report)  91,
    133, 134
Barnes, Alfred [Transport Minister]  111
Barnett, Corelli [historian]  112
Bath, 'Two Tunnels' Greenway  155,
    156, *157*
Bath–Bristol cycleway  159–160, 161
BBC  194–195, 196
Bechtel Corporation  151
Bedford Estate  35, 37
Bedford Square [London]  35
Belgravia [London]  36
Bendixson, T.  130
Bergin, Sue [Sustrans employee]  162
Bermingham, Anne  56
Berne Gauge [railway] standard  139
Berners-Lee, Tim [computer scientist]
    82, 214
Best, Michael [economist]  102
biotechnology companies, Cambridge
    93, 96–97
Birkenhead  63
    growth of  64
    Mersey Tunnel  109
    tramway system  64
Birkenhead Improvement
    Commissioners  66, 67, 70, 175
Birkenhead Park
    architectural features  62, *68*, 69
    [case study]  **18**, 19, 60–70
    compared with Central Park [New
    York]  62–63
    government's role [absence]  173–
    174

official opening [1847]  66
restoration [in 2007]  70
role of individuals  67, 69, 175
Bishop, Jeff, academic view of Milton
    Keynes  127
Blair, Tony [Prime Minister]
    centralizing tendency  204, 205, 207
    on civil service  185, 186, *187*
    Millennium Dome project  156
Bletchley new town  124, 125
    *see also* Milton Keynes
Bletchley Park [Buckinghamshire]
    73–74
    [case study]  **18**, 19, 71–79, 82–83
    code breakers  75, 77, 117
    government's role  74, 173
    informal style  76, 177
    location  73–74
    role of individuals  74–75, 82, 175
Bloomsbury Square [London]  34–35
'blue sky' science  89
Boeing 737 airliner  10
'Bombe' [electromechanical code-
    analysis machine]  77, 81
Bor, Walter [planner]  123
Bostock, Mark [economist]  148
botanical gardens  50
Bovis [house builder]  127
Bradford, Manchester Road Bridge  *162*
Braudel, Fernand [historian]  98
Brewer, J.  198
Bridgeman, Charles [garden designer]
    47
Bristol, formation of Sustrans  159–160
Bristol–Bath cycleway  159–160, 161
British cities
    growth in 19th century  64–65
    revenue sources  204
British institutions, autonomy of  83,
    194–196
British [national] Library  6
British planning style  209–210, 214
    polycentric governance in  216

British professions, independent status
195
British Rail
and Channel Tunnel rail link 142,
144–146, 148–149, 172
joint venture with Arup 147–148
Broadgate estate [London] 40
Brodie, James [Liverpool City
Engineer] 109
Brown, George [Chancellor, *then* PM]
125, 190, 204, 206
Brown, Lancelot ('Capability')
career and contribution 46–51, 58,
67
clients 55–57, 175
influences 51–55, 178
style 46–47, 175
Bruzelius, Nils 11
Buchanan, Colin [town planner] 84
building control, early [17th c.] form
27, 43
bureaucratic state, early beginnings 197
Burgin, Leslie [Transport Minister]
110
Burlington, Richard Boyle, 3rd Earl of
54
Butterfield, John, quoted 84, 92

Cabinet Office 184, 185, 210
CAD Centre [Cambridge] 95–96, 176
CAD technology 95–96, 98
Cairncross, [Sir] Alec [economist] 142
Caligula [Roman emperor] 140
Callaghan, James [Labour PM] 128, 158
Cambridge
Addenbrooke's Hospital 97, 176
CAD Centre 95–96, 176
[case study] **18**, 20, 84–103
as cluster of innovation 93–97, 98,
178
collegiate buildings 91
discouragement of mass production
[in Holford plan] 90–91, 92, 98

high-technology companies 85,
92–96, 98–99
Holford–Wright plan/report [1950]
85, 89–92, 174, 176
population 85, 90
as university town 85, 89–90
Cambridge Biomedical Campus 93, 97
Cambridge Interactive Systems 96
'Cambridge Phenomenon' 85, 92–93
explanations 98–99
factors affecting 101
Cambridge Positioning Systems 96
Cambridge Science Park 98
Cambridge Scientific Instrument
Company 93, 99
Cambridge, University of
attitude to innovative activity by
staff 100
aversion to commerce and industry
86, 89
Cavendish Laboratory 87–89, 93,
97, 176
Church of England bias 85, 86
compared with Oxford 87, 89
Computer Laboratory 95
Department of Physics 94, 96
Institute of Technology 96, 97
Mathematical Laboratory 95
origins 85
reforms [19th c.] 86, 101, 176
scientific excellence 87–89, 176
staff contracts 100
Campbell of Eskan, 1st Baron 121,
125–126, 127, 176
'Capability' Brown *see* Brown, Lancelot
('Capability')
case studies 19–20, 25–168
achievement criteria 17
Birkenhead Park **18**, 19, 60–70
Bletchley Park **18**, 19, 72–79, 82–83
Cambridge **18**, 20, 84–103
Channel Tunnel rail link **18**, 19–20,
138–154

characteristics **18**
landscape design **18**, 19, 45–59
London's roads and squares **18**, 19, 25–44
Milton Keynes **18**, 19, 119–137
motorways **18**, 19, 104–118
National Cycle Network **18**, 20, 155–168
Casson, Hugh [architect] 84
Castle, Barbara [Transport Minister] 113, 117, 174
Catherine II the Great 50
Cavendish Laboratory [Cambridge] 87–89, 93, 97, 176
central government
and innovation 214
role of 171–174
staff numbers 211
Central Policy Review Staff 182, 184, 192
centralization
local government affected by 203–206, 211
wartime activity 203
Centre for Cities, statistics on Milton Keynes 130
Centre for Environmental Studies 121
Chadwick, G.F. 68
Chamberlain, Joseph [Board of Trade President] 141, 172
Chamberlain, Neville [Prime Minister] 133
Channel Tunnel
early proposals 140–141
French government initiative 143, 172, 176
nuclear device proposed? 141–142
official opening [1994] 138
opposition to 140–141
pilot tunnels [1880, 1973] 140, 141–142
traffic forecasts 145, 179
Channel Tunnel Act [1987] 144

Channel Tunnel Committee 141
Channel Tunnel Group (CTG) 143
Channel Tunnel rail link 13
1899 route 138–139, 140
[case study] **18**, 19–20, 138–154
cost 151–153
eastern route 148, 150–151
Heseltine's role 150, 154, 172, 177
London terminus 40, 144, 151, *152*
south-eastern route 148, 150
Channel Tunnel Study Group 141
Charles I [King of Britain & Ireland] 198
Charles II [King of Britain & Ireland] 26–27, 33, 34
Charles, Prince of Wales 164
Chatsworth estate [Derbyshire] 67
Cherwell, Viscount *see* Lindemann
Chinese gardens 53
Church of England bias, Oxford & Cambridge Universities 85, 86
Churchill, Winston
and Reith 134
wartime Prime Minister 183
City of London ['the City'] 43, 195
City of London Corporation, landholdings 37
Civil Service
criticisms 180, 181, 185, 186–189
Fabian Society report [1964] 188
Fulton Report [1968] 189, 192
independence of 195
Institute for Government reports 184–185
McKinsey report 187
recruitment basis 188, 189
reforms 186–188, 210
staff-reduction proposal 211
*Civil Service Reform Plan* [2012] 186, 187, 210
Civil War, English 43, 198, 199
Clarke, Bill [Cyclebag Secretary] 160
Clarke, Kenneth [Transport Minister] 161

Clarks [shoe company], grant by 159–160
Cobham, Lord 47–48
code-breaking operations 73
  sources of information 75, 76, 77
  staff ('code breakers') 75, 77, 117
Coke II, Thomas [agriculturist] 56
collective action, logic of 200
Collingwood, [Admiral Lord] Cuthbert 4–5
Colossus electronic computer **18**, 19, 79–81, 175–176, 177, 178
  postwar use 80
  role of individuals 79–80, 175–176
  technical details 80
Colvin, Brenda 52
Combe Down tunnel [near Bath] 155
Combined Authorities 212
Comfort, Nicholas [journalist] 144
Committee on Unhealthy Areas [1920] 133
Community Enterprise projects 161, 162
computing, British 81–82, 95
Concorde airliner 6
Consett & Sunderland Sculpture Trail 166
Cook, Frederick [Chief Engineer, Ministry of Transport] 108, 112
Coombes, Alan [electronics engineer] 80
Copeland, B.J. 80
cost benefit analysis
  characteristics 12
  examples of use 113, 145, 178–179
Cotton, C. 93
County of London Plan [1943] 28
County Surveyors Society
  motorway plan [1938] 109, 113, 114
  road network report 107
Covent Garden [London] 34
Cowper, William [poet] 51

creative chaos
  Arup Group 147
  Bletchley Park 76–77
creative scientific thinking
  Bletchley Park 76–77
  John Butterfield on 84
Crick, Francis [molecular biologist] 97
Cripps, Stafford 183
Cromwell, Oliver [Lord Protector] 198
Cromwell, Thomas [chief minister to King Henry VIII] 197
Croome Park [Worcestershire] 48, *49*
Crossman, Richard [Minister for Housing & Local Government] 121, 125, 127
  on working of government 180–181
Crown Estate 37, 39
Cubitt, Thomas [builder] 36
Cunningham, [Admiral] Andrew 3–4
Cyclebag campaign group 159, 160
cycling
  in Cambridge 90
  in Milton Keynes 122, 123, 131
  *see also* National Cycle Network; Sustrans

D-Day landings [1944] 71–72
  [decoded] German message about 72, 80
Dahrendorf, Ralf 83, 190–191, 194–196, 197, 202
Davies, [Sir] Howard, London Airports Commission 6
de Gamond, Aimé Thomé [mining engineer] 140
decentralization of government 211, 212–213
Declaration of Rights [1689] 198
Defence Committee 181
demand [economic] management 128
Denniston, Alistair [Head of Code & Cypher School] 75

Department of Economic Affairs 125,
190, 192
Department for Transport 144
and Channel Tunnel rail link 150,
172
Derby Arboretum 66
development corporations
for new towns 128, 131, 135
for regeneration projects 149
*see also* London Docklands
Development Corporation; Milton
Keynes Development Corporation
developmental state(s) 6, 12, 191
Japan as 191–192, 209
devolution 212
Diglis [cycling/walking] bridge
[Worcester] *163*
Dimitriou, [Professor] Harry 13
'disjointed incrementalism' 16, 179
Disraeli, Benjamin 64
Dissenters Academies 86
dissolution of monasteries 85, 197
disused railway lines, potential as cycle
routes 160, 161
Dollis Hill Communications Research
Establishment 19, 78–80, 176
'Dongas Tribe' 116
Drake, James [civil engineer] 109,
110–111, 117, 176
Duchy of Cornwall landholdings 37
Duchy of Lancaster landholdings 37
Duke of Devonshire 88, 89, 176

East Thames Corridor 149, 150, 153
*see also* Thames Gateway
Easton, Mark [journalist] 211
Eddington transport report [2006] 108,
172
'edge city' developments 130
Edgerton, D. 202
Edward I [King of England] 131–132
Edwards, Michael [planner] 130–131
Eight19 [solar panel company] 94

Eisenhower, Dwight
[US President], and interstate
highway system 112–113
[wartime General] 71, 72–73, 81
electronic computer, world's first **18**,
19, 73, 79–80
electronics companies, Cambridge
94–95
Elizabethan garden design 51
Elliot computers 82
employee-owned firms 147
English Civil War 43, 198, 199
'enigma' coding/decoding machines 77
environmental objectors, town
planning shaped by 33–34, 203
Euro rail 148
Evelyn, John 26, 52, 175

Fay, Sam [Great Central Railway's
manager] 139
Ferguson, George [architect] 159
Ferranti computers 82
First Garden City Limited 132
'fiscal-military' state 198
flexibility, in Milton Keynes master plan
120, 121, 129, 131
Flowers, Thomas [telecommunications
engineer] 78–79
computer designed by 79–80, 82–
83, 176
work style 79, 82
Flyvbjerg, Bent 11–12
Ford Foundation, funding from 121
Ford Motor Company 15
'forecasting doubters' 8–11, 17
Forshaw, J.H. [LCC Chief Architect]
28
Fowler, Norman [Transport Minister]
142
Foyles bookshop building [London] 42
freedom of choice, in Milton Keynes
master plan 120, 121, 127, 129, 131
Friedman, Milton [economist] 128

Friend, J. 7
Fulton, John [university administrator] 189

Gamble, Andrew [political scientist] 199
Garden Cities Association 132
garden city, characteristics 123, 133
Garden City Pioneer Company 132
garden suburbs 133
'gardenesque' style 67
Germany, motorways 106–107
Gillespie Graham, James [Scottish architect] 64
Glorious Revolution [1688] 54, 196, 198
'golden age'
    for motorway building 116
    for technocratic planning and mega-projects 7–8
Goldsworthy, Andy [sculptor] 165
Gould, Philip [political strategist] 130
government, central opposition to motorways 108, 110, 172
Government Offices for the Regions 212
Grace, W.G. [cricketer] 140
Grafton, Duke of 48
'great British plans', meaning of term 5
Great Central Railway London Extension 138–139
    financial failure 139
    opposition to 140
great estates 36–40, 175
    new estates 40–43
Great Packington [Warwickshire] 48–49
Greater London Council (GLC), road and motorway plans 30, 31, 44
Greater London Development Plan 30
Greater London Plan [1944] 28, 91, 134
green belt concept 28, 29, 43, 134

Greenwood, Antony [Minister for Housing & Local Government] 126
Grimshaw, John [Sustrans, civil engineer] 159, 160, 161, 162
Grimshaw, Nicholas [architect] 144
Grosvenor Estate 38

Haldane Report [1918] 182
Hall, [Professor Sir] Peter
    on agglomeration economics 99
    on Milton Keynes 131
    on planning disasters 6, 7, 30, 31
    on redevelopment of London 40, 149, 154
    on Victorian slums 65
Hampstead Garden Suburb 133
Hanson, Julienne [architect] 127
Haussmann, Georges Eugène 31
Heath, Edward [Prime Minister] 116, 141, 158, 182, 184
Henderson, [Sir] Nicholas [former UK Ambassador to France] 143
Hennessy, Peter [historian] 185, 201–202
Henry VIII [King of England] 197
Heseltine, Michael [Environment Minister] 149
    Channel Tunnel rail link 150, 154, 172
    East Thames Corridor/Thames Gateway 149, 150
    Milton Keynes 129
    planning advisor 149, 154
Heseltine, Michael [Lord Heseltine], *No Stone Unturned* report [2012] 212–213
high-rise buildings 29–30
high-speed rail system [UK] 12, 152
high-technology companies, Cambridge 85, 92–96, 98–99
Hill, Christopher [historian] 199
Hillman, Mayer [social scientist] 158–159

Hilton, Steve [PM's director of strategy] 185, 211
Hoare, Henry [banker] 56
Holford, William [town planner] 84–85
  Cambridge plan/report 85, 89–92, 174, 176
Holmes, Isaac [Liverpool councillor] 69, 175
Honda 10
Hooke, Robert 26
Hore-Belisha, Leslie [Transport Minister] 108
Howard de Walden estate 38
Howard, Ebenezer 132
  garden city concept 28, 132–133
Hubbard, E. 68
Hussey, Christopher [architectural historian] 55

IBM computers 82, 98
improvisation 177–178
incremental approach to public policy 16
indicative planning 188, 189
individualism 174–177, 203
individuals
  change driven by 209
  role of 174–177
Industrial Revolution 192, 196, 202
informal style of working 76, 177–178
infrastructure planning 6, 13, 143
  Armitt's review 5, 211
innovation 178
  central government and 214
  serial innovators 214–215
Institute for Government reports [2010, 2011] 184–185, 210
Institution of Civil Engineers 157–158, 177
instrument engineering companies, Cambridge 93, 99
intellectual property, Cambridge University's attitude to 100

Inverness-to-Dover [cycle] route 163
'iron triangle' evaluation [of project management] 14
IT infrastructure, development of 73, 80, 81–82
Italy, motorways 106

Jackson, Kenneth 63
Jackson, [Sir] William [businessman] 67, 69, 175
Jacobs, Jane 115
James I [King of Britain & Ireland] 198
James II [King of Britain & Ireland] 198
Japan
  as 'developmental state' 191–192
  Ministry of International Trade & Industry (MITI) 191
  post-war economic 'miracle 191–192, 208–209
Jeffery, R. 127
Jenkins, Roy [politician] 181, 190
Jenkins, Simon [journalist/author] 196
Jessop, W. 7
Jobs, Steve 10, 214
Johnson, Chalmers 6, 190–192, 202, 209–210
Jones, Inigo 34, 43
Joseph, Keith 29–30

Kay, John [19th c. reformer] 65
Kay, John [economist] 10
Kelly, G. 191
Kemp, David [sculptor] 166
Kemp, Edward [Birkenhead Park Superintendent] 67
Kennedy, Paul [historian] 20, 21
  quoted 208
Kennet & Avon Canal towpath *156*
Kent County Council, and Channel Tunnel rail link 144–145, 145–146
Kent Rail [joint venture] 147–148
Kent, William [landscape architect] 47–48, 54, 175

Keynesianism 128
King's Cross development [London]
    40–41, 175
    and Channel Tunnel rail link 147
Kirk, K. 93
Knight, Frank 10
Knight, Valentine 26
Kropotkin, Peter 132

Laird, William [shipbuilder] 64
Lamont, Norman [Chancellor] 150
Lancashire County Council, road plan
    [1949] 110–111
Lancaster bypass 111
landowners, increasing influence
    55–56
landscape design
    [case study] **18**, 19, 45–59
    development in England 51–53
    in London 27, *38*, 39
    political messages 56–57
Lang, Charles [CAD group at
    Cambridge] 95
Langham Place [London] *39*
Layfield Report [on local government
    finance, 1976] 204
LDA Design [landscape architects] 46
Le Nôtre, André 27, 51
Leasehold Reform Act [1967] 38
leasehold system [in London] 32, 34,
    35, 36
Letchworth Garden City 109
Lichfield, Nathaniel [planner] 131
Lincoln's Inn Fields [London] 33–34,
    44, 175, 203
Lindblom, Charles [economist] 16,
    179
Lindemann, Frederick [scientist] 183
Lipton, Stuart [developer] 40
Liverpool
    East Lancs Road 108–109
    Mersey Tunnel 109
    pioneering developments 69

population growth 64
    Queens Drive 109
    wealth [in late-19th c.] 69
Llewellyn Davies, Richard [architect/
    planner] 121, 126
Llewellyn Davies, Weeks, Forestier-
    Walker, Bor planning consultancy
    126
Lloyd George, David 106, 182, *183*
local enterprise partnerships 213
local government
    effect of centralization 203–206
    loss of control 203–204
    loss of financial independence 204,
        205
    role in new towns 124
    role in road construction 110–111,
        113, 117, 174
    staff numbers 211
    support by 161, 164–165, 209
Local Government Act [1933] 203
localism 213
Lock, David [planning consultant] 130
Locke, John [philosopher] 55
London
    Abercrombie's plans 28, 91, 134
    Act for the Rebuilding of the City of
        London [1667] 27, 33
    airports 6, 10, 126–127, 210
    City Surveyor(s) 33, 37
    as collection of 'villages' 31–32
    compared with Paris 31, 36, 44
    elected mayor 212
    great estates 36–40
    Great Fire [1666] 19, 25–26
    Greater London Plan [1944] 28, 91,
        134
    motorways 6, 7, 28–29
    opposition by objectors 30, 44
    Olympic Games [2012] 153
    plans for rebuilding 26–27, 172
    roads and squares [case study] **18**,
        19, 25–44

squares 33–36
Vauxhall Gardens 65
Westway 31
WW2 Blitz 27–28, 173
London Building Centre, Great Estates exhibition [2013] 36–37, 42–43
London & Continental Railways (LCR) 151
Loudon, John Claudius [landscape designer] 66, 67
Low, William [engineer] 140
Lowe, Chris [biotechnologist] 96
Luberoff, D. 115
Lucasian Chair of Mathematics 87, 101

M1 motorway 113, 114
M2 motorway 114
M3 motorway 114, 116
M5 motorway 114
M6 motorway 104, *105*, 110, 114
M11 motorway 116
M25 motorway 30, 31, 173
M40 motorway 45, 115
M60 motorway 111
M62 motorway 114
Macgregor, John [Transport Secretary] 151
McKinsey consultants, report on civil service 187
Macmillan, Harold [Defence Minister, *then* PM] 104, *113*, 141, 184
McNamara, Robert 15–16
Magna Carta 197, 198, 208
Major, John [Prime Minister] 149, 162, 204, 205–206
Manchester University computers 82
manufacturing weaknesses [in Britain] 82
'market', meaning of term 194
Marks & Spencer 10
Marples, Ernest [Transport Minister] 113
Mars, Tim 122, 123

Marshall, Alfred [economist] 99
Marshall Plan 181, 188
Marylebone High Street [London] 38
Marylebone Station [London] 139
Mathias, Peter [historian] 6
Mathieu Favier, Albert [mining engineer] 140
Mauroy, Pierre [French PM] 142
Maxwell, James Clerk [physicist] 88
Mazzucato, Mariana [economist] 214
Medical Research Council, Laboratory of Molecular Biology 97
Medway Viaduct *150*
mega-projects
    characteristics 153
    misrepresentation by professionals and consultants 11, 30
    reduction of risks 12
Meller, Helen [historian] 133
Menzies, Stewart [Head of Secret Information Service] 75, 82
Mercer, [Alexander] Cavalié 36
Mersey Tunnel 109
Microsoft Cambridge 95
middle-class politics 130
military computers [post-WW2] 82
Millennium Commission 162–163
Millennium Dome [London] 156, 164
Millennium Lottery funding 156, 163
Milton, John [poet] 52, 175
Milton Keynes
    [case study] **18**, 19, 119–137
    central shopping centre 129–130
    characteristics 122–123
    compared with American cities 122
    conceptual basis of master plan 131, 178, 179
    government's role 125–126, 174
    Great Linford 127
    modernist vs vernacular designs 127
    Netherfield district 127
    private sector investment 127, 128–129

role of individuals 120, 121, 125–126, 127, 128, 129, 135, 176
sewerage plant 126
success 130–131
transport modes 126
Milton Keynes Development Corporation 126, 127
Chairman 125–126
consultants' report to Board 126
strategy after Thatcher election 128–129
Ministry for Housing & Local Government 125
Minister 121, 125, 126, 180
Permanent Secretary 180
Ministry of Technology 96, 101, 192
Ministry of Town & Country Planning 84, 134
Minister 89–90, 135
Ministry of Transport
opposition to motorways 108, 110
*see also* Department for Transport
Ministry of Works & Planning 134
Mishan, Edward [economist] 115
Mitterand, François 19–20, 142, 143, 172, 176
modernist architecture 29
monetarism 128
Montagu of Beaulieu, 2nd Baron 105–106
Morton, Alistair [Eurotunnel chief executive] 145
Moses, Robert [urban planner] 107
motor car, compared with public transport 119–120, 122, 126
motorways
[case study] **18**, 19, 104–118
central government opposition/indifference 108, 110, 172
first proposals 105–106
Germany 106–107
Italy 106
local government support 110–111, 174

London 6, 7, 28–29
opposition by objectors 30, 44, 115–116, 175
role of individuals 110–111, 176
Mowl, T. 55

Nairn, Ian 32, 124
Nash, John [architect]39 *38*, 40
National Cycle Network
[case study] **18**, 20, 155–168
compared with other great plans 167
description 156
funding for 156, 163, 164
government scepticism 157, 172
health benefits 157, 166–167
mileage targets 163, 165
objectives 157, 163–164
as outdoor sculpture park 165–166
role of individuals 159–160, 175
*see also* Sustrans
National Health Service 174
Thatcher's reforms 205
National Health Service Act [1946, 1973] 204
Nazi regime, organizational characteristics 76
Needham, Roger [director of Cambridge University Computer Laboratory] 95
Nelson, [Admiral Lord] Horatio 4–5
Network Rail 151
new towns
20th-century 28, 29, 91, 125, 134–135, 203
historical examples 131–132
*see also* garden cities; Milton Keynes; Washington New Town
New Towns Act [1946] 135
New Towns Act [1965] 125, 126
New York City
Bronx River Parkway 107
Central Park 60–63

road system  107

Newbury bypass, road protest tactics
116

Newell, Dick [software technologist]
96

Newham [London Borough]  148, 154

Newman, Max [mathematician]  81

Newton, [Sir] Isaac  87

Nobel Prize winners  88, 214, 215

Noel-Baker, Philip [politician]  110

non-hierarchical institutions  178–179

'non-place urban realm'  120, 123

nonconformists *see* Dissenters

Normington, David [civil servant]  187

Norris, Steven [Transport Secretary]
157

Northern & Western Motorway
[1920s]  106

Northern Ireland, cycle network plans
164, 167, 177


objectors
Lincoln's Inn Fields  34, 44, 175,
178
motorway/road construction  30, 44,
115–116, 175, 178
role of  178

Official Secrets Act  73, 75

oil crisis [1973], effects  114, 158, 192

Olmsted, Frederick Law  61, 63

Olsen, Donald J. [historian]  18, 25, 32

Olson, Mancur [economist]  200–201

Omega Centre study  13–14, 18

Osborn, Frederic J.  133, 176

Ostrom, Elinor [political scientist]
215–216

Otmoor, road protest tactics  115

Oxford, University of  85, 86
compared with Cambridge  87, 89


Paris, compared with London  31, 36,
44

parkway roads  107, 109

Parliament
first formed  197
growing power of  197–198, 199

Paxton, Joseph  67
design of Birkenhead Park  63, 66,
67–69, 175

Peasants Revolt [1381]  197

Pepys, Samuel  25, 173

personal initiatives
Birkenhead Park  66–67
Bletchley Park  74, 75, 79–80, 82–83

Pevsner, N.  27, 68

Phelps, Edmund [economist]  214

Phibbs, John [landscape architect]  46

physical activity, Commission on
166–167

Pickles, Eric [communities & local
government minister]  213

'plan rational state'  191, 192
*see also* developmental state

planned restraint, in Cambridge  89–92,
174

planning
British style  209–210, 214
cost benefit analysis techniques  12,
17, 145
as decision-making style  12, 13, 14,
16–17
lack of comprehensive strategic
framework  5–6
systems approach  8

planning environment, uncertainty
related to  7

Platt, J.  130

Platts, George [founder of Sustrans]
159, 160
quoted  155

pleasure gardens  65

Plowden, [Sir] Edwin  184

pluralism
and London squares  35
opposition to absolute power  197
rise of  196–198

police commissioners 213
political values, expressed in landscape
  parks 56–57, 175
poll tax 205
polycentric governance 215–216
  and British planning style 216
Pompidou, Georges 141
Pooley, Fred [Buckinghamshire
  Planning Officer] 124, 131
Pope, Alexander [poet] 52–53, 175
Popper, Karl 10–11
Portillo, Michael [Junior Transport
  Minister] 144, 145
Post Office
  Communications Research
    Establishment 19, 78–80, 176
  work on DARPA computer network
    214
Pound, [Admiral Sir] Dudley 4
power, commercial/political split 43–44
Prescott, John [Labour Deputy PM]
  151, 192, 206
pressure groups 133, 159, 160, 203
Preston bypass 19, 104, 111, 113
Price, Richard [of Birkenhead] 64
Priestland, David [historian] 115
Priestley, Joseph [chemist] 86
Prime Ministers, lack of support staff
  for 184, 210
Princes Park [Liverpool] 67
'project doubter' 11–12
'propaganda society'
  planning by 135–136
  TCPA as 133
Public Improvements Act [1860] 66
public park(s)
  first in North America 60
  first in world 63, 66
public transport, compared with car use
  119–120, 122
Pye [Electronics] Company 93, 96, 99,
  176
Pye, William 93, 176

'quangoes' 196, 206

Radio Security Service (RSS) 76–77, 173
Radio Society of Great Britain 76
radio transmissions, monitoring of
  76–77
Radley, Gordon [Director of Dollis Hill
  Research Establishment] 79
Railtrack 151
Rasmussen, S.E. 27, 28, 32, 35, 43,
  121–122, 202–203
rational comprehensive approach to
    public policy 16, 177
  criticisms 17, 177
rational planning
  cost benefit approach 12, 17, 178
  as decision-making style 12, 14,
    16–17, 178–179
Raymond, Paul [nightclub owner &
    entrepreneur] 41, 175, 178
  granddaughters 41, *42*, 175
redbrick universities 86
Reformation and Dissolution of the
  Monasteries [1530s] 85, 197
Regent Street [London] 37, 39–40
Regent's Park [London] 37, *38*, 39, 68
Regional Assemblies 212
Regional Commissioners [WW2] 202
Regional Development Agencies 192,
  212
regional government 202
regulatory centralism 203–207
'regulatory state' 191
  Britain as 202, 208
  United States as 191, 209
Reid, Bob [British Rail Chairman] 150
Reith, John, 1st Baron 134, 135
  and Churchill 134
  and new towns 135, 176, 203
Repton, Humphry [landscape designer]
  67
Restoration of the Monarchy [1660]
  85, 198

Rifkind, Malcolm [Transport Secretary]
150, 151
Road Board 106
Road Construction Units [central
government] 113, 117, 174, 204
Robinson, James [political scientist]
196, 197, 200
Roche, Fred [architect] 127
Roosevelt, Franklin D. [US president]
10
Roskill Commission 126–127
Roth, Philip 61
Rothengatter, Werner 11
Rowse, Herbert [architect] 109
Royal Commission(s)
on distribution of industrial
population 133–134
on transport/roads [1931] 108
on universities 86
Russell, Francis [4th Earl of Bedford] 34

Sahashi Shigeru [MITI Minister,
Japan] 191
St Pancras station 40, 151, *152*
Salmond, Alex [former SNP leader] *212*
Sanderson, M. 89
Sandhurst, Lord 76
Sawday, Alistair [writer] 159
Schreyer, Helmut [computer engineer]
76
Schumacher, E.F. 115
Scotland
cycleways 161
tree planting 52
Scottish Government 212
Scottish National Party 212
sculpture, commissions for National
Cycle Network 165–166
Sea-to-Sea [cycle] route 163
Secret Intelligence Service 73, 75
Head of 74, 75
Segal Quince Wicksteed reports [on
Cambridge] 92–93, 98, 100

Select Committee on Public
Administration, quoted 180
Select Committee on Public Walks
(SCPW), Report [1833] 65–66, 173
Select Committee on Roads 112
Select Committee on Science and
Technology [1999], memorandum
from Cambridge University 99–
100
Self, P. 12, 13, 14, 179
serpentine lakes/paths/rivers 48, 62, 67
Sharp, Evelyn [Permanent Secretary,
Housing & Local Government]
180, 184
Shore, Peter [Environment Minister]
128
Shostak, Lee [planner] 121, 128
Silkin, Lewis [Minister of Town &
Country Planning] 89–90, 176
Simmons, Jack [historian] 139, 140
Simmons, Martin [planner] 10
Sinclair, [Admiral Sir] Hugh [Head of
Secret Information Service] 74, 75
Sinclair Radionics 94
slave trade 200
smartphone technology 96
software development 96, 99
Soho Estate [London] 41–42, 175, 178
Somerset & Dorset Railway, Combe
Down tunnel 155
South East Regional Study [1964] 125
Special Roads Act [1949] 112, 117
Sproxton, Dave [film maker] 159
Sri Lanka, Peradeniya Royal Botanic
Gardens *50*
Stagg, John [meteorologist] 71
Stannard, Colin [banker] 147, 148
Stourhead [Wiltshire], landscape park 56
Stowe Landscape Park
[Buckinghamshire] 47–48, 175
statues and buildings 56–57
strategic planning, scepticism about
benefits 8, 192

strategic thinking, central government
182–184
Stratford [east London] 148, 151
Stretford bypass 111
Stroud, Dorothy [landscape historian]
58
success(es)
Cambridge 101–102
Colossus computer 81
examples 6, 10
meaning of term 6
Milton Keynes 130–131
National Cycle Network 166
Thames Gateway and Channel
Tunnel rail link 153
Summerson, J. 43
Sustainable Transport Limited 160
Sustrans
as charity 161
early projects 160–162
funding for National Cycle
Network 163, 164
membership numbers 162
origins 159–160, 177
support from local authorities 161,
164–165, 178
Sydney Opera House 147
systems approach to planning 8

Taleb, Nassim Nicholas 8–9, 10, 179
targets, spending 206
disadvantages 206
Taylor, A.J.P. [historian] 182, 201
technocratic planning
first developed 15–16
'golden age' 7–8
scepticism about benefits 8, 115
telecommunications
Cambridge companies 96
Dollis Hill Research Establishment
19, 78–80
Temple, William [philosopher] 53
Tetlock, Philip E. 9, 21n[1]

Thames Gateway 149
and Channel Tunnel rail link 149–
150, 153
success 152
Thames Gateway bridge 153
Thatcher, Margaret 128, 149, 158, *205*
centralizing tendencies 204, 205
and Channel Tunnel 20, 142, 143,
172, 176
and Milton Keynes 128, 129, 130
and motorway construction 116
thermionic valves
British expertise 78, 79
first use in computers 79, 80
Thompson, E.P. 56
three-day working week [1973–74] 158
Todt, Fritz [German General Inspector
of Roads] 107
toll roads/motorways 106, 108, 113
top-down planning 214
topiary [in gardens] 51–52
Town & Country Planning Act [1947]
84, 174
Town & Country Planning Association
(TCPA) 132, 133, 176
reports 5–6
Town Development Act [1952] 124
Train, George Francis [entrepreneur] 64
Trans Pennine Trail 161, 163, 164
transparency 12
transport mega-projects 13
'era of transition' for 115
transport policy, and pedestrians/
cyclists/public transport users 116,
158–159, 163–164
Travers, Tony [economist] 204
Treasury
on Channel Tunnel and rail link
141, 145, 150
coordination role 210
cost benefit analysis used by 12, 145
and Department of Economic
Affairs 190

opposition to motorway scheme 108–
112
tree planting 52
'trial and error' approach to policy 9,
17, 177, 178, 179, 209
Trunk Roads Act [1936, 1946] 204
Tudor England 197
garden design 51
Turing, Alan 75, 77, 79, 81–82
'thinking machine' concept 80, 95
Turner, R. 55
'Two Tunnels' cycleway [near Bath]
155, 156, *157*
Twyford Down, road protest tactics
116
Tyme, John [motorway/road protestor]
115, 158

uncertainty, sources 7
Unemployment Assistance Board 204
United Kingdom, high-speed rail
system 12, 152
United States
application of Japanese
developmental planning 209–
210
as 'regulatory state' 191
urban public investment 8
universities, funding of 195, 196
Universities of Oxford and Cambridge
Act [1877] 88
urban countryside, Milton Keynes as
123
utilities, control removed from local
government 203–204

value judgements, uncertainty related
to 7
value-for-money considerations 12–13
Vaux, Calvert [architect] 61, 62
Vietnam War 15–16
voluntary organizations/workers 77,
159–160, 173, 195, 196

Wakefield [West Yorkshire], parkland
design 48
Walker, Derek [architect/planner] 120,
127, 128, 129
Walpole, Horace 48
War Cabinet Secretariat [WW1] 182
war socialism [WW2] 201–202
Washington New Town 120
Wass, [Sir] Douglas [Treasury
Permanent Secretary] 190
Water Act [1945, 1973] 204
Waterloo station [London] 144, 151
Watkin, [Sir] Alfred [railway
entrepreneur] 138–140, 141, 172
Watson, James [molecular biologist] 97
Watts, Arthur [radio amateur] 77
Webber, Melvin [urban planner]
119–120
and Milton Keynes 121, 131, 178, 179
Weber, Max [political economist] 190
Welchman, Gordon [mathematician]
79
Welfare State 174
Wells, H.G. 105
Welsby, John [British Rail Chief
Executive] 145
West, N. 77, 173
Whig Party 199
Whitman, Walt 60
Wilkes, Maurice [Head of Cambridge
University Mathematical
Laboratory] 95
William of Orange [King William III of
Great Britain] 198
Wilson, Harold [Prime Minister] 96,
124–125, 141, 181, 189, 190, 192
'Winter of Discontent' [1978–79] 128,
158
Winterbotham, F.W. 73
Wolseley, [General Sir] Garnet 141
World War 2
airfield construction programme
110, 174

Battle of the Atlantic  19, 81
Cambridge University's role  89,
   101
code breakers  72–78, 82–83, 117
D-Day landings  71–72, 80
London blitz  27, 173
state-directed action  201–202, 203
Taranto naval attack [Italy, 1940]  3
US bombing strategy  15
Wren, Christopher  26
   plan for rebuilding of London  26,
      27, 44, 172, 174

Wright, H. Myles [town planner]
   84–85

Yates, Richard Vaughan [of Liverpool]
   67
Youngman, Peter [landscape planner]
   123

Ziegler, Philip [biographer/historian],
   quoted  171
Zuse, Konrad [computer engineer]  76